SECRETS

OF BECOMING A

LATE BLOOMER

"This fine book reminds us that this land of opportunity extends to the middle and later years of life, when we can still invent new possibilities for ourselves."

— ROBERT N. BUTLER, MD
PRESIDENT AND CEO
INTERNATIONAL LONGEVITY CENTER—USA

"Secrets of Becoming a Late Bloomer *is a warm, caring, inspiring book and we who are old can use as much of that as we can get!*"

— EDA LeSHAN
FAMILY COUNSELOR AND AUTHOR OF *It's Better Over the Hill than Under It* AND *I Want More of Everything*

"*A potpourri of wonderfully provocative examples of folks who respond creatively to the changing conditions in the later years of their lives.*"

—RAM DASS
AUTHOR, LECTURER, AND SPIRITUAL TEACHER

"*With this brilliant book Connie Goldman and Richard Mahler have given me a rewarding shove, convincing me that I am Eddie "Late Bloomer" Albert. Thank you. This is a valuable book.*"

— EDDIE ALBERT
ACTOR

SECRETS
OF BECOMING A
LATE BLOOMER

STAYING
CREATIVE,
AWARE,
AND
INVOLVED IN
MIDLIFE
AND BEYOND

CONNIE GOLDMAN

RICHARD MAHLER

Fairview Press
Minneapolis

Published by Fairview Press, 2450 Riverside Avenue, Minneapolis, MN 55454.
Fairview Press is a division of Fairview Health Services, a community-focused health
system, affiliated with the University of Minnesota, providing a complete range of services,
from the prevention of illness and injury to care for the most complex medical conditions.

For a free current catalog of Fairview Press titles, call toll-free 1-800-544-8207,
or visit our Web site at www.fairviewpress.org.

Originally published by Stillpoint Publishing, 1995. Published by Hazelden Foundation,
2000. First published by Fairview Press in September 2007.

Printed in the United States of America
12 11 10 09 08 07   5 4 3 2 1

Library of Congress Cataloging-in-Publication Data

Goldman, Connie.
    Secrets of becoming a late bloomer : staying creative, aware, and involved in
midlife and beyond / Connie Goldman, Richard Mahler.
        p. cm.
    Previous ed.: Center City, Minn. : Hazelden Information and Educational
Services, 2000.
    ISBN 978-1-57749-170-5 (alk. paper)
    1. Aging—Social aspects. 2. Aging—Psychological aspects. 3. Older people—
Psychology. 4. Older people—Biography. 5. Retirement. I. Mahler, Richard. II. Title.
    HQ1061.G643 2007
    646.7'9—dc22
                                2007023731

Cover design by Laurie Ingram

DEDICATION

To my children and grandchildren, who will come into midlife and their later years at a time when, I am hopeful, our world will understand that sixty-five is the speed limit, not the age limit.
— Connie Goldman

For my father, Donald, and late mother, Mary, both inspiring role models for creative, positive, and good-humored aging.
— Richard Mahler

CONTENTS

FOREWORD

IN *Secrets of Becoming a Late Bloomer,* Connie Goldman and Richard Mahler confirm in a striking way what I have believed for some time: *we need an updated image of aging.* The antiquated view of maturity as a period of stagnation and decline must be replaced once and for all with the reality that the latter part of life is an exciting time of growth, productivity, and newfound pleasures—if we know the secrets of becoming a Late Bloomer.

The good news is that more and more people are celebrating their maturity as a wonderful period of life. In fact, many older members of society are truly turning their lives around. In this delightful book, Connie and Richard show us that a new generation of older men and women are finding ways to make their later years remarkably rewarding. Through the authors' many captivating examples of late blooming from all over the country, we are inspired to begin thinking about aging as a much more positive experience than perhaps we realized previously.

Some of the people whose stories are recounted in these pages, like the now-departed founder of the Gray Panthers, Maggie Kuhn, and late actress Jessica Tandy, are extraordinary people who continued to blossom as they aged. Others might be described as "ordinary people"—the kind of individuals you might encounter at your supermarket or doctor's office—who have broken through previous patterns or shifted lifestyles in order to accomplish astonishing things in their maturity. These Late Bloomers are single, married, or widowed; they live in apartments, cottages, condos, campers, retirement communities, single-family dwellings, and non-traditional group homes. They do all sort of things, from making music to growing vegetables, from acting and modeling to writing and teaching, from becoming social activists to starting their own businesses. They are people who have made up their minds how they want to live their later years and who have found the courage to take on entirely new challenges. Many have made up their minds to explore fresh ideas or try out new activities that they've always wanted to explore.

How have these Late Bloomers managed to make such a rousing success of what used to be thought of as "retirement years?" That's the question Connie and Richard answer in these pages, and you'll be inspired by what the stories reveal about the potential that each of us has for continued growth and development.

Those who find later life rewarding have grasped the truth that to find their particular niche they must begin by addressing important aspects of life, including health, humor, creativity, spirituality, and intimacy. They realize at some point in their quest that they must find out not what society expects of them but what they as individuals really want to do to fulfill themselves.

Secrets of Becoming a Late Bloomer thoughtfully examines how in maturity people sometimes unintentionally stand in the way of their happiness, and how some simple shifts in attitude and behavior can help set them free. The book tells us, by example, how powerful and profound changes can—and do—occur at any point in our lives.

One of the fascinating revelations of these Late Bloomers is the way their mental *and* physical health often improve dramatically soon after they discover how they really want to live and begin taking "action steps" to reach their goals. As I pointed out in my book, *Age Wave*, older people can manage their health a lot better than we thought in the past—when they are following their heart's desires and living life with gusto.

Prepare yourself. Once you begin reading *Secrets of Becoming a Late Bloomer*, the rest of life will never look the same again!

KEN DYCHTWALD, PH.D.
President and CEO
Age Wave, Inc.

ACKNOWLEDGMENTS

WITHOUT THE MANY "extraordinary ordinary" Late Bloomers who generously shared with us their inspiring stories of growth and satisfaction in their later years, this book would never have come into being. The observations of recognized experts in the field of aging have been helpful, but the depth, richness, and texture of our stories derive from the real-life experiences of the many inspiring sixty-, seventy-, eighty-, and ninety-year-old persons we've been privileged to meet and interview. Even though we cannot acknowledge each of them here by name, we thank and honor them all.

We extend special gratitude to our Fairview Press editor, Lane Stiles, whose support and guidance were instrumental in bringing this new edition into print. We tip our hats to other enthusiastic Fairview staffers involved in this project, whose guidance and hard work are much appreciated. Thanks also goes to Stillpoint Publishing for their belief in the inspirational value of the stories of others and their support in publishing the first edition of *Secrets of Becoming a Late Bloomer,* and to Hazelden Educational Services for their contributions to our second edition.

Finally, we wish to reiterate our hope that the "secrets" revealed in these pages will inspire and guide our readers in their search for positive personal transformation, greater happiness, and deeper spiritual meaning in midlife and beyond. We thank you in advance for embarking with us on this journey.

DARE TO EXPLORE

WE CALL THIS BOOK *Secrets of Becoming a Late Bloomer* not only because we think it's a catchy title but because it describes exactly what we wish to share with you. We hope that by reading the stories of successful Late Bloomers, you will develop the awareness, tools, and techniques that will make your later years the richest and most fulfilling of your life.

First, let's clarify that phrase "late bloomer." Rest assured, you don't have to be in any specific age group to qualify. In fact, the most important secret of becoming a Late Bloomer is that anybody can be one, because no matter what diverse and rewarding realms you've explored in your earlier years, there's always room to experience growth and creativity. By late bloomer, we simply mean anyone who defies the notion that his or her best years are over, someone who responds to the later stage of life not as a crisis but as a quest.

It's important to understand that this book is not necessarily about aging but about personal growth and transformation. Our Late Bloomers aren't so different from their peers, except when it comes to attitude. What Late Bloomers believe and value has a direct impact on the way they live.

No matter what else you may have been taught or led to believe, the basic truth is that *you* are the one in control of your future. Your views and principles have a strong influence on what will happen in your life. No one seems able to explain scientifically why this is so, but daily observation confirms that when people hold positive attitudes and strong beliefs, their energy reservoirs and potential for change appear virtually inexhaustible.

Natalie G., for example, longed for a life of service and adventure. At age sixty-seven she joined the Peace Corps, learned Spanish, and became a schoolteacher in Peru. Spurred by the determination to become choir director of his church, Sidney K. eventually met that goal and won additional acclaim as a tenor soloist. At age seventy-one, Martha B. transformed her lifelong love of stamp collecting into a successful mail-order business. Seeking a satisfying leisure lifestyle, Sid and Ramona M. sold their home after retirement, bought an RV, and are now systematically touring each of America's national parks.

We know your interests, needs, and circumstances will differ in various ways from those of other Late Bloomers. After all, people tend to become more individuated as they age—more like themselves instead of like a group. With that in mind, we offer inspiring role models, uncomplicated exercises, practical hints, and time-tested "action steps" that have proved useful in finding out what path or project is best suited to late blooming. Through them, we'll help you assess needs, examine values, set appropriate goals, and formulate a workable plan to nourish your continuing growth and self-actualization.

Each chapter relates stories about Late Bloomers we've gotten to know and admire. We include them as a way of illustrating a specific situation, along with practical suggestions and action steps designed to help you respond when a similar theme or circumstance arises in your own life. Each chapter considers the importance of life-affirming attitudes, as demonstrated by the consequences of action, formation of identity, release of judgments, need for risk taking, creation of intimacy, benefits of humor, rediscovery of past pleasures, satisfactions of gardening, development of late-life spirituality, and the challenges wrought by changes in health, lifestyle, relationships, or work.

As researchers, we're convinced that there is always a positive, life-affirming place to grow. The Late Bloomers we've met have generously shared with us their personal tales of sadness and joy, frustration and satisfaction, struggle and survival, challenge and change. We regard the spirit demonstrated, victories won, and positive attitudes shown by these individuals as validating examples of the beliefs espoused in this book.

Although a few locations, names, and quotations have been altered slightly in the interest of clarity or to protect privacy, each of our Late Bloomers is either a person we've interviewed personally or, in a handful of cases, a composite of several people who've expressed similar thoughts, feelings, and experiences. In the latter instances, we felt that the use of a single character made our points stronger.

The use of real Late Bloomers—including composites based on several individuals—is crucial to our underlying premise: *knowing and understanding what others have done can help us take control of our own lives.*

Incidentally, we use the word "secrets" in our title because we believe that too much of the positive stuff about aging has been kept hidden, while the so-called disadvantages and drawbacks of getting older have received far too much attention. It's high time somebody let at least a few life-affirming, life-enhancing secrets out of the bag.

Bear in mind that the kind of blooming we envision has as much to do with play as it does with work, with self-enrichment as much as self-examination, and with contentment as much as striving.

We like to call *Secrets of Becoming a Late Bloomer* a "how-do" rather than a "how-to" book. Our approach is distinctive because it reflects our experience and point of view. We're not trained social workers, gerontologists, or psychologists. We're journalists who find it most rewarding and effective to report so-called human interest stories.

In writing this book, we are simply passing along the insights that hundreds of wise Late Bloomers have so kindly shared with us in the hope that they will encourage and guide positive change and growth in you. This book is full of the stories of remarkable individuals who have tackled the challenges of life and come out on top, using strategies that are creative, inspiring, and effective. Late Bloomers regard each day as a chance for new growth, satisfaction, and happiness—built on what life has already taught them. Their focus is not on limitations but on constantly expanding horizons.

Being a Late Bloomer is about being *realistic.* It's about honestly assessing your interests and skills, accomplishments and aspirations, values and lifestyle. It's about understanding both the limits and advantages of your financial situation.

It's about daring to explore what life can be like in the "adult-lescent" years that lie ahead.

Somewhere in midlife or beyond, many of us realize that the priorities we set in our younger years have gradually shifted. Swiss psychologist Carl Jung noted the impracticality of responding to the afternoon of life in the same way we did during its morning. As one Late Bloomer put it, "It's time for me to figure out who I am, now that I am no longer who I was!"

Philosopher Henry David Thoreau observed more than a century ago that "we are constantly invited to be what we are." This book seeks to celebrate those who already have accepted that invitation and can inspire the rest of us to follow their examples. Becoming a Late Bloomer, we've found, is its own reward.

CHAPTER ONE

THE SECRET OF ATTITUDE

Some Late Bloomers are legendary. Grandma Moses didn't start painting until she was nearly eighty. Winston Churchill was in his seventies when he led Great Britain through World War II. At sixty-five, Groucho Marx started a brand-new career hosting a TV show.

Every one of us, famous or not, at any age or stage of life, has the potential to become a Late Bloomer or continue blooming as the years roll by. One of our favorite relatives took her first camping trip at sixty-eight and has been regularly (and happily) heading off to the woods ever since. We know an eighty-two-year-old former cartoonist who taught himself silk screening after retirement and now enjoys a successful new career. A friend in her early sixties put her considerable bookkeeping skills to use as a volunteer income-tax counselor for neighborhood senior centers. You, too, can blossom, experiment, and head in new directions, no matter what your chronological age or circumstances.

Declaring that each of us can be a Late Bloomer is not the same as saying "anything is possible" or "life has no limits," however. If you've read popular personal-growth and self-help books, you may have come away with the mistaken impression that there are really no restrictions on what one can do.

Let's be realistic. No one over fifty-five is going to try out for the Los Angeles Lakers basketball team or ask to be a space shuttle pilot. Nor are we likely to become ballerinas or climb Mount Everest. Our bodies change as we get older, and age inevitably begins to have an impact on our choices, not to mention our spirit and emotions. We may feel sadness about not having the stamina, agility, or resilience that we enjoyed when we were teens and young adults. Along with an accompanying sense of loss, there may be flashes of irritation and even anger. We're reminded of a conversation we once had with actor Hume Cronyn, then seventy-seven, on exactly this subject: "I have only one eye," he grumbled. "But even with two, I simply don't see as well, and I don't hear as well either. I've always been very active and taken a lot of exercise. It just *infuriates* me that I cannot do the physical things that I did twenty-five years ago."

During our interview with the "first couple" of American theater, the late Jessica Tandy reminded her husband that he still swims, dives, water-skis, and spearfishes in spite of these complaints. While it's true that Cronyn has modified his activities somewhat, he hasn't eliminated them and continues to enjoy their many benefits in moderation. He may not be blooming in exactly the same way he did fifty years ago, but he's still blooming.

As longtime observers of Late Bloomer behavior, we see a crucial difference between being *young* and being *youthful*. In our view, being old is just fine. In fact, we're convinced that aging offers many praiseworthy "gifts" and some distinct advantages. It is in our later years that we are often able to give our most meaningful consideration to values, to refocusing our priorities, shifting our outlook, and developing a sense of gratitude for the richness of life.

One couple we know, seventy-one-year-old Phyllis M. and her husband Bill, operate a sixteen-seat snack bar at one of the largest hospitals in South Florida. While eighty-year-old Bill makes sandwiches in the kitchen, Phyllis waits on customers in a dining area just off the main visitors' lounge. They turn their substantial profits over to a scholarship fund, which the couple established ten years ago after Bill was rushed to the hospital's emergency room for open-heart surgery. "I collapsed on the golf course," recalls the former restaurant manager. "They had me on the operating table within twenty minutes."

Phyllis credits the hospital's medical team with saving her husband's life and changing hers forever. "This is our way of giving something back," she explains. "We have enough money invested so that we don't need the snack bar for its income. There was nothing like this for visitors or staff when Bill was admitted, so we know we're providing a unique service." Bill and Phyllis put more than fifty hours a week into their small business, doing everything from accounting to food shopping, serving to cooking. A plaque on the wall testifies to their ten thousand hours of dedicated work.

Choices like these aren't made in a vacuum, of course, and the consequences of aging are among the many factors influencing our decisions. The context in which change occurs in the lives of older people like Bill and Phyllis is, by definition, complicated.

During our "retirement" years we undergo more dramatic changes in a shorter span of time than at any other period in our lives except childhood or adolescence. We're often dealing with major shifts in work and leisure. Our later years bring the loss of loved ones and, frequently, a limitation of abilities we've always taken for granted. The latter may be minimized by proper exercise and eating habits, but at some point the vagaries of time begin having an impact on our bodies. We're more vulnerable to disease, joints tend to ache, and our bones heal more slowly if they've been broken.

Having said that, let's consider the almost endless possibilities that remain and the vast number of opportunities that are now open to us. This is where our energies can be directed most productively in our later years. Let's praise age, not condemn it.

Many of our Late Bloomer stories are about growth and enrichment. We all know that good sometimes comes out of bad, that a negative and stressful experience often leaves us stronger and wiser. In this same vein, you may have noticed how many things change after children leave home, a nine-to-five job ends, a mate dies, or a serious illness threatens. New possibilities may suddenly open up.

Humorist Erma Bombeck tells the true story of an eighty-four-year-old man "with one foot in the grave" who announced suddenly that he was taking a trip around the globe. When a friend asked him why, the fellow replied, "I haven't got long for this world, and when I get to the pearly gates and the Lord asks me, 'How did you like that planet I made for you down there?' I'd have to say, 'Sorry, Lord, but I didn't have a chance to see much of the place!'" That old man was afraid God would be disappointed in him for not taking a closer look at his beautiful

4

handiwork. "I figured I ought to take the trouble to see it while I still had my health," he concluded.

We've met many Late Bloomers who are a lot like this fellow. Their remarkable accomplishments occurred *after* doors seemed to swing shut on their choices. In their passion to be the most they could be, they saw these events as stepping-stones, not roadblocks.

Even in his late seventies, Willard G. was an avid bowler with an average score of 182. When a hip replacement and several bad falls threatened to doom his participation in the sport, Willard taught himself to bowl from a sitting position. Within months, he boosted his average to 185.

Our Late Bloomers have shown us how they are able to see beyond "limitations" or "handicaps" in order to get what they want. Instead of holding them back, such factors become pathways toward a new way of living—and thinking. As you read this book, think about ways in which you may have allowed various kinds of limitations to influence your own way of life. Keep in mind that our intention is not to have you imitate the behavior of anyone we describe but simply to inspire you to explore possible choices of your own.

One of our favorite Late Bloomers is a native New Yorker named Jacob L., who didn't let heart disease and retirement put a damper on his future.

Jacob grew up wanting to be teacher. In 1934, he began earning $4.23 a day as an apprentice teacher at a Brooklyn grade school. Jacob married a few months later and, in order to support his growing family, set aside teaching to become an administrator, which paid better. He became a guidance counselor, then a school principal, and finally a Manhattan school district official.

"I was in charge of a tremendous amount of money," Jacob marveled, looking back on the active years of his first career. "We had almost a quarter of a billion dollars coming in.

"Then I had the first of a series of heart attacks. The job was too demanding, and I had to leave," this small, dignified man told us, speaking in a calm but emphatic voice. "I felt a loss of control and power, as though I didn't have a place in the world anymore." Jacob was only fifty-nine years old at the time and not content to merely sit at home. For six years he taught education courses in the graduate division of a prestigious university. But even the lessened stress of this work was too much for him.

"I had open-heart surgery, which was not entirely successful," he explained. "I had a quadruple bypass of the four main arteries and was quite ill for a long time—it took me almost a year to get back on my feet. Being sick made me feel old and even more out of touch with the workplace." Predictably, Jacob became restless. Wanting to take advantage of his many years in education, he decided to become a part-time consultant.

Three years later, Jacob still felt there was something essential missing from his daily routine. He couldn't quite place what that certain "something" was, and it depressed him to think that his health problems would prevent him from trying anything risky. "I spent a lot of time thinking about when and if a new challenge would come along," Jacob continued. "It slowly began to dawn on me that I was going to have to take on the responsibility of finding it, whatever 'it' might be."

For the next several weeks Jacob mulled over his options, which still seemed terribly limited. "The family had Thanksgiving dinner at my home," remembered Jacob, setting the scene for a conversation that would ultimately change his life. "We were all sitting around talking, and I felt very envious of my daughter, who was telling us about her experiences in law school.

"I said, 'I wish I could do that!' And she asked, 'Why don't you?' I answered, 'How can I? I'm aged and decrepit. What college would want to accept an old man in his dotage?'" Jacob offered the usual reasons one gives when one doesn't want to do something. But his daughter was insistent, and the exchange became more heated:

"Look, if you really want to do it, you can do it!"

"Well, no school is going to accept me at the age of sixty-seven."

"You don't know that for a fact! You just *hope* that's true so you'll have an excuse for feeling like a victim, but you don't really know it. Why don't you find out?"

Jacob realized that his first impulse had been to become defensive and to invoke the same rationalizations he'd always used for not pursuing the study of law. "Okay, then," he finally blurted out. "I'll do as you say. I'll check into it."

After accepting her challenge, Jacob thought all weekend about his daughter's words. He was filled with the heady, excited, and slightly woozy feeling many of us have when we step beyond long-maintained boundaries, when we realize that there's no backing away from our new commitment, that our lives have already changed forever. You may have felt this when you got the promotion you always wanted, joined the Army, or learned you were pregnant for the first time.

By Monday, Jacob had decided he couldn't live with himself without at least satisfying his newfound curiosity. Although apprehensive, he was still determined to explore the possibility of becoming an attorney, whatever the odds might be. He called the university he'd attended many years earlier and asked point-blank whether it would be possible for him to attend law school there. "Why not?" the admissions officer replied. "There's an antidiscrimination law. We can't turn you down solely because you're old."

"I hadn't thought of that," Jacob mused. "Is it too late for me to take the exam?" When he learned there would be one the following Saturday, Jacob rushed to the university and filled out the necessary papers to become a walk-in applicant. Next he stopped at the school bookstore and bought background materials. For the next three days and nights he crammed for the test.

"Much to my surprise, I did very well on the exam," said Jacob, still flushed with pride. "I applied and was accepted to law school."

As Jacob shared his story, we were reminded of a lesson many other Late Bloomers have taught us in the course of our interviews. A first step, even a small one, often mobilizes a reservoir of energy that sets us on a course with the potential for changing our lives completely. At a certain stage all your other plans and excuses melt away. You are led to the point where, as the expression goes, "nothing does it like doing it."

As soon as Jacob received news of his test results, he shifted into high gear. He started planning his study habits, figuring out which room would be the best to read in and which hours would be most productive for studying. From the start, Jacob looked upon law not as a hobby but as a new career. His daughter and son, who were both attorneys, served as role models.

In the beginning, Jacob found that fellow students at his school tried to baby him. "It was as if to say, 'Here's this elderly gentleman, and we have to be nice to him.' But after a while they forgot about that. They argued and debated issues with me, just like everybody else."

The proudest moment of Jacob's life came during the commencement exercise at Carnegie Hall. "I had a lot of family there: my wife, brothers, sisters, children, grandchildren, and other relatives. Some of my retired friends came too. The dean had cautioned the audience against applauding or doing anything disruptive in the middle of the ceremony, yet when my name was called, *everybody* got up and clapped. I was so pleased by that gesture that if I had won all the awards passed out at graduation, it would still not have meant as much to me."

It wasn't long before Jacob, like his classmates, found himself pounding the pavement in search of a job. He sent out one résumé after another but received no offers. One day, a reporter from *The New York Times* came around to interview this newly minted, senior lawyer. Someone at the newspaper had heard Jacob's story and thought it would make an interesting feature article. Within days of the article's publication, one of the city's biggest legal advocacy organizations offered Jacob a job handling cases involving older people.

"Considering my health needs and desire to set aside some time for leisure, I wanted to work no more than twenty or twenty-five hours a week," Jacob told us. "I wanted to go into the office no more than four days a week and be able to take long vacations if I wanted to. The company agreed, as long as I got the job done." So Jacob took off on a long-promised month's vacation to Europe with his grandchildren and then reported to a midtown office building to begin his new career as a lawyer.

Jacob's is a success story created through planning, risk-taking, determination, and hard work. And even though his is not a folk tale, it does have an almost "happily ever after" ending. Over the last several years Jacob has become a specialist in Medicare and other public benefit programs, often lobbying lawmakers for better use of such funds. He also gives a great deal of legal advice to social workers and others who have direct contact with the elderly poor and disabled. "It seems to me that the least my country and state can do for seniors is to guarantee them that their standard of living will be equal to what the government agencies have themselves defined as the poverty level," Jacob emphasized, clearly relishing the battle he wages to protect client rights.

Instead of acting like a victim, Jacob is now a victims' advocate. Instead of telling himself, "I can't," he says, "I can." As soon as Jacob stopped using his heart ailments as a justification for a rigid approach to life, his health stopped being a major influence on his choices and lifestyle.

"I don't think I'm essentially different from most people," Jacob concluded. "Perhaps I'm more academically minded or have a bit more willpower, but I think each person is a combination of different elements. As you get older, some elements naturally deteriorate or diminish. The basic human being, however, remains unchanged. Our basic desire to do things for ourselves and with or for other people is still there. I think that most of us have been brainwashed to believe that at a certain age we must turn up our toes and prepare to die."

Jacob then spoke with quiet passion about his dream of living in a country in which older people who still wish to do so are allowed to work part time or share a full-time job with another person. He talked about a society in which an individual is evaluated not on age but on what he or she can accomplish.

"Right now most of my friends are resting comfortably in

Florida or Arizona," he smiled, as an anxious client waited on the telephone for legal advice. "They think I'm a little odd because I'm still working. They find it somehow difficult to accept. And yet the happiest people I know are those who are doing what I'm doing: being active and involved in their own way."

For years Jacob had let a negative voice inside him dictate decisions; the fear of risking something new held him back. It took encouragement and loving support from his family for those interior messages to begin changing. By conceding his own initial resistance to his daughter's challenge, Jacob took the necessary first move in replacing that repetitive, inner-most "I can't" chant with one that says "I will."

Are there new activities that your spouse, family, or friends have encouraged you to try, only to be confronted by your nay-saying? Would you, like Jacob, secretly like to take on a fresh challenge? If the answer is *yes*, you're already on your way to becoming a Late Bloomer.

Many Late Bloomers, including Jacob, have never attended a personal-growth class or read a self-help book. They've never heard the psychological jargon that's bandied about every day in hundreds of achievement-oriented seminars and workshops. And while these Late Bloomers may not recognize their own ideas in the carefully refined exercises served up by the experts, they've unwittingly applied many of these same methods and processes toward making their lives more diverse and satisfying.

If you've ever made a list of New Year's resolutions, you know what it is we're talking about. Or maybe you've smiled when you didn't really feel like it, either to improve your own sour mood or the cranky disposition of a frazzled store clerk. Perhaps you have found yourself discounting a negative remark as soon as it escaped your lips (or somebody else's). These are the kinds of things we do every day without even thinking about them, yet they can be powerful tools when applied to our own self-growth.

A basic belief held by our Late Bloomers is that *attitude affects outcome*. If you think you're going to fail, you almost certainly shall. If you decide you can accomplish something, your optimistic and upbeat attitude will support you in the direction of that accomplishment. Yes, thoughts are just that potent. When we asked the author of *The Power of Positive Thinking* about this, Norman Vincent Peale immediately quoted the Bible: "As he thinketh in his heart, so is he."

Most of us know someone who's tried to stop smoking and failed. The person may without success have tried nicotine gum, support groups, hypnotism, and acupuncture. Yet we all are aware that if you feel deep down that you *can't* quit smoking, you'll probably continue to smoke no matter what strategies you apply. Once you reach the point where you honestly believe you can quit, you'll finally be able to stop.

The responsibility of making a choice is always yours. Your truest feeling about what your future can be is a major ingredient in the process of actually creating and expanding that future. Such is the power of belief. "Whatever you can do, or dream you can do, begin it," wrote the German philosopher Johann Wolfgang von Goethe. "Boldness has genius, power, and magic in it. Begin it now."

Many of our Late Bloomers make the same point with elegant simplicity. "You *always* have a choice," ninety-one-year-old Rebecca told us as we watched the nimble widow put up apricot jam in the kitchen of her Wisconsin farmhouse. "In the end, how you live your life is up to you. You don't have to cross some make-believe finish line to be a winner. Whatever it is you want to do, just go out and do it!"

Compare this positive outlook with the kinds of "safe" responses we've heard (or uttered ourselves) when the suggestion surfaces that it's time to try a different approach. "I can't go to the Wednesday club meetings because I have no way to get there," complains Henry, an arthritic but avid bridge player who's often invited to join a group that convenes weekly at a neighborhood community center.

"I used to enjoy literature," shrugs Muriel, a once-avid reader, "but my eyesight has gotten so bad I've just given it up."

"Since I lost my wife, I've felt guilty and embarrassed about wanting to go square dancing again," sighs a quiet homebody named David.

Many of these limitations may seem to the rest of us like minor inconveniences that are easy to resolve. After all, a fellow card player would probably be happy to give Henry a lift, Muriel could rent or buy audiotapes of classic and best-selling new books or find out about free recordings that are offered to people with limited vision. A relative or friend of either sex might easily join David in the resumption of his favorite social activity.

Little things like losing your driver's license or having to give up salt may not seem to be of the same magnitude as recovering from open-heart surgery or taking radiation therapy treatments. Yet when it enters your life, a barrier that seems small to others can seem to threaten your independence. And each such hurdle challenges us to make life-affirming choices.

So now we'll share another secret, one that can make all

the difference in your life at any age: How you *respond* to events is much more important than what the events actually are. The Late Bloomer's secret, reinforced in every interview we've conducted, is that if your attitude is affirmative, open, and flexible, you can make your life work differently. Even seemingly "negative" situations or events contain possible opportunities for growth. Remember that at first Jacob's health problems seemed disastrous, but ultimately his heart attacks, surgery, and introspection led to new joys and satisfactions.

Bringing about growth *does* require faith, confidence, dedication, and commitment—to *yourself.* Our Late Bloomers have all shown that you must take responsibility for your own life and recognize that it is within your power to create change and move ahead.

Jacob, for example, was at a major crossroads when he made the decision to alter his lifestyle drastically. But the rest of us certainly don't have to wait until we're faced with a physician's dire warning, a daughter's rebuke, or some other challenge before making changes that put us in the driver's seat. We have the opportunity to make such choices every day. Recognizing and accepting those challenges and responsibilities can bring about wonderful and amazing changes at any time in our lives.

Many of us, for example, may feel trepidation about taking a public speaking course or learning to use a computer. Such activities may involve making our way through unfamiliar surroundings, changing daily routines, finding transportation, responding to intimidating technologies, or making new commitments of time and energy. In our individual lives, these presumed "barriers" may grow to proportions that loom as large as those Jacob dealt with.

Here's how some other Late Bloomers have dealt with these challenges.

Amanda F. was determined to overcome the stage fright she'd felt since grade school. She was convinced that this paralyzing fear hindered her career as an affirmative action officer, since it prevented her from advancing to a supervisory position. Amanda decided to build her confidence by giving brief lectures on African American history, a subject in which she was well versed, to small groups of children at the local library. Gradually, she became relaxed enough to speak on the same topic before high school assemblies. Today she is an adept public speaker and, as head of her department, trains up to a hundred recruits at a time.

In one large city, a nonprofit group called The Balding Bytes teaches computer skills to seniors. The organization was founded several years ago by retirees who felt intimidated by the computer science classes being offered at local community colleges. The Balding Bytes use a foundation grant to hire their own private tutor, who teaches members on high-tech equipment donated by a local manufacturer. The nurturing environment that members provide has produced several crops of older students skilled in word processing and using spreadsheet programs.

Here's the story of another Late Bloomer whose experience, like Jacob's, supports our conclusion that "If you can dream it, you can do it!" The secret is to adopt an affirmative attitude that nurtures the dream and encourages it to grow into a reality through purposeful action.

Sylvia K. is a widow living alone in a small house in a popular resort area of a northeastern state. She lives modestly on her Social Security checks and savings. An outgoing woman with many friends, Sylvia has always taken pride in keeping active and meeting the goals she sets for herself. She is careful in her spending so that she can take a trip each year to Europe, Canada, or Mexico.

Yet whenever she came home from vacation, Sylvia always had the same reaction: "I wish I had a garden," she'd sigh, lamenting the fact that the hillsides behind and in front of her otherwise attractive home seem much too steep to grow anything and the cliffs on either side of her house are strewn with jagged rocks. "I'd love to plant some beautiful flowers and watch them grow," Sylvia told herself. "It just isn't sensible," she'd mutter to no one in particular. "Nobody could grow *anything* on this property."

Still, Sylvia often found herself reading gardening manuals and talking about horticulture with her friends. She loved to buy flowers and always kept a fresh arrangement in the vase on her dining room table. In her mind's eye, she could see herself puttering around in a carefully tended garden, wearing a straw sun hat and quietly humming Cole Porter tunes to herself. It was a pleasing yet seemingly impossible fantasy.

One spring day Sylvia visited a woman known throughout the neighborhood for her especially healthy and attractive rosebushes. This time, Sylvia couldn't contain her envy. "You're so lucky," she stammered. "I don't have any room to grow things, so I'll never have a garden."

"That's 'poor me' talk," the neighbor replied, in a firm but loving voice that was more encouraging than critical. "Listen to you! If you really want a garden, you'll find a way to have one."

For the first time, Sylvia wondered whether she had given her excuses the power to shut off every possibility of creating a garden. Perhaps there was a way to realize her dream.

Then one evening after supper, Sylvia was doodling on a piece of paper as she chatted on the phone with one of her grown children. At one point in the conversation, Sylvia found herself writing down this sentence: "I want a beautiful garden of my own." Next to these words she drew a picture of flowers growing, sun shining, and a figure holding a watering can. Above the drawing she added the bold-lettered caption, "MY GARDEN!"

After doing this, Sylvia felt silly and a little bewildered. She didn't know where this strange impulse had come from, but it seemed curiously appropriate. The possibility of a garden now seemed more real than she'd ever imagined possible. She still didn't know how to make it come about, however.

Through the simple act of writing down her vision, Sylvia had done something very important: she had set in motion an unconscious process that gradually strengthened her belief that such a vision could become reality. Confidence and hope began to swell inside her.

These shifts in her thinking led to other changes as well. Sylvia posted what she had written on her bedroom mirror and read its message several times a day. It became an insistent echo in her mind, popping up while she was doing the dishes or driving to the grocery store. Once or twice, when no one was around, she even dared to say the words "I want a beautiful garden of my own" right out loud.

After a few weeks, Sylvia had a clear mental picture of what kinds of flowers she'd have: petunias, zinnias, tulips, poppies, and roses, of course. She envisioned a purple wisteria vine climbing over an arbor and a birdbath full of splashing robins. Then one day, she heard herself say the sentence differently: "I am standing in a beautiful garden of my own."

A possibility for the future had involuntarily moved into the present. Her last vestiges of doubt were beginning to evaporate. Later that week, Sylvia wrote a list of ways to meet her goal. It included such tasks as "buy gardening books" and "talk to experts at a nursery."

Although Sylvia didn't yet dare discuss her fantasy with friends, she found herself getting less defensive with them when the subject of gardening came up. She caught herself before the "I can't" phrase was out of her mouth and rephrased it into something more positive, such as, "What would you do to create a garden if you had a yard like mine?"

Then one of Sylvia's neighbors casually suggested that she ask the local Boy Scout troop to voluntarily terrace her hilly slopes as a group project, building retaining walls and bringing in topsoil for her to fill with flowering plants. Response from the local Scout leader was as enthusiastic as it was immediate. Within weeks, Sylvia's garden had become a reality. She could hardly wait for the sun to come up before she rushed out in her old clothes and strawhat to weed, water, and fertilize. With all the new exercise, Sylvia lost five pounds in the first four weeks. Her heart soared when the first new buds began to appear.

The last time we visited, the local garden club had found Sylvia's backyard so attractive that it had become a frequent setting for the group's monthly get-togethers. The garden is the new hub of Sylvia's social life. "I've made so many new acquaintances that I have to start writing Christmas cards in October in order to get them all mailed on time," joked Sylvia, sipping tea amid her backyard blossoms. "I can't believe I waited so long to plant these wonderful things." Sylvia now concedes that it was her own resistance that first kept her from realizing her dream of creating a garden. As soon as she accepted it as a possibility, she began to feel herself supported toward fulfilling that goal. For Sylvia, a dramatic shift in lifestyle was the eventual outcome of a change of heart.

We hope your creative juices are flowing now and that you're ready for "doing." And that, like Jacob, Sylvia, and our other Late Bloomers, you will experience an invigorating energy bringing new activities, acquaintances, and satisfactions into your life.

Keep in mind that an important part of successful aging is accepting that there are some things you realistically can't do. Your choices may be limited slightly, for instance, if you've had a heart attack or suffered with cancer, or if you use a hearing aid or reading glasses, care for an invalid spouse, or have recently lost a loved one. But the range of possibilities for rewarding activity remains enormous. If you focus on a goal that is realistic and important to you, you've made the first big step toward accomplishing it.

Taking full advantage of life's options isn't simply a matter of adopting a positive outlook, of course. Much still depends on persistence and planning. In upcoming chapters we'll discuss other "building blocks" in greater detail, but suffice it to say here that everyone, not just those who have a certain physical ability, financial security, or lifestyle, can grow and change in later life.

THE SECRET OF ATTITUDE

A key to becoming a Late Bloomer is the secret of attitude. Many of the happiest and most fulfilled older people we've met maintain a state of mind that, rather than clinging fearfully to the past, accepts change and encourages growth. This optimistic point of view, whether conscious or unconscious, affects their behavior and outlook in a positive way, allowing them to realize all manner of life-affirming possibilities through their actions.

An attitude that accepts change and encourages growth can be a guiding force in remaining healthy, upbeat, and invigorated, whatever the date on your birth certificate. The sensation of being fully alive, spirited, and aware is not a function of being young in the chronological sense. We might label the somber working children of Charles Dickens's novels as "old before their time," for example, and in the next breath speak of today's peppy seventy-year-old aerobics enthusiasts as "young at heart."

The secret of remaining truly youthful means tapping into the best energies and qualities we associate with being young, all of which relate to attitude. Our Late Bloomer friends manage to mesh the winning combination of a fresh, optimistic outlook with the kind of wisdom and self-knowledge that comes with each passing day.

We've all been told (especially as we get older) that "you're only as young as you *feel*." Don't be misled by this glib catchphrase. Too often it's translated to mean "you're only as young as you *act* and *look*." A "young" attitude, however, is not a young look; it's what allows us to take calculated risks, tackle new projects, and try fresh approaches.

Some Late Bloomers are fortunate enough to adopt a life-affirming approach early and rely on it to support their continued blooming. Others recognize this principle in their later years and proceed to unlearn negative habits, behaviors, and ways of interacting. Yet both groups share a secret that gives them the necessary energy, strength, and courage to explore life at a time when much of society expects them to slow down, or even stop altogether. It's all in their attitude.

The secret of attitude among Late Bloomers has four main dimensions. First, learn to appreciate and respect your age, whatever that chronological number happens to be. Second, understand and respect the reality you find yourself in, including whatever circumstances you haven't the power to change. Third, recognize what's within your power to change and learn effective ways to accomplish this. And finally, remember that what is *always* within your power is the ability to modify your attitude toward a person, circumstance, or an event.

HOW TO ACT ON THIS SECRET

Consider applying to your own life some of the same approaches the Late Bloomers in this chapter have used. These individuals sometimes intuitively employed a couple of powerful tools that are often used in personal-growth seminars and workshops. We urge you to try them also, since these techniques have proven effective in modifying attitudes.

Although our Late Bloomers were probably unaware of the prevailing psychological terms for what they did, their actions fit the definitions of affirmation and visualization. Affirmations are verbal statements that provide a vivid image of your dream, fantasy, or plan as a present-day reality. Visualizations are mental pictures of that same dream, fantasy, or plan. These images have even more power if they describe, as specifically as possible, how you feel or show what you want.

Here are some examples of affirmations that have been phrased effectively: "I *have* new friends that I see often and enjoy very much." "I *have* an income-producing business of my own that makes me happy."

Another way of stating an affirmation is, "I *am* raising pedigree Yorkshire terriers and am having lots of fun with them." Or, "I *am* learning to speak French and have made reservations for a trip to Paris with my favorite aunt."

Write or repeat out loud your goal or dream in a sentence that begins with the words "I *am*" or "I *have*." Your statement should always be couched in the present tense so that the possibility feels alive. Passive verbs are not as effective, and use of the future tense "I *will*" implies that your goal hasn't been attained. When you say "I *am*" or "I *have*," a subtle but powerful change often occurs that opens the door to opportunities. When you begin acting as if your goal is already a reality, opportunities for accomplishing this goal often surface.

Once you have affirmed your goal or dream in this way, you can begin to nourish it by bringing it into your mind and repeating it several times a day. You may feel a little embarrassed with what feels like talking to yourself, but we urge you to stick with it. Within only a few days, the results are likely to surprise you.

Once you have learned how to phrase an affirmation, you may be ready to try visualization: using the same concept but employing *imagery* rather than *words*. Not everyone finds this an effective technique, since some of us are less visually oriented than others. Nevertheless, it's at least worth a try. Here's how to begin:

Close your eyes and imagine yourself somewhere else, doing something you've often dreamed of. Don't worry if this flight of fancy seems far-fetched or unrealistic. Simply picture yourself in your mind's eye. Do this even if capturing your heart's desire has always seemed impossible. Since this is a kind of game, don't worry about whether your fantasy is "obtainable"; merely pretend for a moment that it is. When visualizing, some people see themselves in a particular place or scene, as if they were appearing in a TV show or movie of the imagination. Others create mental pictures like those conjured up in dreams.

Do you see yourself touring Australia? finding new friends to form a Friday night get-together? walking a mile every morning before breakfast? learning to cook on a Chinese wok? getting a part-time job doing office work? riding a motorcycle? Maybe you imagine yourself composing a letter to your daughter suggesting you make a cross-country trip to visit your grandchildren. Can you see yourself surrounded by smiling faces as you emerge from an airplane at their hometown airport?

Visualization and affirmation are proven empowerment tools that can be extremely effective when repeated over time. They've brought many people closer to living out their fondest desires. This occurs not by magic but through the creation of a more receptive and fertile state of mind for achieving success. We suggest reactivating your affirmations and visualizations with some regularity. Early morning is a good time, or just before going to sleep at night.

Don't expect immediate changes. Be flexible. Accept the process that's slowly taking place inside. The seed you've planted will germinate on its own, growing into possibilities you weren't aware of.

While engaged in these exercises, it's helpful to begin examining the responses that pass through your mind when somebody suggests you do something you've previously postponed, avoided, or discounted. Listen carefully to your wording as you speak. You may realize that you've been placing the responsibility for your indecision somewhere other than on yourself. Listen to these examples of "yes, but" excuses. Does any one of these sound familiar?

"I'd like to go on a Caribbean cruise, but I have no one to travel with."

"I feel so useless without a job, but nobody wants to hire a guy who's over the hill like me."

"I want to visit my son, but he lives in Chicago, and I'm terrified of flying."

Even if these aren't the exact words you'd use, there are times when you've probably expressed similar feelings. This "negative languaging" is the opposite of positive thinking. Without realizing it, you've blamed other people or other situations as a way of masking your own pessimistic expectations. Repeating these rationalizations makes you believe them, and before you know it, you've created a self-fulfilling prophecy. So we suggest that on your way to becoming a Late Bloomer you concentrate on shaping your language in a more positive way. Try approaching each of the above examples in a more affirmative spirit:

"I've found a delightful traveling companion, and we're going on a Caribbean cruise."

"I have located a part-time job where I feel productive and useful."

"I'm taking the train to Chicago and will enjoy the scenery and fellow passengers en route."

Did you notice the difference in the speakers' implied attitude as compared to their earlier statements? Your attitude is always revealed in the way you respond to the opportunities life presents you. Ask yourself whether you create unnecessary problems for yourself or become part of your own solutions. Determining the answer to these questions is often as simple as listening to the words you use, whether they are spoken out loud or confined to the inner dialogue of your mind.

You have the power to set in motion a chain of events that can enrich your life profoundly. We cannot guarantee that changes will occur simply though a shift in attitude, but we assure you that such a transition will expand and improve your range of options and that you are taking the action that accompanies personal growth.

CHAPTER TWO

THE SECRET OF "WHO AM I NOW?"

RETIREMENT AIN'T WHAT IT USED TO BE. Who wants to sit in a rocking chair reminiscing about the "good old days" when so many other possibilities beckon?

We think it's time to permanently retire society's prevailing stereotype of older people as unmotivated has-beens. After all, more than 65 million Americans already belong to the "over 50" club, and another six thousand people join them each day. The vast majority lead stimulating, rewarding, interesting lives during their so-called "retirement years." Thankfully, we're in an era in which the most offensive depictions of older people, like "the absent-minded geezer" and "the eccentric blue-haired lady in tennis shoes," are yielding to more accurate images.

In the course of our Late Bloomer interviews, we've met people who are enrolled in Elderhostel classes, working out for the Senior Olympics, tapping at keyboards, and playing in Ping-Pong tournaments. Some go off to part-time jobs or the new businesses they've started. Others study transcendental meditation, practice yoga, drive dune buggies, or splash around in water ballet classes. Still others volunteer at children's cancer wards, trek through the Himalayas, tap-dance in the living room, or fall in love all over again.

How did these older folks reach the point where they'd try these things? What motivates them to be so adventurous? And what can you do to be more like them? We'll begin to answer these questions through the story of a native midwesterner who shamelessly and wholeheartedly loved what he did for a living, only to have his world turned upside down.

For the better part of forty years, Henry S. worked up the corporate ladder of a nationally known food manufacturer based in Minneapolis. After starting out as a teenage stock boy, Henry moved from one important position to another, inching his way toward the wood-paneled suites of the firm's highest-ranked executives. "By my late fifties, I'd finally 'arrived,'" Henry told us. "I spent the last nine years of my career as a special assistant to the company president, plotting corporate takeovers and negotiating multimillion-dollar business deals. Boy, those were exciting times for me!"

Those times came to a screeching halt at age sixty-five, when Henry was forced to comply with a then mandatory retirement policy. He was honored with a magnificent farewell party, generous bonus, and verbal commitment that his services would be put to use as a consultant. "My colleagues were truly wonderful," Henry said, gazing wistfully into the distance. "I felt very much appreciated and was absolutely certain I'd be seeing them often while working on important projects."

In the short run, that's exactly what happened. After a restful trip to Hawaii with his wife, Sandra, Henry was called in to troubleshoot a subsidiary that had been losing money. A few months later, his former boss sent him to Europe to smooth the ruffled feathers of a valuable client who'd been miffed by a deal gone sour. Henry was also pleased to receive several speaking invitations involving professional organizations he'd long been associated with. Everyone still smiled at Henry and called him by name whenever he showed up at company headquarters. His former colleagues offered to share a noon meal or to get together sometime for coffee.

"But y'know what happened?" he whispered in an incredulous tone. "After about six months, the phone stopped ringing. I was never called in as a consultant again. There was no explanation; they simply stopped calling." Everyone was still delighted to see Henry whenever he stopped by the office, and his former co-workers were eager to find out what he'd been up to, but they gave not the slightest hint that his services were needed or even missed.

Months later, Henry was able to see that his associates meant nothing personal in all this; they had concluded logically that Henry no longer had his finger on the industry's pulse and was therefore no longer the best choice for critical assignments. Henry conceded that he would have acted the same way if he'd been in their shoes.

At the time, of course, Henry felt rejected. And the more spurned he felt, the needier he became. He began timing his errands so that he'd never be away from the house during working hours, just in case someone from the company called to make a request or ask a question. He also began snapping at Sandra, who, in turn, was peeved by Henry's indifference to her feelings. Although Henry found enough projects around the house to keep occupied, he approached these tasks without energy or enthusiasm. "I fixed up the garage as an art studio," Henry said. "Painting had always been a hobby I'd enjoyed. But once I devoted all my spare time to it, something seemed to be missing. I was playing, not working."

Henry spun into a dark spiral of depression. He became listless, grumpy, and withdrawn. Nothing excited him anymore. When his wife or children suggested he try something new, the first words out of Henry's mouth were, "Why bother?" This situation went on for almost two years.

"I'm embarrassed that I didn't figure things out sooner," shrugged Henry. "When I retired, I no longer felt valuable as a person. All my self-esteem had been tied up with my belief that I was somehow indispensable to the company. What a shock it was to discover, after thirty-eight years, that although my colleagues still liked and respected me, they could get along fine without me."

What Henry learned in this moment of revelation was that it was up to *him* to determine his own value as a person. It dawned on Henry that if he could do that, he could let go of the judgment he'd made in his own mind about how unimportant a person Henry was. "I had to accept the fact that I was no longer a pivotal person in the domain of my former employer," Henry said. "That wasn't my world anymore."

The question became: "Who am I, if I'm not the guy I was on the job?" He began to realize that his position in the workplace had almost entirely constituted his self-image. Henry's co-workers had been a kind of surrogate family, filling him with a sense of belonging, power, and prestige. He'd defined himself by his position at work.

Henry apologized to Sandra for handling the transition so badly and for making unreasonable demands on her. Together, they thought about ways to fill the enormous void that loomed in Henry's life. The process wasn't easy, although in many ways it was similar to the kind of problem solving Henry had often engaged in on the job. The difference was that this time he was applying the process to his *own* needs, not those of the corporation.

Henry knew that he'd always been able to think better when he walked through the pristine forest that surrounded the family's summer cabin in Wisconsin. Its solitude and serenity seemed to put things into a sharper focus. An avid bird-watcher, Henry would rise at dawn to watch the many species of waterfowl on a nearby pond. Somehow, the familiar calls and feeding habits of the ducks and geese gave the world order again, and when he got back to the house for breakfast, Henry's life at last seemed manageable.

"It came to me that I really needed to find an activity that both fascinated me and made me feel important," said Henry. "Involvement in the daily world of work was what I missed the most. Even though I was retired, I needed to somehow create something that in a sense became my 'work.'"

But first Henry needed to accept himself in his jobless environment. Over time, he learned to see that he was still worthwhile, creative, and talented. Following many discussions with his wife, children, and friends, Henry decided nature conservation was a field that met his criteria of meaningful, purposeful work. He'd always loved animals and had cataloged scores of species in the woods surrounding his cabin. Henry was alarmed by the decline in wetlands and other prime wildlife habitats in Wisconsin and Minnesota and had read about the efforts being made to save the remaining habitats. He knew that big business was pitching in to help acquire and preserve such precious lands.

"So I've become very active in several regional and national conservation organizations dedicated to preserving or restoring bird and animal habitats," said Henry. "I specialize in lining up large companies for contributions that can be used to create land trusts and conservancies. I speak to corporate boards and trade associations, basically asking for money. I'm proud to say I've raised more than $10 million to make this country a better place."

Henry has recreated the world of work at home by dividing his garage workshop into an art studio and an office. Three mornings each week he reports at nine o'clock to a big oak desk where he writes reports, answers correspondence, makes telephone calls, and receives visitors. His in-home office has a sophisticated computer, photocopier, and fax machine. On work days, Henry takes a lunch break at noon, then heads back to the office for the rest of the afternoon. On his off days, Henry retreats to his studio, where he loves to paint naturalistic watercolors, several of which have been reproduced in national conservation magazines. Every summer he spends at least six weeks with Sandra at their Wisconsin cabin, observing waterfowl, listening to the sounds of the forest, and *enjoying* retirement!

When we asked what advice he had for other executives stepping down from high-powered appointments, Henry had a quick reply: "Being retired involves change and adjustment. The way to accomplish this with success is to acknowledge the responsibility of taking charge of your own choices. You must let go of your past life and have faith that there's something even better out there, even if you don't know exactly what that 'something' is yet."

As Henry discovered, the seemingly simple idea of keeping

self-esteem high is a vital first step on the path to discovering *what* you want to do and *how* you want to do it. Once you acknowledge love and respect for yourself as part of the full appreciation of the person you are, beyond the world of work and child-rearing, you'll find it much easier to explore fresh options and make appropriate changes. This is the fertile topsoil in which fulfilling experiences and new relationships can put down roots and grow.

We've had conversations with other individuals whose situations were different from Henry's, yet who describe similar experiences during dramatic transitions in their own lives. Their varied responses reinforce our belief that there is no single pathway to becoming a successful Late Bloomer— or to acquiring and sustaining a good sense of who you are. Late Bloomers follow their own recipes, to be sure, but their success stories all have a few ingredients in common, including generous doses of self-confidence, a positive self-image, and a healthy level of self-esteem.

Most of us have a pretty full storehouse of these essentials much of the time. They are the inner reserves we depend on to get through the various traumas, hardships, and crises that test us over the course of a lifetime, but we can't always count on our feelings about ourselves remaining constant. Everybody has "off days" when even a sideways look from one's spouse is interpreted as an insult, or a careless lane change by the foolish driver ahead of us feels like a personal affront. A dramatic change like retirement or a major illness can throw our emotions into a tailspin. Sometimes no matter how carefully we've put our lives in order, something knocks it out of kilter. Such changes may open the door to vulnerability and insecurity, so that we're unsure what to do next. Although it's basic human nature to adapt to change, our opinion of ourselves may falter when making post-retirement decisions.

When we asked the late musician and composer John Cage, then seventy-two, what he considered to be the secret of his busy and successful later life, he recounted the story of his father, an inventor. "My dad was always happily self-employed," explained Cage. "Father never had a 'job' in the traditional sense. One morning he got up and puttered around in his workshop until noon, ate a simple lunch, and stretched out for a nap. Then he made a funny sound and died, without ever waking up."

For the senior Cage, because there was never any sharp division between work and "everything else" in his life, he never suffered through the loss of identity and self-esteem often associated with retirement. His son John adopted a similar lifestyle, which kept him busy and satisfied until the day of his own death. "I recommend that everybody experiment with some form of 'self-employment,'" Cage told us, "especially if they hold down some kind of full-time job. This way you'll learn how to work for yourself when that job comes to an end."

John Cage learned, in a very different manner than Henry S., how important it is for all of us to feel somehow that we matter. Most of us are not as fortunate as Cage and other self-actualizing artists, of course, and we usually spend our lives getting those "I matter" feelings from our work or from people we're close to. Unfortunately, largely because of social conditioning, we often feel it vain, selfish, or immodest to seek out this kind of positive feedback from *ourselves*. Try thinking of these "I matter" feelings—whether they're derived from yourself, your work, or from other people—as a kind of "self-love sunshine" that you store up for a rainy day.

If you do this, you can tap into your store of radiant, ego-boosting energy whenever you need it.

Actively seeking "I matter" feelings may feel strange at first, since many of us have made it to our fifties, sixties, seventies, and beyond without ever consciously appreciating ourselves. Henry, for instance, hadn't really thought of himself as a well-connected conservationist until two years after his identity as a businessman became obsolete. Yet once Henry accepted the fact that he deserves recognition for who he is *in his own right*, retirement didn't seem nearly as awkward.

A man named Bob S. sent us a note describing how, after five years of retirement from the insurance business, he'd at last found something that reinforced his conviction that he was still an expert in his chosen field. Through his church, Bob now helps fellow seniors understand Medicare benefits, long-term care insurance, and complex health-related financial issues. "I lived and breathed this stuff," he told us. "I've kept current and feel good about sharing my knowledge with others."

Coincidentally, a few days later a letter arrived in our mailbox from a Virginia attorney named Susan K. who shared the story of her seventy-six-year-old mother, Muriel. "Mom was a very traditional housewife," Susan's letter began, "at least until Dad died and she retired from her teaching job at our small-town high school." Susan explained that Muriel had always viewed herself primarily as a homemaker and teacher. "My mother was raised to be a lady, and a lady she was," the daughter wrote. "She was shy and uncomfortable in any kind of controversy, doing all she could to avoid either confrontation or the spotlight." Yet during her mid-sixties, Muriel began experimenting with the long-suppressed adventurous and outgoing side of her inquisitive nature. She won a seat on the local school board and was eventually appointed to the state board of education.

"She now zestfully tackles each challenge as it comes along," Susan explained, "whether it be a fanatical group of ice hockey parents, the teachers' union (which she faced down), or the governor when Muriel felt he wrongly tried to pin the blame on her board for a political slip-up." This "traditional" Southern belle has taken up sailing and, in what little remains of her spare time, recently took a ride in a glider and joined a friend on a walking tour of England. Somewhere along the line, both Bob and Muriel looked inside and decided they still had a lot to contribute, even in "retirement."

For yet another perspective, we'd like to introduce you to Elsie L., an attractive and bright-eyed seventy-two-year-old, whose healthful, glowing radiance seems to emanate from within. She introduced herself to us after one of our speaking engagements in her home state of Arizona. We were intrigued by this forthright lady with the infectious air of enthusiasm, and she readily agreed to tell us her life story.

"I grew up in a small Michigan town," Elsie began. "I married my high school sweetheart, an assembly-line worker at an auto factory. We settled down and raised a family of nine children. I worked hard and made a nice home."

Throughout her life, Elsie explained, she's been gregarious, sociable, and active. She's always loved serving other people, in whatever capacity seemed appropriate at the time. As her children got older, Elsie obtained a real estate license and began selling houses on a part-time basis. She also became involved in volunteer church work, a rewarding activity that continues to occupy much of her spare time. "I take to church the folks who can't drive, make potato salad on bingo nights—that sort of thing."

After his retirement, Elsie's husband bought a travel trailer, and the couple toured the national parks of Canada and the United States. They camped out for several months before eventually settling down in a suburb of Phoenix. "I'm afraid George just didn't take to the desert," Elsie continued. "Some people don't. After two years, he returned to Michigan, and I decided to stay. I'd started selling real estate again and gotten to know a lot of people here in Arizona. I just couldn't see myself going back East. You know what those winters are like!"

Other problems in Elsie and George's relationship had been building up for a long time. The two had grown apart, and although they'd sought help from their minister and a marriage counselor, their many differences kept getting in the way. Eventually, the couple went through an amicable divorce. "It was a big change for me when George left," Elsie recalled, pulling from her wallet a well-worn photo of her children and grandchildren at a family reunion. "I was so used to taking care of others. I always felt worthwhile and useful as long as I had other people around, so I took in an elderly boarder and his dog to keep me company. I knew that having them around would make me feel better."

Elsie enjoyed making meals for Don, a pensioner in his nineties, and twice a day they walked his old beagle, King. As the real estate market cooled, Elsie found herself spending more and more time at home. She gave up selling houses entirely, so she found plenty of time to look after Don, who was alert and companionable but in fragile health. Elsie had not had the opportunity to care for her parents when they were old and frail, and in a way she regarded Don as a kind of father figure. Within the year, however, he was gone.

"He died quietly in his sleep," she explained. "Just worn

out, they told me. I missed him terribly at first. Still do."

After Don's death, Elsie found herself going through the built-up grief and sadness she felt for her husband George as well as for her boarder. Her sense of loss, which she hadn't allowed herself to feel before, seemed overwhelming. She found herself completely alone in the rambling ranch-style home with no one to take care of, no one to give to or to serve. She realized that she'd always relied on others to nourish her sense of worthiness.

"I guess everybody goes through black times," she sighed, then looked aside and paused a moment before continuing. "That's what those days were like for me. I didn't feel like I was *anyone*. I felt kind of like I wasn't even there." Elsie needed a pat on the back, and her own arms didn't reach that far. Now there was nobody else around who could lend her theirs. She floundered in her loneliness, searching aimlessly for something that might help her feel that she was making a contribution to the world—and to herself.

Some well-meaning friends suggested she get more involved in the church, take a part-time job, or go off on a trip—anything to occupy her time and engage her energy. Despite their pleas, Elsie preferred keeping to herself. When she did go out, she felt as though she were living underwater, in a dull, dim environment full of muffled sounds and gray landscapes. "This seemed like my time for reflection and solitude, things I'd never made much time for," she explained. "I'd always kept so busy helping others—George, our nine kids, Don, my real estate clients. It was a time to find *me*."

Elsie allowed herself to experience the depression she felt. By nature and temperament, however, she had always been a friendly, talkative person, and her desire to communicate was still there. Yet talking out loud to herself, listening to the words bounce off the walls of the big house, seemed foolish. One day, Elsie remembered that talking to others had always brought her out of blue moods in the past. "So I did the next best thing I could think of," said Elsie. "I started writing." First she sat at the kitchen table and wrote simple verses, all expressing the faith she felt in the value of her own life. "I don't know why, I just had to put some of my thoughts down on paper and focus on my feelings about myself. It had been so long since I had someone I could really talk to. It was a start in making friends with myself."

Over the next six months, Elsie shaped her thoughts into polished poems. She'd never written anything more than a personal letter before and certainly had no ambition to become a published poet. Elsie's simple, unadorned verse merely reflected her homespun philosophy, belief in God, and the intrinsic positive value of people, including herself.

Although she'd begun writing as a way out of her depression, the activity quickly became a means of getting in touch with her inner self. Through the process of affirming her own positive qualities and accomplishments, Elsie felt nurtured from the inside out. "I wrote my first poems to help me feel good about myself, to appreciate my value as a special individual. I became aware of my uniqueness and my ability to continue growing."

Here are a few stanzas from a verse our friend has written on precisely this theme. "It's called 'I'm Important,'" Elsie explained before reciting the words to us, "because that's what my message is all about."

Everyone needs to be important.
That's not the least bit wrong.
It's our God-given value
Needing to be actualized.

How shall I manifest this—make it happen?
To start with, I can make today count.
To see to it that each day I do
Something that I feel good about doing.

All these things—and you'll think of many more—
Can make one feel important
And realize one's true worth
In the great harmony of the Universe.

Heartfelt reflections like these helped validate Elsie's sense of self-worth. "I know that writing these poems helped bring me out of my depression," she said. "I remember when I started to feel like I wanted to get up in the morning again. I was coming back into the real world."

Elsie told us that when she felt brave enough to begin sharing her poetry with some neighbors and friends, they urged her to assemble it in a booklet. One self-published volume led to another, as Elsie turned her attention to childhood memories, humorous anecdotes, nature stories, and spiritual meditations. Now our friend has a stack of photocopied, hand-stapled pamphlets she hands out to friends, relatives, and anyone else who seems interested. She carries extra copies of "I'm Important" in her purse wherever she goes. "I can tell when people aren't feeling very positive about themselves, and I like to give them a copy of my book," Elsie explained. "It's a boost for them and a boost for me."

The urge to express feelings on paper ultimately led Elsie into a love affair with writing and a new and fulfilling lifestyle. On her own, Elsie did something that many counseling professionals and facilitators advise their clients to do. She used an external process to acknowledge, support, and build up a feeling of deservedness. Instinctively, Elsie found a way of reinforcing her sense of self-worth.

When she designed the cover of her first collection of poetry, Elsie decided to use very large, boldface type for the booklet's title: I'M IMPORTANT. She wanted to make sure everybody who picked up a copy knew what her poems were all about. The words she picked were exactly what she herself needed to hear.

Elsie's story demonstrates how important it is to recognize when you need a little reinforcement in life, especially at times when your self-confidence and self-image are shaky or downright negative. Since boosting our self-confidence isn't always something we can do for ourselves, we suggest you keep in mind that outside help is available. Counselors, psychologists, and therapists are trained to support you at times like these, should you feel professional help is appropriate. You may also want to see your medical doctor, who can discuss the advisability of prescription medicine.

THE SECRET OF "WHO AM I NOW?"

There's no more powerful secret involved in becoming a Late Bloomer than cultivating a positive opinion of yourself. When you don't view yourself as worthy and deserving, it's hard to feel nourished, supported, and respected in life. On the other hand, if you maintain a confident self-image, your very outlook encourages affirmative change and healthy growth.

Knowing you're an essentially good and decent human being comes from seeing and accepting who you are, warts and all, at this point in time and space. The secret lies in your ability to look beyond your own flaws and imperfections—and those of others—in order to live more fully and compassionately. The idea is to neither ignore shortcomings nor gloat on accomplishments but to take it all in as the essence of what a person is: a special being, unlike any other. This process of nonjudgmental acceptance, holding yourself in high regard and seeing yourself as a worthwhile person, becomes a fundamental building block for personal growth. It isn't something you necessarily go around repeating every day: it becomes, ideally, part of the weave and fabric of who you are and what you're becoming.

In her book *You Could Feel Good*, psychologist Suzanne Harrill defines self-esteem as "a place of knowing yourself, accepting yourself, loving yourself, enjoying yourself, and being yourself." In short, self-esteem grows from loving yourself unconditionally.

If you want to feel better about your life and its late-blooming potential, learning to build and nurture your self-esteem is a goal deserving of your very best efforts.

HOW TO ACT ON THIS SECRET

Late Bloomers discover and act on the secret of deciding "who am I now?" in a variety of ways. For Henry, involvement in a cause he believed in—one that made excellent use of his considerable talents and skills—became a way of being good to himself and supporting his positive sense of worth. For Elsie, the act of writing and publishing her innermost thoughts became a way of affirming and nurturing herself.

For others, similar results may come through such varied activities as tutoring an underprivileged child, enrolling in a French cooking class, organizing a church picnic, playing a set of tennis with old friends, or spending quality time with family members.

Your positive self-image might be further enhanced by giving in to "indulgences" you've felt you didn't really deserve, like going to the beauty parlor, shopping for a new car, taking yourself to a movie, or sharing a gourmet meal with a favorite friend.

Building self-esteem is like putting nickels and dimes into a piggy bank: taken one by one, the wealth of image-building activities may seem insignificant, but when the container is finally opened, you'll discover a significant nest egg. Habitually reminding yourself that you're a worthwhile person in small ways, day by day, can add up to a big boost in self-esteem. Take time to get in touch with yourself, to experience and express approval, affection, and appreciation for who you really are. The process can make an enormous difference at any stage of life, but it's especially valuable in our later years, because society often discounts the worth of an older person, dealing blows to our self-esteem.

As we age, we are sometimes hard on ourselves for reasons that are complicated and deeply rooted. This harsh self-judgment often grows out of the empty spaces that were left unfilled when our careers ended, our children left home, or our marriages changed.

One effective way to replace these negative self-judgments with more productive and positive emotions is through use of the visualization techniques described in chapter 1: using the mind's eye to conjure up a fresh outlook that can nourish present-day experience. This approach replaces "bad stuff" with "good stuff," trading negative images for positive ones.

To start, we encourage you to take a few moments to recall a time, place, or circumstance when you felt you were truly at your best. Imagine being fully at peace, in tune with your body, and filled with the joy of simply being alive. Remember how it felt to really *like* who you were (and still are)—to feel fully content and confident? Perhaps your wedding day fits this description (judgment: "I'm attractive and worth loving"), or the moment you got your first big raise or promotion at work (judgment: "I'm a valued asset"). Maybe these memories involve a bygone love affair (judgment: "I'm sexy and appealing"), birth of a child (judgment: "I'm a giver of new life"), completion of a dream house (judgment: "I've managed my affairs well and deserve a fine home"), or the experience of a relaxing vacation (judgment: "I've earned this holiday").

If we transfer these warm, supportive feelings from the past to the present, our whole outlook on life can change dramatically. The secret is to hang on to these nurturing images of ourselves as we go about our daily lives and to recreate them whenever we need them. In other words, put them to use for real and tangible benefits.

Focusing on the positive emotions anchored in our past may become difficult as we get older, when we perhaps feel burdened by a lifetime's accumulation of miscellaneous travail and woe. Keeping our attention on the times we felt in top form is like putting out a welcome mat for the kind of self-renewing energy that allows us to become Late Bloomers.

CHAPTER THREE

THE SECRET OF FORGIVENESS

REMEMBER FIBBER MCGEE'S CLOSET in the old *Fibber McGee and Molly* radio series of the 1940s and 1950s? The tiny space was so overstuffed that whenever an unsuspecting McGee opened the door to put something inside, an enormous pile of long-forgotten junk rained down on the hapless fellow's head. This pack rat never threw anything away and preferred to simply stuff everything back inside, so the problem kept getting worse. Because he never got around to cleaning up his mess, McGee went through the same humiliating experience every time he cracked open the closet door.

Like McGee's closet, our minds fill up, year after year, with unsupportive psychological baggage that we don't necessarily need or want yet can't quite bring ourselves to deal with, let alone dispose of. Too often we cling to this baggage without really knowing why. In fact, we may have no clear recollection of what's packed inside.

Frequently, our mental baggage is packed with all sorts of

negative judgments about ourselves and others that we've been squirreling away for years. These judgments relate to things we've done that we wish we could somehow make right, once and for all. What gnaws at us are the uncomfortable feelings we create with our judgments.

Often, we're not even consciously aware of the existence of these dark thoughts and repressed emotions. Sometimes we can't steel ourselves to get rid of them in any event, since that would entail confronting memories that make us uncomfortable. Some of us are convinced that nothing we could do would make up for the perceived injury that's been visited upon us or that we have caused another. Instead of dismissing or dealing with these judgments, therefore, we cling to them with an iron grip. When that happens, they wind up shaping the picture of ourselves (and others) that we take with us everywhere.

"It was so stupid to make that investment," you may find yourself scolding (judgment: "I make rotten decisions"). Or, "How could I have treated my mother so badly?" (judgment: "I'm a lousy son"). Or, "Why did I say such a mean and nasty thing to my best friend?" (judgment: "I'm a petty person").

These negative judgments are not always directed at ourselves, of course. They are just as often aimed at others:

"How could my spouse divorce me and neglect his children?" you ask a friend (judgment: "My former husband deserves my angry wrath"). Or you wonder, "Why is my boss so unfair to me?" (judgment: "I deserve better treatment by my insensitive employer"). Or, "That drunk driver ruined my life when she ran into my car" (judgment: "I'm a victim of someone else's careless behavior").

These heavy, unresolved feelings are like cumbersome steamer trunks. They weigh our spirits down, take up valuable space in our heads and hearts, and keep us from letting go of the past and moving forward. They are a major hindrance to becoming a Late Bloomer, since they tend to stunt or distort our personal growth. Here are two examples of the way criticism of self can stand in the way of late-life blooming.

Edward B. retired ten years ago from his position as a New Jersey plumbing contractor. Looking back on the intervening decade, the seventy-two-year-old former businessman confided something to us during our interview that left him feeling pretty ashamed. "I haven't done much with my retirement time," Edward announced. "Most of my friends are happy and have projects that keep them busy, or groups of people they get together with on a regular basis. I guess I just never bothered to figure out my retirement plans. I've always been hopeless when it comes to taking that kind of responsibility." He shrugged his shoulders and continued talking. "I don't like this about myself, but I guess I'm just lazy. I feel doomed. Anyway, it's too late now for me to do anything about retirement." Edward's self-judgment: "I'm not as good as other people in planning things, and it's impossible for me to change."

Another acquaintance, a widow in her seventies named Judith L., told us she had given up traveling, including making trips to see her grandchildren, because the wheelchair she had recently started using made it difficult for her to get around. "My kids have enough to worry about as it is," she sighed. "Why should I make their lives even more complicated? I don't like being such a shut-in, but let's face it, I'm better off staying at home." Judith's self-judgment? "I'm a nuisance and a burden to others."

In order to clear out the excess baggage blocking personal

growth, it's important to recognize the central role that judgment of self and others plays in our lives, then learn to forgive ourselves and others for these judgments. It is only through forgiveness that we can achieve the inner peace that, in turn, frees us to embrace the present fully without the need to reenact or hold on to our past. Although the two processes are similar and interrelated, we'll deal with *self*-judgment and *self*-forgiveness separately from judgment and forgiveness of *others*. First, let's look at the way we judge—and can subsequently forgive—ourselves.

The *American Heritage Dictionary* offers "censure" as one definition of "judgment," and this is the one we'll be using here. To "forgive," the dictionary suggests, is "to excuse a fault or offense; to give up or let go." The process central to this chapter, therefore, involves letting go of censure. Or, put another way, forgiving a judgment on oneself or others.

In our examples, Judith and Ed are tripping over mental steamer trunks that inhibit them from fully exploring late-life options. Their self-judgments, though logical and pragmatic in their own minds, are needlessly limiting. With a change in attitude, Judith could be seeing more of the people and places she loves, while Ed could be exploring a wide range of fulfilling retirement options.

When we hold on to such negative attitudes, making way for positive self-evaluation becomes nearly impossible. Until we do something—*anything*—the old stuff keeps getting in the way. Like Fibber McGee, we often find it easier to shut the door and walk away with a fatalistic shrug, saying, "That's just the way I am." Sadly, we are thus settling for a negative self-image, one that stifles growth and ignores opportunity.

It's important to understand that having a positive

self-image doesn't mean that we're faultless people, that we don't have significant limitations, or that everything we've ever done is absolutely wonderful. After all, if we acted like saints all the time the world would be pretty boring. We're not any less worthy because we occasionally goof up or do dumb things. "I'm so stupid," we may scold ourselves after berating a loved one, bouncing a check, or burning the toast. We are not really stupid, although what we *did* may have been.

Consider our friend Audrey, a seventy-three-year-old mother of four grown children who lives in Rhode Island with her seventy-five-year-old husband, Tom, a retired electrical engineer. "Almost from the moment Debbie, my youngest child, left home, I began to heap blame on myself for being a lousy mother," Audrey recalled during a conversation in her suburban home, "not just as far as Deb was concerned, but with regard to all my kids. I just couldn't stop finding fault with myself for things I'd done—or didn't do."

Audrey conceded to us that each of her children turned out "basically fine," with fairly successful marriages, happy offspring, and rewarding careers. Yet certain things still troubled her. "I see Donna, the oldest girl, being a real drill sergeant with her twins, Joshua and Jennifer," Audrey explained. "I can't help thinking, *Was I too strict with Donna when she was little? Is this the role model I became for her?*" Audrey's two sons, Randy and Roger, raised a different set of concerns. "Neither of them seems to know how to handle money," she explained. "They run up huge credit card bills and can't seem to save a dime. I say to myself, *If only I'd resisted the temptation to spoil them.* But my tendency when they were growing up was to give the boys everything they asked for, because I wanted their lives to be easier than mine.

I didn't want them to suffer the deprivation that I did, growing up so poor in the Depression."

With time and self-discipline, Audrey said, she's been able to let go of her anxiety and guilt about her parenting. As a young married couple, she and Tom were preoccupied with all sorts of problems, including conflicts in their own relationship. They learned to raise children as they went along. "We were practically kids ourselves," Audrey laughed. "We did the best we could. If mistakes were made, they weren't intentional. So many factors form a child's personality that I know now I can't take responsibility for everything."

For Audrey, part of the self-forgiveness process relates to her newfound role as grandmother. With her three grandchildren, Audrey feels she is applying the wisdom of experience, taking time and exercising patience in ways she could never appreciate as a harried young mom forty years ago. "I know I'm still not perfect," Audrey smiled, "and I can forgive myself for that."

Self-judgment over parenting is one of the most common examples of the way in which older people sometimes paralyze themselves with the baggage of unresolved feelings. At some point, all parents need to realize that they are no longer responsible for the behavior of their adult children. Forgiving themselves for any real or imagined shortcomings can relieve mothers and fathers of enormous burdens that may make it difficult for them to move forward.

"If you were wiser and more aware, you could have done something very different, but you weren't," points out Bill Ferguson in *How to Heal a Painful Relationship*. "You only knew what you knew at the moment. . . . Sometimes the way we see life and what we know is not enough to avoid making mistakes. We need to forgive ourselves for that."

Audrey's story raises important questions about human behavior that defy easy answers. Why are we so quick to condemn ourselves? Why does our judgment of one act often become our total judgment of ourselves? Why do we make overgeneralizations about ourselves, concluding that we're inept or stupid? And, as a corollary to this, why do so many of us have a negative reaction to the concept of self-love, the idea that we deserve a *positive* judgment of ourselves as opposed to a *negative* one?

Perhaps because, for many of us, self-love conjures up images of ego and conceit, like the loud braggart who can destroy an otherwise pleasant dinner party with interminable stories about how marvelous he is. Understand that we're using self-love in a very specific sense here: not to mean narcissism or vanity but as the positive image we have of ourselves when we're feeling good about who we are underneath it all. Feeling self-love is simply having a healthy appreciation of ourselves, including "the good, the bad, and the ugly." Self-love, by our definition, is unconditional acceptance of ourselves.

Even this concept of self-love is difficult for many people to accept fully and implement in their daily lives. Haven't we been taught that it's immodest to say nice things about ourselves within earshot of others? Isn't it better to be self-effacing, always directing compliments to other people and catering to their needs first? Do we dare say, "Gosh, maybe I'm a good person too"?

Self-love means treating yourself as well as you treat other people you care about. Or, to turn the Golden Rule inside out: "Do unto yourself what you would have yourself do unto others." It may sound odd, but as someone once pointed out,

"If we treated our friends the way we treat ourselves, we soon wouldn't have any!"

Self-love is not only about appreciating yourself, it's about letting yourself know that this is how you feel, knowledge most often demonstrated by small gestures like praising yourself for a special talent or accomplishment. When you cook a delicious meal, for instance, give yourself credit for the pleasure it brings others. Are you a loyal and generous friend? Then by all means acknowledge these qualities in yourself. Plan your activities so you get to display your value to others. It's like being president of your own fan club.

Most of us engage in negative self-judgment so often that we're rarely aware we're doing it, perhaps because we frequently use rote phrases like "I'm giving myself a hard time" or "I'm really beating myself up." You'll notice how your friends frequently counter with suggestions of their own, admonishing you to "be gentle with yourself" or "lighten up."

Negative self-judgment is such an ingrained response that we sometimes need constant feedback in order to break the habit. One of our Late Bloomers, who says she began to appreciate herself only after age sixty, sent along a copy of the following reminders. Catherine keeps this list taped to the front of her refrigerator, where she can read it every day. We include it here as a wonderful example of positive self-judgment and helpful affirmation:

Because I am the only person I will have a relationship with all of my life, I choose:

• To love myself the way I am now.

- To always acknowledge that I am enough just the way I am.
- To love, honor, and cherish myself.
- To be my own best friend.
- To be the best person I would like to spend the rest of my life with.
- To always take care of myself so that I can take care of others.
- To always grow, develop, and share my love of life.

One of the benefits of truly knowing we're okay is the ease with which we can forgive past actions and let go of negative judgments from the past. It's impossible to simultaneously accept yourself as being an inherently "bad" person and a "good" person. One self-assessment drives out the other.

"When my marriage began I was a compulsively neat housekeeper," our friend Marianne, age seventy-seven, confided to us. "Somehow I was convinced that if a neighbor saw a ring around my bathtub, she'd never speak to me again. Fortunately, I realized eventually that being a mediocre housekeeper doesn't make one a mediocre person."

Another person we interviewed, sixty-eight-year-old Stephen, a retired accountant, confessed that he'd spent many years berating himself "for being a lousy father" after recognizing that he'd neglected his children during their formative years. "I hated who I was for who I'd been," Stephen explained. "Over time my kids helped me accept the fact that my behavior had changed, and they really liked the man I'd become . . . and that I should too."

If we are to grow and change in later life, we must learn to forgive ourselves. This means not forgetting or ignoring things we may dislike about the past or our personalities but finding ways to accept and release them. Self-forgiveness involves more than letting go of the past; it allows acceptance of praise as something you genuinely deserve and the redefinition of *selfish* as legitimate concern for yourself. It means feeling basically okay about simply "being you" and recognizing that you're a person you enjoy knowing, now and for the rest of your life. Remember, we all make self-judgments about what we are and what we aren't, what we did and what we didn't do. But we don't need to hang on to them; we can forgive, let go, and move on. "It took me two years of thrashing around," the late-blooming retired executive Henry S. told us, "but finding out I was still a person I really liked outside the world of work was one of the great turning points of my entire life."

The close connections between self-acceptance, self-esteem, making changes, and risk taking are very important. Why? Because they tend to reinforce and feed off each other. It is helpful to think of them as the cornerstone of attitude: the foundation of our most basic feelings about ourselves. And, as noted, our attitude has a tremendous impact on our willingness to take healthy risks and make life-affirming changes. If we can't forgive ourselves and others, our resentment and anger darkens our feelings like an umbrella, shrouding the pathway to personal growth. Once we let go, through the process and practice of forgiveness, we are free to live a new way.

Now let's examine what's involved in judging and forgiving others. The subject is important, because freeing ourselves from angry or hurtful feelings toward others opens our lives to wonderful new possibilities. In short, it allows us to bloom.

Television personality Hugh Downs, interviewed at age seventy by Connie Goldman and Phillip Berman for their book *The Ageless Spirit*, concluded that one of the best things about aging was realizing he didn't "have to hate anybody" anymore. "When I was very young," said Downs, "I had a lot of hatreds that came from fears. Now there's nobody I fear, and therefore there's nobody I hate. That's a great freedom, because hate, as somebody said, is a weapon you wield by the blade and it just cuts you up. But if you don't fear, you don't hate. There's a great liberty in [that]."

The act of forgiving others often connects us with profound emotional or physical pain. The source of this pain can be a psychic or emotional injury so deep and long lasting that our whole life has been affected. This is why releasing such pain may change our outlook on everything.

You probably have known couples who, after thirty or forty years of marriage, broke up because one partner or the other was restless or simply didn't feel love anymore. A woman we know named Clara was filled with bitter hatred and seething rage when Gus, her husband of thirty-eight years, left her abruptly, saying he'd been bored with Clara for a decade. "I have to find another life," Gus told her. "I can't stand being with you."

Clara was so hurt and angry that she refused to allow her children to mention their father's name in her presence and did her best to turn them against Gus, who eventually remarried.

Beverly Flanigan, a professor of social work at the University of Wisconsin and author of *Forgiving the Unforgivable*, notes that such wounds can deform and distort one's personality for life, if they're allowed to. In an article for the newsletter *Bottom Line Tomorrow*, she cites the example of Ann, the mother of two small children, who, when she drove home from work one day, found a moving van full of family belongings parked in her driveway. Ann's husband, Jerry, walked out of the house and announced calmly that he was abandoning her and the children for a woman with whom he'd been having a secret love affair. Jerry climbed into the van and drove away, leaving Ann speechless and bereft.

These kinds of incidents don't always involve couples, of course. We are reminded of two women who lived in the same neighborhood and became intimate friends. Denise told Margaret everything, including the family secret that her oldest son had recently been sentenced to prison on a drug charge. When Margaret carelessly betrayed this confidence during a casual coffee klatch, Denise felt deeply hurt. It became impossible for her to trust any of her woman friends. She stopped seeing not just Margaret but her other neighborhood friends as well. "Injuries like these seem unforgivable," Flanigan concedes, "but it is vital to forgive them. If you don't, the aftereffects of anger can poison your whole life. . . . They change your whole outlook on the world—and other people."

Accepting responsibility for yourself—and dealing with your past and future—is an ongoing process. It is not the sort of thing you do once and then forget about. It is, rather, a continuous unfolding that demands adaptability. It needs to accommodate sickness as well as health, bad times as well as good, age as well as youth. Forgiveness and acceptance require humility because we do not always conform to our preferred image of ourselves, nor do others. "There is everything to gain and nothing to lose in forgiving," Dorothy Larsen writes in *A*

Touch of Sage. "When we forgive those who have offended us, we are not doing it for them, but for ourselves."

The Bible, too, reminds us that forgiveness is its own reward. "Forgive and you will be forgiven," Christ advises his followers in Luke 6:37. "For the measure you give will be the measure you get back."

Each morning and each evening, Barry M. gives thanks for the power of forgiveness, which has helped keep him sober and drug-free for nearly a decade. At age fifty-seven, Barry feels like he is "living a dream." The life that the recovering alcoholic and drug addict once fantasized about has become real.

Barry's journey wasn't easy—and he is the first to admit that his own dogged perseverance and tenacious temperament helped bring him success after twenty-five years spent in and out of treatment facilities. Although he was raised as a member of a wealthy, privileged Indiana family, Barry found himself in an ongoing cycle of drinking and drug using that he seemed unable to control. And once the highs wore off, his unhappiness always returned.

"I finally realized that I had unresolved, painful issues with family, self-image, self-esteem, and negative reinforcement that I'd grown up with. My father, for example, was an alcoholic who told me at the age of nine that I was no good, would never amount to anything, and that the only reason people would ever like me was because of my money."

As a child, Barry's father beat him regularly, often flying into unpredictable rages during bouts of drinking. "The attacks came whenever I did anything that displeased my dad," Barry recalls, adding that his father was also verbally and emotionally abusive. "I never knew when he would attack me. What might be a transgression one day would bring praise the next. There was no consistency." Barry's birth mother divorced and moved away when her son was four years old. The stepmother who arrived soon after did not know how to handle the situation, which only intensified Barry's alienation from his father. At the age of eight, Barry began smoking cigarettes. At twelve he started drinking and at twenty-one he began a love affair with marijuana that lasted twenty-seven years, eventually leading to abuse of cocaine, heroin, and other drugs.

"I grew up evading unpleasant situations," Barry remembers, noting that his family's affluence and high profile encouraged authorities to handle his drug-related problems with kid gloves. "Because I had money, I didn't need or want to have a career. I got the message from my father from an early age that I couldn't do anything right, so I figured, *Why do anything?* It became a self-fulfilling prophecy."

During periods when he wasn't drinking heavily or abusing drugs, Barry enjoyed some successes. He became a firearms expert during a three-year hitch in the Army and later earned a college degree. Yet his addictions always got the better of him. An embarrassment to his parents, he eventually moved from Indiana to California, where it was easier to buy marijuana, LSD, cocaine, and heroin. Barry was in and out of seventeen drug treatment programs—as well as two failed marriages and numerous jobs—before he hit bottom in his midforties.

"In 1989, I met a Sister of Mercy nun who was a recovering alcoholic and a drug-abuse counselor. It was Sister Monica's firm intervention that really saved my life. She simply decided that it was her job—maybe even her mission from God—to protect me and to get me sober. She was my virtual guardian angel and wouldn't take no for an answer."

For more than eighteen months, Barry allowed Sister Monica to handle the logistics of his daily life. She found an apartment for him, took control of his money, and gently urged him to change his self-destructive ways. Barry couldn't understand her unwavering faith in his ability to get off booze and drugs, since he himself wasn't sure if he could conquer his addictions. In time, Sister Monica's optimism became contagious. Barry's thinking began to shift, even though his self-defeating behavior often prevailed.

"One day in June of 1990, I was sitting on my couch watching TV, my empty bottle of wine on the floor. Sister Monica came in and said, 'Barry, don't you think it's time for you to take some responsibility for yourself and stop hiding from the world?' I tried to ignore her, but I just couldn't. I surprised myself by focusing instead on the motivation and strength that had been building up inside me. I knew I didn't want to hide from myself any longer. So I simply got up and went to the phone and called [a treatment facility] and I said I needed help. Sister Monica drove me up the next day and that's the last time I had a drink."

His mentor's strong support had inspired Barry to believe in himself in a way he never had before. For the first time, the possibility of a new way of life began to seem real. Although he would have been the last to admit it, a seed of hope was beginning to grow in Barry's heart.

Besides Monica's persistence, what made the difference for Barry was his eventual willingness to come to terms with his past. "During the next four months, those who treated me were smart enough to ask the right questions, and I was honest enough to answer them truthfully."

Barry came to a better understanding of his upbringing through private psychotherapy sessions and treatment at the live-in rehabilitation center. In time, he was finally able to forgive his father and others in his life who had contributed to his downward spiral. Most important, Barry was able to forgive himself for not having taken responsibility for his self-destructive attitudes and behavior. "I had been ashamed of who I was and I didn't know why," he explains. "I had to go back to ground zero, reassessing myself and how I related to other people. My treatment gave me a start; the people at the center became my new family."

Barry was able to acknowledge that he had participated in previous treatments mainly to get people off his back. "I was afraid to drink and I was afraid not to drink," he says, recalling how his various bosses and wives pestered him into getting help. "Eventually I became sick and tired of the life I lived, and I figured that the only way I was going to change things was to understand why I was doing them in the first place. I had to face the negative emotions I'd been avoiding and learn where they came from—what caused all my pain and fear in the first place. I slowly made inroads into some of those keys issues. Day by day, my life was changing for the better."

After his discharge from the treatment center, Barry spent three months in a halfway house, plunging headlong into the Alcoholics Anonymous program. He later moved to a new city where he could begin his new life. Determined to pursue his long-neglected education, which Barry had abandoned under the assumption that he would never amount to anything, he enrolled in a nearby college. Barry's impressive 3.96 grade point average eventually earned him a master's degree and certification in counseling.

Another way Barry built his self-esteem was by volunteering twenty hours each week at the center where he received his addiction treatment. He discovered that the more he gave, the more he got back. "I've been helping people through their own recovery processes," Barry explains. "I'm proud of what I do, and if I keep doing it, I doubt that I'll ever drink again." He now has a paying job as a clinical advisor and program developer for people in recovery.

Besides being happy, gainfully employed, and drug-free, Barry has been able to expand the circle of understanding and forgiveness to his two sons, aged twenty-nine and thirty. "We've worked through a lot of stuff," says Barry, conceding that he was either absent or high on drugs during most of his sons' formative years. "There was resentment and anger, but recently we've really developed a support system for each other."

Barry is the first to point out that when it comes to personal transformation, there are many different ways to get to the same place. Because each person and problem is unique, direct intervention by a treatment center or therapist is not necessarily appropriate for everyone who is dealing with addiction. Barry dismisses the idea that those who are wealthy have better access to such care, noting that financial aid is often available for addicts. What are more important than money and clout, Barry says, are motivation and diligence. In order to make lasting and meaningful change, we must take our fate into our own hands. Such changes don't simply happen in the head, but in the heart and spirit as well. For Barry, the deep-seated avoidance and lifelong denial of his deepest feelings finally led to the healing and transformative power of forgiveness.

"I've forgiven myself for those many tough years, and I've redefined a time in my life that others might label as failure as a time of preparation for recovery instead," Barry says. "Viewed in that light, I'm very grateful, and I know in my heart that I, personally, needed to experience all that tragedy in order to do what I am doing today, which is helping people who not very long ago were in the same shape I was.

"Something in me wanted to conquer my problems—not only to survive but to reinvent myself and really thrive. I can't explain it. Maybe I was simply meant to do this work and perhaps that is what kept me trying, again and again, to beat my addictions. Whatever the reason, it sure feels like a miracle."

It took seventeen treatment programs for Barry to see his miracle. It's important to recognize that the insights and changes we've been describing in this chapter won't always strike you like the proverbial "bolt of lightning" or "ton of bricks." Let's be realistic. We're not talking about white lights or high drama here. The changes we're talking about are subtle and gradual, yet very powerful. You may feel more open, trusting, willing to experience and acknowledge whatever comes your way. You may notice that you are taking better care of yourself: standing up straighter, getting more physical exercise, speaking up for yourself with more assurance, seeking quiet time for contemplation, and perhaps saying no, politely but resolutely, to people who make unwanted and unproductive demands on you. You may hear yourself talking about your accomplishments and needs in a different way or risking new things you've always wanted to try but kept postponing. These changes will open the door to a life that's more comfortable and, at the same time, more dynamic and exciting.

We are reminded of the story of an eager student of the

world's religions who climbed a high mountain to question a legendary and venerable guru. After completing his ascent, the callow young man rushed to the side of this wise old teacher and demanded, "Please tell me what my life will be like after I attain enlightenment!"

The meditating sage opened his eyes and blinked down at his visitor, then responded in a calm, even voice: "Before you are enlightened, you chop wood and carry water. After enlightenment, you will also chop wood and carry water."

So it is with us. We will still have the joys, fears, angers, and familiar details of our lives. We'll just approach them in a different way, with an updated attitude, as we begin feeling better about ourselves.

All the shifts in thinking, feeling, and behaving that we have discussed in this chapter will take some exploration, effort, and persistence on your part. After all, we each carry around a whole lifetime of habits, resentments, hurts, conditioning, and social expectations that must be dealt with on an individual basis. We think you will be pleasantly surprised, however, in learning how far along you already are and how much expertise you already have for letting go of self-judgment and judgment of others. Changing our views of past events is often a matter of getting sufficiently motivated, then having the courage and desire to put these latent skills to use.

Our judgments about ourselves are among the most important we make in life. This is because our *outer* reality mirrors our *inner* experience, and the way we proceed in the world is a direct reflection of what we're feeling about who we are. If we fully embrace and celebrate the knowledge that we're really okay—manifested in loving and caring for ourselves unconditionally—our mature years may indeed prove to be the best of our lives.

THE SECRET OF FORGIVENESS

Forgiveness of negative judgments about ourselves and about others is one of the most liberating secrets of becoming a Late Bloomer. Learning and practicing forgiveness is a powerful healing technique and an effective tool for achieving personal growth. It is what happens inside us when we love and feel compassion. An antidote to the pain and separation caused by negative judgments, forgiveness recognizes that we are all human and, as such, sometimes fall short of our ideals and aspirations.

The process of forgiving gives us a way to distinguish and affirm the fundamental essence of who we are—right here, right now—and who we have the potential to become. The parallel, and often simultaneous, process of making positive judgments about ourselves (and others) fulfills a deep-seated human need for the nourishment of self-esteem and reassurance that we deserve to pursue happiness. When self-esteem is high, the positives in our lives have more power than the negatives. Conversely, when self-esteem is low, the negatives have more power than the positives.

"Free yourself of your baggage and you lose none of your personal power," clinical psychologist Judith Sills writes in *Excess Baggage: Getting Out of Your Own Way.* "You just bring yourself back into a healthy balance . . . [and] you free your strengths to work for you."

Why is forgiveness such an important secret? Because

without it, our negative judgments tend to knock big holes in our self-esteem. And when our self-esteem is full of holes, it's hard to feel happy, fulfilled, and at peace with ourselves.

At one time or another, we've all muttered to ourselves something like *I'm too fat, I'm cold and calculating,* or *I have a temper I can't control.* When we did, these harsh thoughts invariably made us feel even worse. Therefore, when we at long last excuse ourselves for making these kinds of negative self-judgments, what we're really doing is cleaning the old baggage out of our mental closets, making space for a new set of positives to move in and for our self-esteem to rise.

When we forgive ourselves and forgive others, we can heal, move on, and lighten our spirits. Through the process of forgiveness, a world of new possibilities and growth begins to unfold.

HOW TO ACT ON THIS SECRET

Beverly Flanigan and other experts insist that forgiveness is a conscious choice that allows *you* to master *your* past instead of allowing your past to master you. Forgiveness—releasing yourself from negative judgments—is usually accomplished through an extended process that, although varying among individuals, generally contains six main elements. The order in which they occur may also be different from one person to the next, and the ease with which they are resolved will vary too:

1. Name the injury—Recall what happened and decide exactly what needs to be forgiven.

2. Recognize your particular injury—Separate what happened to you from what happened to others, such as your children or friends. Only they can forgive what was done to them.

3. Determine who is to blame—Weigh your own role in the situation and consider the excuses offered by others. Try to be fair and objective as you assign responsibility for what happened.

4. Balance the scales—If you feel punishment is necessary, consider talking or writing to your injurer, or withholding something he or she wants from you. You might also do something symbolic, like burning his or her photo.

5. Choose to forgive—Accept that you'll be better off after forgiving the injurer and letting go of the hurt or resentment you feel.

6. Let your new self emerge—Put the past behind you. Move ahead, knowing you are stronger and happier for the forgiveness you've granted.

What follows are some tried-and-true approaches for making the secret of forgiveness a reality in your life. These action steps will often help the above-described process move faster.

You've probably felt some reluctance, however, when somebody asks you to write something down or find somebody to complete a spoken exercise with. Maybe it's human nature to resist anything that smacks of a school assignment or deals with such weighty topics as forgiveness.

Having acknowledged that, we nevertheless urge you to participate in these exercises. Think of them as hammers and nails, tools that can be used to build something very useful. Some are like games, while others may seem rather silly and unrelated to your particular aging process—but they don't take very long, and they have worked for many people.

It may be helpful, before starting, to discuss the issues that are important to you with people you know and trust, such as a spouse, friend, counselor, or minister. These individuals can often provide important feedback within a context that feels safe and welcoming. There's nothing wrong with making yourself comfortable!

The first exercise has to do with the way we talk, both to ourselves and others. One very basic way of letting go of negative self-judgments from our past is to forgive ourselves out loud for making them. Practice this exercise by sitting face-to-face with another person in a quiet room and forming self-revealing sentences that begin with the phrase "I forgive myself for judging myself." We recommend you do this with a relative, friend, or neighbor. The two of you can take turns, allotting about five minutes for each person. (It helps if the one doing the listening keeps a record of the judgments being acknowledged. If they're written down, these notes can later be referred to.)

Once you tune in to your "inner voice," you'll begin acknowledging a lot of self-imposed verdicts from the past. You may, for instance, hear yourself saying something like this: "I forgive myself for judging myself a lousy parent." Other endings for that sentence might include "a fool in front of my boss," "a coward for once having an abortion," "a procrastinator for not getting my will written," "an unfair person for not loaning my daughter money," or "inefficient for wasting so much valuable time." Repeat your sentences over and over until they sound as if you really mean what you're saying.

If no one else is around to join in, you can achieve much the same result from this exercise by looking directly at yourself in the mirror as you talk. Remember, it's helpful to write your comments down in addition to saying them out loud.

Here is a variation on the preceding exercise. This one is designed to help you forgive others and was developed by the Reverend Roberta S. Herzog of Wyalusing, Pennsylvania. For at least two weeks, immediately after waking up or before retiring for the day, sit and be still. Close your eyes and picture someone you feel ready to forgive. It could be a spouse, relative, co-worker, friend, or even someone who has long been dead. Imagine the person smiling and happy. Then say the following out loud to the picture of him or her in your mind's eye. "I forgive you for everything you've ever said or done to me in thought, word, or deed that has brought me pain, resentment, or anger. You are free and I am free. And I ask that you forgive me for anything that I have ever said or done to you in thought, word, or deed that has brought you pain, resentment, or anger. You are free and I am free."

When you experience a true sensation of release, you will know it is time to stop repeating these phrases on a daily basis. This may manifest itself as crying, laughter, relief, happiness, or some other emotion, but you will know intuitively that your attitude has changed, profoundly and irrevocably. The process will help release the pain, resentment, or anger you have felt, while at the same time infusing you with a sense of peace and well-being. Your heart and spirit will feel lighter and happier.

At the conclusion of this process, you may want to post an affirmation in a prominent place, where it can remind you of the new frame of mind you've adopted. Here's one we found posted on a refrigerator door: "I am easily letting go, trusting, and lovingly accepting myself and others."

The object of these exercises is to release the destructive negative judgments that are chipping away relentlessly at our sense of worthiness, slowly eroding the good feelings that boost our self-esteem, and invariably clouding our perceptions of others. Taken together, these responses distort the world so that we are unable to move freely, seize new opportunities, and grow. In order to release these imprisoning judgments, we need to learn to practice forgiveness of ourselves and others.

"Forgive," concludes psychologist Judith Sills, "and we free all the energy we are currently using in reviewing old injuries, fantasizing revenge, and craving justice. Forgive, and the piece of our being that was tied up with rage and hurt is free to be much, much more."

CHAPTER FOUR

THE SECRET OF RISK TAKING

PEOPLE USED TO REGARD GETTING OLD the same way early explorers viewed the earth. You got to the edge and fell off, never to be heard from or seen again. Everyone back in the Old World learned to assume there was nothing out there except pitch-black emptiness.

If you think about it, those "Dark Ages" weren't so long ago. When you went to grade school, for example, didn't science teachers insist that the human body starts deteriorating irreversibly at age thirty-five? Maybe your civics text described retirement as "a well-deserved rest" for those tired souls who finally huffed-and-puffed their way to age sixty-five. Was your idea of a "successful senior" anyone who could make it across the street without assistance?

Contrast those stale and misleading images with today's aerobic grandmothers, un-retiring business executives, and gray-haired world travelers. Why, we've even had a seventy-eight-year-old president!

Thankfully, society's long-standing perceptions of its older citizens are becoming more varied and realistic. Today's children encounter "retired" folks behind fast-food restaurant counters, zipping down the street on motor scooters, swimming laps at the community pool, and engaging in all manner of other activities that would once have raised eyebrows but no longer merit so much as a second glance.

Seniors are increasingly likely to view their lives with optimism. A 1990 Marriott Corporation survey found that half of those interviewed over age sixty-five felt they were enjoying "the best years" of their lives. More than 68 percent said they felt an average of twelve years younger than they actually were. The majority of those questioned labeled themselves "excited" about the future, whether they were seventy years of age or ninety. "For the first time in my life, I can do exactly as I wish," one Late Bloomer told us in our own informal survey. "I don't have to worry about pleasing anybody except myself." Like those early explorers, she (and we) think it's pretty exciting to find out our planet isn't flat and that there's a whole new world out there waiting to be discovered. Instead of life turning dark and mysterious as we move toward the earth's outer edge, it can just as easily be thought of as opening up and growing brighter, with more opportunities for adventure.

We compare the Late Bloomers we've met to those brave and inquisitive European explorers who pushed themselves to take chances, even when that meant putting their own lives in jeopardy. Because these men and women took risks, the history of the world was altered irrevocably.

Risks that offer the best odds for success are those undertaken with a clear sense of purpose or a specific goal in mind.

The Vikings were looking for new pastures for their goats and sheep when they bumped into Greenland and Labrador. Columbus was in search of a shorter route to the Spice Islands when he ran aground in the New World. And while they didn't exactly find what they were looking for, the important point is that they wouldn't have found *anything* if they hadn't had a goal of some kind that motivated them to set sail into uncharted, shark-infested waters.

In this chapter, you'll meet Late Bloomers whose fearless gumption led to new experiences that have in turn made their mature years rewarding and satisfying. Like the early explorers, the chances they took were not made blindly or in a vacuum; they reflected a sense of purpose. The diversity of their individual choices underscores the important fact that there is no right or wrong way to go about risk taking. What worked for them may not work for you. We offer their stories as examples of what's possible and to share with you their energy, spirit, and determination.

At the age of seventy-one, for example, our friend David B. realized his lifelong dream of taking a safari through the jungles of east Africa. Helen H. started going to college when she turned sixty-eight—as she put it—"just for the thrill of learning." Herbert K. combined his enthusiasm for baseball and young people by becoming a Little League umpire in his midseventies. Karen and Alvin T., both eighty, spend half of each year traveling the country in a cozy recreational vehicle, the other half relaxing at their South Carolina beachfront condo. Recently retired nurse Mary V. has turned her hobby of refinishing antique furniture into a part-time business.

The roster of Late Bloomer examples seems endless. With so much to choose from, how did they know where to start?

What was the process each went through in sizing up potential fields of interest, making appropriate choices, and sticking with a commitment day after day? Obviously, no single approach is effective for everyone, and some techniques may work well for you in one situation and not at all in another. Picking and choosing is the name of the game.

Here's how our Late Bloomer friends Barbara and Bernard S. went about answering some of these questions for themselves. Like many of us, Barb and Bernie had only a vague idea of what they were going to do after retiring from a family-run printing business in an East Coast city. They owned a large home, where they'd raised three children, and had bought a smaller house in Florida, where the two spent their vacations. During their early sixties, Barb and Bernie agreed that they'd sell their printing business and principal residence when Bernie turned sixty-five, then invest their profits in such a way that they'd be assured of a modest but reliable monthly income. "We weren't sure exactly what we were going to do when we got to Florida," explained Barb, an energetic woman with expressive hands. "But we both knew we wanted to relocate there permanently."

Having owned the Florida property for three years, Bernie and Barb were already familiar with the community. Nevertheless, they had few friends in the area, and that circle didn't widen much until they began going to their new church regularly and attending various social events like coffee klatches and bingo games.

Then one morning they stared at each other across the breakfast table and asked simultaneously, "Okay, what now?" They gathered pencils and paper together and began to prepare an important set of lists. At the top of a blank sheet

Bernie wrote the word "GOALS" in big block letters. He divided the space beneath it into three equal columns labeled "MINE," "YOURS," and "OURS." Barb and Bernie spent several hours discussing activities or subjects that attracted them, both as a couple and as individuals. When they decided which would be targets or interests, Bernie added them to whatever list was appropriate. "For example, we both like to see and do things in places we've never been before," he recalled, "so we wrote 'travel' under the heading of 'OURS.' I like to read detective novels, something my wife has no use for, so I put that under 'MINE.'"

"And I put down things in my column that I knew Bernie wasn't keen on," Barb interjected. "I've always been interested in collecting rocks and studying geology. I thought I might take up waterskiing. I also wanted to see if I liked being in a women's support group."

Some of the items were very specific, like replacing their ten-year-old car and getting the house painted. Other categories were broad, headed by such words as "exercise" and "history." Over the next few weeks, they found themselves coming back to their list for an hour or more each day, adding new objectives and removing others that seemed to lose their priority status. They speculated on new adventures they'd create together, new places they'd visit, and new satisfactions that might come to them as they expanded their horizons. "By the end of the month, our piece of paper was filled with ideas," said Bernie. "So we sat down again and tried to figure out if there was any kind of discernible pattern to what we'd written."

"It seemed to us that two overriding themes kept coming up again and again," Barb continued. "Those were travel and learning. And by learning I don't mean going to college and concentrating on a single subject, but finding out a little bit about a lot of different things. You know, we both have a kind of general curiosity about the world."

Feeling a step closer to realizing their goals, the pair began investigating options that would fulfill their very diverse interests. They discussed possible activities with their friends, took books out of the library, and scanned articles in magazines and newspapers. They made phone calls, sent in requests for brochures, and checked the bulletin board at a nearby community center.

Then one day Barb and Bernie happened to see a TV news story about a national education system catering to those over age sixty. According to the reporter, the Elderhostel program offers academic classes of limited size, duration, and cost to seniors at college campuses and other locations across the country. The reporter explained that the courses do not lead toward a degree but are simply dedicated to the joy and excitement of learning. Barb and Bernie learned that topics ranging from "Appalachian Bird Life" to "Zither Playing" (and hundreds in between) are presented by Elderhostel instructors, all experts in their chosen fields.

Bernie and Barb requested a copy of the Elderhostel catalog by mail, and when it arrived they were amazed not only by the diversity of available courses but also the appealing settings in which they were offered. Classes are frequently scheduled at mountain summer-camp sites, national parks, and rural conference centers as well as on university or college campuses. They learned that participants eat communally and stay in comfortable bungalows, hostels, or dormitories. "We knew instantly that Elderhostel was perfect for us," said Barb, as her husband nodded in agreement. "It combined our interest in travel with our desire for lifelong learning."

Over the last several years, Bernie and Barb have completed more than a hundred Elderhostel courses and eagerly await the updated course list, which is published several times a year and contains more than a thousand offerings. "We plan our whole year around it," Bernie said. "We immediately go through the new directory and pick out all the classes and locations we're both interested in. Then we look at a calendar to see how many of these we can reasonably expect to fit in over the next twelve months."

The couple shutter their house while they head off to explore the parks, recreational sites, and cities that are close to their next planned Elderhostel experience. If they're signed up for classes in the Denver area, for example, they may plan excursions into the nearby Rocky Mountains either before or after the scheduled Elderhostel activities begin. "We've panned for gold in Arizona," elaborated Barb, when we asked her to describe some of the activities she and Bernie have shared in the Elderhostel program. "We've dug up Indian ruins in Tennessee. We've made pottery in Oregon. We've toured Civil War battlefields in Pennsylvania. I guess you could call us Elderhostel groupies."

Not all of the classes take place outdoors. Barb and Bernie have also attended academically oriented lecture courses that delve into formal disciplines like anthropology, history, political science, and literature. And they continue to spend considerable time at their home in Florida, where each partner pursues separate interests. Barb has learned to make jewelry from the rocks she collects during their trips, and her husband can still spend hour upon hour absorbed in an Agatha Christie mystery. "Now it feels like we have the best of both worlds," Bernie concluded, with a satisfied chuckle.

Barbara and Bernie agree that the act of writing down a list of objectives was extremely effective in clarifying their personal and collective goals. It not only helped pinpoint fields that held the greatest degree of interest for them but also made the possibility of pursuing those interests seem a lot more real. "Once I saw the words on paper," concluded Bernie, "it seemed for the first time like those activities might actually come alive."

On their own, these Late Bloomers discovered the "anchoring" power of the written word. It's something that self-help experts and personal-growth facilitators have known about for years. In fact, many professionals suggest that writing down a goal, purpose, or objective—call it what you will—is the most important first step in the process of ultimately reaching one's destination. The act of writing is a tool, a way of making things clearer to ourselves.

Think of goal setting as your first move toward the land of commitment. Commitment, by definition, implies some action and responsibility. If you're a serious explorer of your own inner territory, it's important that you find your goal(s), set your course, and create a support process that moves you forward.

Most of us aren't as direct in our approach as were Barb and Bernie, who sat at their kitchen table and made lists on a notepad. A lot of people sort of back their way into goal setting with their own creative approaches, many of them unintentional. Seemingly random thoughts may arrive unbidden in the shower or bathtub. A friend or relative may, over coffee, tell an inspiring story that suddenly gets the mind racing. And while there's certainly no right or wrong method, we know from Late Bloomers we've talked to (and our own experiences) that discipline and determination can help bring things into focus. One also needs patience, since answers don't always come when or how we want them.

A particularly effective way to explore feelings and organize thoughts about late-life plans was demonstrated by our Late Bloomer friend Esther S., who lives in New York City. Like Barb and Bernie, she approached her "retirement" years without any real sense of purpose or direction.

A Hungarian immigrant who came to the United States by steamer at age twenty-seven, Esther spent most of her married life in a small New Jersey town raising four children and managing a household that always seemed filled with activity. It was at first a fulfilling existence but gradually became less and less satisfying as one by one her sons and daughters moved away and started families of their own.

Following the death of her husband a few years ago, Esther felt the need to bring a sense of fulfillment and accomplishment back into her life. "I'd been what you'd call 'a typical happy suburban housewife,'" she told us as we sat on the balcony of her fifth-floor Manhattan apartment. "I was devoted to my children and volunteered for many organizations in our community. I took great pride in these things. Now I wanted something to replace them—I wanted to feel needed again."

Esther's husband had seen to it that she would have no financial worries for the rest of her life, and she could easily have spent her remaining years relaxing or traveling. Nevertheless, Esther felt that kind of lifestyle wouldn't meet her internal needs; yet she was unsure what she wanted to do. "I didn't have much confidence in myself at that time. After all, I hadn't taken any paid job during my entire thirty years of marriage, and I felt a little intimidated by the accomplishments of other women my age."

One day, while looking at a magazine, Esther noticed an article about a nonprofit community organization that provided free counseling services to teenagers. It was illustrated by a photograph that showed a friendly middle-aged volunteer counselor in animated conversation with a sixteen-year-old girl. Esther couldn't take her eyes off this picture. The counselor seemed so wise and maternal, the teenager so grateful for having someone to talk to. Esther remembered how a longtime friend of hers named Tanya, a fellow immigrant, used to take pictures out of magazines that represented things she longed for. It seemed childish to Esther at the time, but Tanya insisted that looking at something she wanted helped her find the means to acquire it. Feeling a bit silly, Esther removed the news account and pinned it to a corkboard in her hallway. During the next week, she found herself stealing glances at the photo several times a day.

"I loved looking at that scene and imagining I was the one seated at the counselor's desk," Esther explained. "Without really knowing why, I think my feelings began to change about what might be possible for me in the future. I felt a new sense of purpose and direction growing within me."

Esther soon found herself cutting other items out of magazines and newspapers: photographs, advertisements, words, and phrases that described what her projected fantasy of a future life might be like. "I spent hours and hours going through piles of magazines trying to find the right words or pictures," she said. "I think what I was really trying to say was, 'the world is my oyster.'"

One Sunday morning Esther spread out her collection of clippings on the living-room floor, arranging and rearranging them into a bright and colorful collage. She then transferred this personal "treasure map," as she called it, to a poster-sized sheet of cardboard, where it became a vibrant jumble of words and images of all colors and dimensions. Esther found that the map made her feel more focused on her emerging goal of going to college. Once the process began moving, she started having fun with what one friend in the advertising business called her "personal storyboard"—a reference to the colorful posters ad agencies use to develop new TV commercials.

"I know it sounds a little odd to sit at home and cut out scraps of paper," Esther shrugged, "but I took my treasure map seriously. I spent a great deal of time on it because it really helped me keep going in the direction I wanted to go."

Over the next several weeks, Esther began keeping an eye out for anything that "supported" her. "I took a large snap-shot of myself that I particularly liked and placed it in the middle of the cardboard. All around my face were pictures and words and other things that I felt good about." These items surrounded her image like a halo. They included a photo of a college classroom and part of a "back to school" advertisement. She cut out pictures of books, the outline of a diploma, and the headline of a brochure asking, "What Do You Want to Be?" Esther added a photo of her grandchildren and the copy of an appreciation certificate she'd once received from her synagogue. Above the treasure map she tacked a sign bearing the words "ESTHER'S HAPPY LIFE."

Soon Esther's display included pictures of vacation scenes, antique furniture, and such phrases as "You're a Success," "Career Move," and "New Graduate." Her treasure map displayed some interesting original creations too. Esther had cut apart the original news photo of the older woman

79

and teenager, inserting her own image in the counselor's chair. Family-album photographs of Esther were imbedded in a picture of a crowded classroom. The word "Victory" was cupped in a pair of outstretched hands, and several individual words had been taped together to form the phrase "Free of Fear." "When I see myself in the middle of this collage," Esther stressed to us, "I feel as though I'm the heroine in my own fairy tale. There's something nice about that!"

Although she wasn't listing her goals in as direct a manner as did Barbara and Bernie, Esther's treasure map had a similar impact. If someone had asked her what she wanted for herself in the next four years, they would have gotten a pretty good idea simply from looking at what she had pasted together on the cardboard. By focusing on her own needs, desires, and aspirations, Esther found the collage gradually drawing her in the direction of preparing herself for a career in social service. Without consciously thinking about it, she began accepting the notion that a big change in her lifestyle was way overdue. She felt as if a door had been opened and Esther was standing at its threshold.

During the six years that she's been adding to (and sometimes subtracting from) her personal storyboard, Esther's life has indeed changed. A few months after the first counseling article caught her eye, the sixty-year-old widow noticed an advertisement in the Sunday edition of *The New York Times*. A major university was promoting a College at 60 program that encouraged older members of the community to continue their education. (Of course Esther cut and pasted the slogan from that ad on her personal storyboard as well.) "I enrolled as a freshman the very next day," Esther told us. "I decided after reading the advertisement that what I really wanted to do was become a social worker, so that I could go into counseling and help others."

Because she had never been to college, Esther had to start with basic courses in the humanities and social sciences. She was delighted to be around younger people, who in turn welcomed her with open arms. She earned a bachelor of arts degree in four years and continued with the graduate courses that allowed her to apply for a position with the city as a social worker. "I was offered and promptly accepted a part-time job as a counselor working with the elderly as well as with teenagers," said Esther proudly.

She has decided to specialize in helping older women who are having trouble making life transitions—a subject Esther knows a great deal about from personal experience. Esther hopes that her life will serve as a role model for some of these women, who often find themselves alone and at loose ends in an empty house or apartment. "I feel comfortable working with women, and expect I will soon set up a private counseling practice in my home," Esther said. "I'm still taking classes and at one time considered going on for my doctorate. But I was too impatient and wanted to start working right away. For me, the most meaningful experiences come from my clients."

Esther said that choosing to start college at her age in order to become a social worker was a choice she'd never even have considered during the years she was married and taking care of a family. "I feel better than ever about myself," she concluded. An important stimulus for Esther's decision to set counseling as a goal was the treasure map she put together out of inspiring magazine pictures, family photographs, newspaper headlines, and original drawings. These reminders helped her formulate a vision of what her priorities were and what she wanted her life to be like. "I've gotten to know other people who have made similar maps for themselves," Esther pointed out. "There seems to be a kind of magic in them. They set in motion an energy that brings you closer and closer to where you want to go. They get your mind focused and working in a way that leads you in that direction."

Since meeting Esther, we've encountered a number of other Late Bloomers who've assembled this kind of collage. Each construction reflects the individual personality and interest of its creator. Sally B.'s treasure map, for instance, consists of a loose-leaf binder that she carries with her almost everywhere she goes (one of the goals she talks of is training for a later-life career in real estate sales). Each page is like a miniature storyboard concerned with a specific topic. One devoted to travel is covered with pictures of exotic destinations taken from travel literature and cutouts of world maps. Another, entitled "My Romantic Companion," shows happy gray-haired couples dining by candlelight and holding hands as they walk along the beach.

Tom G. pasted an advertisement for a late-model automobile on the six-foot treasure map he's mounted on his bedroom wall. Tom's been saving money for a roomier car and has already picked out a model and color that's identical to the one in the ad.

Eleanor W. added some unique touches to her personalized "wish board": a toy rabbit's foot, a restaurant menu, and a real $100 bill. She's a retired restaurant manager who's always wanted to run a breakfast-only diner and recently made a down payment for the purchase of just such a business within walking distance of her home. In case you're wondering, Eleanor told us the $100 is on her wish board in order to "seed" her success and that of her employees. She claims it's already prompted generous tips from customers for her hard-working servers.

THE SECRET OF RISK TAKING

Late Bloomers take risks. They know that being cautious and passive doesn't always bring them what they want. Late Bloomers enjoy the rewards of direct, assertive action. Experience has taught them that some chances are worth taking, even though such risks will occasionally yield disappointment and pain. Sometimes they also bring satisfaction and joy.

"Everything you really want in life involves taking a risk," declares psychiatrist and author David Viscott, who notes that uncertainty is involved in everything from getting married to asking for a raise to making an investment to starting off in a new direction after retirement.

The secret of successful risk taking, as the Late Bloomers in this chapter have demonstrated, is making choices that are reasoned, affirming, and appropriate. If we've taken the time to carefully and thoughtfully consider the potential benefits an action may bring us, chances are good that we'll get what we're looking for, even if we're not sure at the outset exactly what that is.

Some of us worry that giving this much attention to ourselves is too self-indulgent. Yet there's another way to gauge the significance of personal development in later life. During our early and middle adult years most of our waking hours—

not to mention income, energy, and concentration—are devoted to others. This is the time when we are often striving to support a spouse, raise children, maintain a household, complete higher education, manage a career, attend to chores, and get on with the so-called necessities of life. By the time we reach full maturity, our offspring are on their own, homes are paid for, housework is simplified, and jobs are winding down. In our later years, there's less compulsion to work long hours or shoulder domestic responsibilities, and many of us have at least some measure of financial security.

Our mature years are frequently the ideal time to concentrate on making life qualitatively better for ourselves. These years may represent the first chance we've had to pursue that goal. Why? Because we've finally gotten rid of the distractions and can sit down to seriously consider the multitude of options available. Now we have the opportunity to decide for ourselves what our ultimate contributions to ourselves and our world will be.

Our stories of the way Late Bloomers have clarified their aspirations and interests reveal only a fraction of the approaches you might apply to your own life. As you mull these possibilities, remember that you don't have to go through this process on your own. All the help you need is there when you want it: from spouses, family members, friends, mentors, teachers, counselors, and others. The important thing is to commit yourself to taking that critical first step. You can start by getting rid of any fuzziness and confusion in your mind about where you're going, so that you can focus and move ahead.

HOW TO ACT ON THIS SECRET

For the next exercise, we'd like you to try making your own list of goals, generally following the model of our self-proclaimed Elderhostel "groupies," Barb and Bernie. Write down everything you can think of that feels like something you really want to do. If, upon reflection, something doesn't seem right, simply cross it off your list. If an important element seems to be missing, try to put it into words so that it can be counted. Don't worry how long your list gets. There are many ways to pare it down, including taking action steps and planning techniques that will move you toward your objectives.

Don't be discouraged if this act of personal writing at first feels frustrating, strange, or downright difficult. Hang in there! Many Late Bloomers have assured us that this strategy was a crucial step in focusing their thoughts.

We don't want you to think this process poses special difficulties merely because you're older. It's hard for *everybody*, whether they're sixteen or eighty-six. Why? Because this kind of introspection can force us to be completely honest with ourselves and finally let go of some familiar excuses. And that can be anxiety-producing at any age.

Creating a treasure map as Esther did is almost like writing down a list of goals. We hope you'll consider it as a focusing technique for yourself. Use the treasure map to let your imagination soar: allow almost anything to become a viable possibility. Because it's part of an ongoing process, feel free to add, subtract, and modify your creation as time goes by and your personal focus changes.

Remember, no hard-and-fast rules apply here. The items

you put on your treasure map can be as individual and as varied as your personality is. We've seen Late Bloomers attach dried flowers, art reproductions, favorite poems, ticket stubs, guitar picks, and matchbook covers to their personal storyboards. Stickers, cartoons, and predictions from Chinese fortune cookies are also perfectly acceptable.

Whether you're writing down your ambitions in list form, cutting out symbols that represent your goals from last month's *Ladies' Home Journal* and *Sports Illustrated*, or even inventing an original method of your own, the fundamental idea remains the same. The more concrete you make your objectives, the further and faster you'll move in the direction of accomplishing them.

Finally, here's another approach that's proven helpful for some Late Bloomers. It's an adaptation of the affirmation technique discussed earlier. Say, for example, that one of your dreams is to go to college. Perhaps you'd be returning after a forty-five-year absence or, like Esther, enrolling for the first time. In either instance, you're probably apprehensive about the way you'll perform among much younger students. You wonder if your classmates will move ahead faster than you or have more effective study habits. You envision them ignoring you in class and rushing past you in the hallways—definitely a picture you don't want to reinforce. Here's an appropriate and positive affirmation that deals with these kinds of negative thoughts: "I am fitting in comfortably with my new classmates and completing my assignments quickly and well."

A positively framed sentence like this one can have a powerful impact on our consciousness without our realizing it, especially when imprinted in our brain through repetition. This can be done by saying the affirmation out loud, writing it down, or displaying it in prominent places. Some Late Bloomers put Post-it notes on the front of their kitchen appliances, atop their car dashboards, inside the pages of books they're reading, or underneath their bed pillows.

Psychologists have confirmed that if we tell ourselves something like, "I'm afraid of not being able to succeed in college," a reinforcement will occur on a very fundamental level of our consciousness. When words that conjure up positive connotations are used, the opposite phenomenon will occur. Thus our use of language can either move us forward or hold us back.

Parents demonstrate a classic illustration of this principle in their bedtime recitation of *The Little Engine That Could*. As you'll recall, this is the story of a small train that tries to pull a heavy load over the top of a steep mountain. "I just can't do it," the discouraged engine sighs, only to slide down the mountain again. But when the engine chants to itself, "I THINK I can, I THINK I can," it glides over the pass with its last puff of steam.

Like the plucky little steam engine, when we change our internal chants from such words as "I'll never make it" to "I'm making it," our focus shifts from fear to optimism. Here's an example that relates to later-life schooling: Suppose your cousin calls to congratulate you on the news that you're going off to college at age sixty-five. "I'm so pleased for you," she cries. "I think it's terrific!"

"Thank you very much," you respond. "I feel excited and happy to be going!" If negative thoughts are in the front of your mind, you might blurt out something like, "Gee, thanks for the encouragement, but I'm so scared. I haven't studied in a long time and wonder whether I'll be able to handle it." By now you can guess which response is more likely to build a solid foundation for success.

This is not to say that the only thing you need to do in order to get what you want is mouth positive words and phrases. That's living in a fantasy world. What it does mean is that positive language can release a psychic energy that moves us closer and faster toward our goals. We're asking you to trust that this "mind magic" can work for you.

The same kind of reinforcement can also occur through the power of repetition. Do you recall when schoolteachers handled misbehavior by ordering you or your naughty classmates to write the same sentence a hundred times on the blackboard? Perhaps it was a phrase like "I will never pull Janie's braids again." Well, don't worry about Janie. She's all grown up now and is taking good care of herself. But you can still teach yourself something using the same principle, simply by writing and rewriting sentences that move you forward, such as "I am fitting in comfortably with my new college classmates and am completing my assignments quickly and well."

We've said it before, but we'll say it again: Negative words and thoughts have power. Get rid of them. Positive words, images, and thoughts have *more* power. Use them.

None of your objectives needs to be engraved in stone. Even if you've affirmed a specific goal by writing it down, including it on a treasure map, or telling your friends or relatives, that goal can easily be changed, updated, or even abandoned if you find it no longer fits or rings true. You're never locked in, and the possibilities are always unlimited. After all, this is *your* life.

"A mind is like a parachute," someone wise once said. "It works best when it's open."

CHAPTER FIVE

THE SECRET OF ACTION STEPS

BLOOMING IS NOT A PASSIVE PROCESS. You can't simply sit around waiting for things to change: you have to *make* them happen. The Late Bloomers in this book were not called into purposeful action by some sort of mysterious or divine intervention. They took the initiative to create positive change in their lives.

First, for any number of reasons, they realized that they wanted something more out of life. Second, they began to actively and narrowly define what that something more might be. Their third step, and the one we're going to discuss in this chapter, was to find ways of putting a little of that something more into their lives in the course of each passing day.

As you've been reading this book, you may have developed some pretty good ideas about what activities or lifestyles you want to explore in your late-blooming years. It could be that you've decided to return in some way to the world of work. Or maybe you want to find out what cruise-ship travel is all about.

Perhaps you're eager to find new companions with whom you can play cards or go to the theater or a movie. You might want to find out what it's like to live in a retirement community.

Whatever your chosen direction, the prospect of moving forward can be stimulating and invigorating. On the other hand, it can also represent a big challenge. Perhaps you've been reluctant to actually get off your duff and start something new. Maybe you find you've been talking about a project and never gotten around to jumping into it. Have you heard yourself saying: "I can't . . . ," "Not just now . . . " or, "I'm not quite ready yet . . . "? No longer! The time has come to get your fondest dreams and desires out of the dusty, overstuffed closet of your imagination and try them on for size. Remember, nothing does it like doing it.

An important but sometimes unpredictable consideration in becoming a Late Bloomer is timing. You can set a goal or draw up an action plan at any age or stage in life, but giving serious thought to your later-life activities before retiring can make a lot of positive difference. If you haven't already done this, remember that it's never too late. Although we strongly support all aspects of preretirement planning, some of our most successful Late Bloomers waited until they left the workplace before considering what they wanted to do after retiring.

Take our friend Charlie V., for instance. When Charlie ended his four-decade career as a chef and restaurant administrator, the sixty-four-year-old bachelor had virtually no postretirement plans. "I left work on a Friday and woke up the following Monday without a clue as to how I'd spend my time," said Charlie during our visit to the small coastal California community where he's lived most of his life. "My future was like a blank sheet of paper. I stared up at the ceiling and thought to myself, *What the heck am I going to do next?"*

During his busy working life Charlie had never developed outside interests or hobbies. He was a shy man who lived alone and had few close friends. And on the first morning of his retirement, it dawned on him that he had never put much effort into creating a vision of what he wanted this part of his life to be like. Charlie realized that almost all of his human contact had been through his job, and without that daily interaction, he felt painfully alone. Confused and isolated, Charlie found himself withdrawing more and more over the next several months. He spent long hours sleeping, watching TV, or simply staring out the window at squirrels playing in his backyard oak trees.

Then one afternoon a neighbor stopped by on his way to a class for seniors at the local community center. Ralph had been worried about Charlie's retreat into his shell and thought he might have found a way to draw him out. "I'm going to a beginners tap-dancing class," Charlie's friend announced. "Why don't you come along?"

"Tap dancing?" Charlie responded in amazement. "You're crazy! At my age?"

"Look at me," Ralph shot back. "I'm almost as old as you are, and I'm giving it a try. I've heard it's great exercise and a lot of fun."

"Naw," said Charlie. "I don't think so. I'm sixty-four years old, and I've never danced a step. Besides, I couldn't stand the idea of making a fool of myself in front of all those folks."

"Come on," Ralph pleaded. "You think I'm Fred Astaire? It'll give both of us something new to do." Despite Charlie's vocal protests, his neighbor persisted, pointing out (correctly) that Charlie had nothing better planned for that afternoon. In the end, they decided to go to the tap-dance class together, on the condition that Charlie, a lifelong wallflower, would be free to leave at any time if he felt uncomfortable.

Although he didn't say anything at the time, Charlie had another reason for his reluctance to check out the dance class. Besides feeling bashful and clumsy around the opposite sex, he also considered himself unattractive. A watermelon-sized paunch hung over Charlie's belt. His arms and legs were thin and flabby. Physical exercise was something he'd always done his best to avoid.

"When we got to the class," Charlie recalled, "the first thing I noticed was that they really needed us men. Ralph and I were the only guys who showed up. A very nice young lady was the teacher, and all the other students were women!"

Although Charlie had accompanied Ralph with the intention of only standing on the sidelines and watching, the instructor quickly pulled Charlie out of the crowd and asked him to follow along with her introductory tap-dance movements. "I felt very awkward when we started and got awfully red in the face. But Terry, our teacher, helped me a lot, and pretty soon I got the hang of it. Because we were all just starting out, the others couldn't really tell when I made a wrong step."

As he gained confidence, the women in the class began asking Charlie to show them what he'd learned, and together they helped each other out. "By the end of the first class I was in paradise. Tap dancing was more interesting than I'd thought, and it felt really good to be included in a group. I'd made some new friends."

As he and Ralph walked home after class, Charlie declared his intention to stick with tap dancing at least through the ten-week introductory course. He still wasn't sure if he could become a successful dancer, but he was willing to try. And although he said nothing about it to his companion, Charlie admitted to himself for the first time that his life had gotten awfully empty and lonely.

Charlie remembers that when the promise to keep dancing slipped out of his mouth, Ralph looked a little skeptical. "He suggested I write this down on a piece of paper, so I'd have that to remind me if I started feeling as if I wanted to drop out. I guess he was afraid I'd come up with some excuse for not going. Ralph said he kept a list of things he wanted to try, and it always gave him something to plan for in the future." The next morning Charlie wrote down his promise to attend the tap-dance classes and practice a little of what he'd learned every afternoon. Surprised at how good he'd felt that first day on the dance floor, he also put down the word "exercise" and placed a question mark beside it.

Within the next few weeks, Charlie underwent an amazing transformation. Every tap-dance class seemed to fill him with youthful energy. Sensing his enthusiasm, Charlie's teacher began working with him after class, practicing routines the two could perform together. "It took a month or so, but Terry and I became a pretty smooth team. After that, I wanted to do solos," Charlie laughed. "And by the end of the course I was invited to do just that in a big variety show at the senior center. Actually, our whole class performed, but they made me the star. I'll never forget the sound of that applause!"

With the sessions over, Charlie looked back at his list of goals. He crossed out the original entries and started over again with a new set of objectives: "Do more tap-dance shows," "Lose weight," "Ride bike," "See if I like to jog." Not only did Charlie soon discover the joys of running on the beach, but his friends from the tap-dance class decided to continue booking the group to perform for school children and nursing home residents.

Charlie knew that tap dancing represented a turning point for him. It was an opportunity to appreciate the precious value of each human being, especially the new friends he's danced with and the appreciative audiences he's performed for. This appreciation was something that he'd never dwelled on much during his long, hectic hours in the restaurant business. "Maybe it's because I remember how lonely I was before I let Ralph drag me out of the house," Charlie mused, "but now I really value the specialness of every individual—and that specialness begins with me!"

Through dancing, Charlie has made friends with some of the nursing home residents who came to performances. Now he visits several of them regularly, taking them for walks and sharing their meals.

While his self-esteem grew, Charlie's paunch shrank. He lost twenty pounds during a six-month regime of jogging, bicycling, and dancing. When his doctor examined him, he declared, "I can't find a single thing wrong with you!"

Charlie's active new life had a noticeable impact on his inner being as well as his physical health. Positive feedback seemed to flow toward him, as strangers marveled at his energy and agility or applauded his onstage performances. He experienced a feeling of accomplishment and camaraderie, as if he'd started accepting and admiring himself for the first time.

As Charlie became more introspective, the items on his list of goals began to change. The physical act of running every morning seemed to take on a deeper, almost spiritual meaning. The rhythmic motion and healthful glow that were part of his jogging often put Charlie in a serene, meditative state of mind. Some time later, when he sat down to re-evaluate where he was headed in life, Charlie realized he had the self-confidence to take some even bigger risks.

"I'd always had a secret fantasy that I could model clothes or maybe act in the movies," he explained. "I figured as long as I was at it, I might as well take a shot at fulfilling those dreams too." So between dance performances, which by now had brought him a trophy and blue ribbon from the California State Fair, Charlie made the rounds of local stores and eventually landed a part-time job modeling clothes for older men. During one floor show, a casting agent spotted him and signed our friend to a nonspeaking role in a movie.

Of course, Charlie keeps on tap dancing and can be found riding his bicycle down along the beachfront bike path every morning. He feels fortunate to be able to keep active and vibrant, although he acknowledges this situation may eventually come to an end. He knows that, should his health or physical abilities change, the confidence he's developed can be transferred to other activities.

"I recently updated my list of goals," he said, as he excused himself to get ready for an outdoor tap-dance performance at the county's annual jamboree. "Now I want to look into country-western singing, or becoming a songwriter like Johnny Cash or Willie Nelson."

Charlie has already become a role model for some of his friends. A couple next door have followed his example by taking up tap dancing. These neighbors say they're especially impressed at how much Charlie has changed in such a relatively short time—quite an accomplishment for a guy who admittedly entered retirement as "a blank sheet of paper."

The transition of this Late Bloomer has been dramatic.

Charlie had assumed that his most productive years were behind him, but with the perspective and wisdom he's garnered during the last few years, his whole attitude has changed. In keeping himself flexible and open to new discoveries, Charlie has developed a sense of well-being and a feeling of confidence.

Not everybody will be lucky enough to fare as well as Charlie if they put off plans until retirement day. Many Late Bloomers we've talked to found happiness and satisfaction in their mature years through careful, step-by-step planning that began years before they left the world of work.

Helen S., for instance, is a divorced Late Bloomer in her midsixties who started laying the groundwork for her retirement a full decade before she closed her private psychotherapy practice in a large eastern city. Helen told us she never put any of her postretirement plans on paper but instead planted in her mind a firm decision that she'd eventually find a small New England village to settle down in. "I'd always taken my vacation during the winter months," Helen explained with a wistful look in her eye. "I particularly loved to visit the Green Mountains up in Vermont when the maple syrup was being harvested and the forests were under a heavy canopy of snow. I broke down my long-range goal into what I call 'baby steps,' " she continued. "Every year I'd do a little bit that would get me closer to where I knew I eventually wanted to be. That way I could see some forward movement with each small change that took place."

The first task Helen assigned herself was to save enough money to buy a small cottage or cabin in the country. Although her therapy practice brought in enough income for her to live on, it was difficult to come up with sufficient money for a down payment. Yet she finally figured out a way. For most of her adult life, in addition to her work as a therapist, Helen enjoyed a small but loyal following as a professional singer of religious hymns and spirituals. She indulged in this activity as much out of love for the music as anything else, but the extra money had always come in handy. After some persistent negotiation with her booking agents, Helen was able to raise her performance fees substantially and set this new income aside for the cabin.

"During one of my winter trips to Vermont, I found the perfect place," Helen said. "It needed a little work, but the size and location were exactly what I'd been looking for." She immediately bought the cabin and leased it to a tenant on a year-round basis, with the understanding that she'd have the place to herself for three weeks every December.

Little by little, as funds became available, she made improvements in the structure. "I replaced the storm windows and fixed the roof during the first summer. The following year I bought a new wood stove and widened the driveway. After that I added a room with a private entrance where I could meet with clients when the cabin became my full-time residence." Her plan was to start a part-time practice once she made the final move to her retirement residence. She had deliberately picked a village close enough to larger towns that could support a part-time counseling practice such as hers, as well as provide her convenient access to an airport where she could easily make connections for her occasional concert tours. "Just as I'd planned, I sold my house in the city and moved permanently to Vermont a few years ago. By then I'd gotten to know all my neighbors and felt very much at home," Helen concluded. "I'm completely happy with the way things turned out for me—it was an easy transition."

Helen's story is a good example of effective preretirement planning. She was so thorough that she made sure her downstairs office could easily be converted into a bedroom—just in case the stairway to her loft someday became too difficult for her to negotiate.

By breaking down her project into small segments, Helen was able to make a major transition without trauma. She was also able to create a sense of excitement that, over an entire decade, sustained her interest in her coming retirement. She took pictures of each addition and improvement, relishing each step of the process and sharing her enthusiasm with friends. Helen's pleasure in the preparations for the move to Vermont kept the project always in the present moment. The process of making her dream home a reality was an adventure rather than a remote and deferred gratification.

The way Helen dealt with her impending retirement was fairly unusual. Not all of us are able to visualize this kind of "happy ever after" for ourselves in such detail and so far in advance, when we're still caught up in the demands of a full-time job and/or raising a family. Helen planned far ahead and made few changes as she moved toward her goal. She was able to derive great satisfaction en route, whether picturing how her furniture would look in her cabin or getting acquainted with the grocer in her new neighborhood.

Helen's story illustrates how the preretirement years in life deserve your special attention. Many of us are reluctant to take much pleasure in preparing for our later years, perhaps because we haven't understood the potential they hold. These stories also demonstrate how many small actions add up to a few big ones. Pursuing goals is a little like climbing the rungs of a ladder. If you take them one at a time, the distance and effort that separate you from the top don't feel unattainable. That's why it's often helpful to take the time to break down a plan into smaller steps that can be tackled one day at a time.

Some Late Bloomers go after their dreams by looking far ahead, while others concentrate on the present. Some write their goals down, others keep them inside their heads. The issue isn't so much *how* you go about doing it but *whether* you do it at all. This principle is illustrated by the example of Jack G., a Late Bloomer who's always lived in the same working-class Boston neighborhood where he was born seventy-three years ago. A widower with grown children who've moved out of state, Jack began dealing with a degenerative health condition soon after his retirement from a long career in state government.

"I was gradually losing my eyesight," he explained to us during our morning visit to his Beacon Hill walk-up apartment. "Because my disease is untreatable, I knew that I had only a few months before I would become completely blind, except for retaining a small amount of peripheral vision."

Jack's doctors told him that other than his eye problems he was in good health and could continue living alone if that was what he wished. "My kids wouldn't hear of it," said Jack, with a rare note of irritation in his normally soothing and gentle voice. "They insisted that I come live with one of them. They were afraid I wouldn't be able to take care of myself." He politely but firmly rejected the idea. "I told them, 'This is my home. I've always lived here. I'm not going anywhere else.'"

Still, Jack knew he had a lot to learn before he could manage alone as a blind person. A proud and independent man,

Jack vowed he would not let his situation place a burden on anyone, especially his children. "I took up my oldest daughter's offer to come here and visit for a couple of weeks," Jack continued. "She was willing to teach me the basic things we both thought I should know before my vision was completely gone."

In the dim fog that now surrounded him, Jack learned how to prepare easy meals, pick out his wardrobe, and move about the apartment with familiarity and comfort. Household tasks as simple as making tea took on complex new dimensions—but also brought him fresh feelings of accomplishment as he mastered them. "There were a lot of things I couldn't take for granted anymore," Jack explained. "For instance, I couldn't test the liquid in my teakettle with my finger to see how hot it was. Instead I learned how to listen carefully to the sound boiling water makes."

By the time his daughter returned to New York, Jack was confident about his ability to get around on the bus, hail a taxi, and take care of necessary errands. Together they arranged for outside help with the chores that Jack agreed would soon become beyond his capacity, such as doing the laundry, grocery shopping, and house cleaning.

In addition to remaining physically active and reasonably independent, Jack was determined to keep his mind stimulated and engaged in projects that would get him outside the apartment regularly. "Right away I thought of two things I wanted to do," Jack told us. "I'd always been an avid reader, so I was anxious to find a way to keep that going. And I also liked helping kids." After many exploratory phone calls and conversations with friends, Jack came up with several possibilities that have since yielded enormous satisfaction. He contracted with a free service, one of several available to the visually disabled, to send him tape-recorded readings of books and periodicals. "I'm getting all kinds of spoken material on audiotapes," Jack explained. "I can listen to novels, short stories, magazines, and even articles from newspapers." Friends and neighbors help Jack order (and subsequently return) the boxes of material, which now overflow his mailbox every morning.

Next, Jack took steps toward accomplishing a long-desired goal of working with children. He was pleased to learn that Boston has one of the most extensive and accessible senior volunteer projects of any public school system in the country. The coordinator of the program immediately came to visit Jack and discuss his skills and interests. "I offered to help out in any area where they needed some extra manpower. They said they'd be thrilled to put me to work. That made me feel just great, because then I'd be able to give something back to the community."

The administrator arranged a meeting between Jack and the head of a grade school not far from his home. The neighborhood principal was eager for Jack's help and told him that what she needed most was a tutor for children with reading difficulties. "But since you're sight impaired," she ventured, "I suppose that idea's completely out of the question."

"Ah, that's where you're wrong," Jack replied. "I've been reading all my life. I can tell just by listening when someone's having trouble." The school set aside a quiet room in the library where Jack now tutors two children at a time, correcting them as they read aloud and helping them expand their vocabularies. If they come to a word they can't identify, Jack simply asks them to spell it for him aloud. "Tutoring is a challenge that I really enjoy," Jack said. "I feel so much more confident and independent just knowing I have this to look forward to."

Jack has made many friends among the students and gets together socially with the administrators and teachers. When the weather is nice, groups of children and adults vie for the chance to walk with Jack the short distance to his home. All have high praise for this Late Bloomer, who wasn't content to let his blindness keep him alone and isolated.

"When the teachers ask their classes how many students want to study with Jack in the library, half the hands go up, I'm told," he said with obvious pride. "They really appreciate my being there."

Although Jack didn't follow a structured series of "action steps" like some other Late Bloomers, his process was effectively the same. He told himself, *This is where I am and what my limitations are. This is where I want to go, and these are the things I am going to do to get there.*

Jack's process may have been informal, but it was anything but random. Although it may bring you limited rewards and satisfactions, a haphazard approach is rarely the most efficient because it fails to allow you to fully explore all the possibilities available. You'll get your deepest and most meaningful sense of accomplishment from having a plan to reach your destination.

Yet even with the most carefully constructed strategy, things can—and frequently do—go wrong. When this happens, you might conclude that you've failed. But there's more than one way to look at "errors in judgment." What makes something a right or wrong choice depends on how you feel about it now, in the present. Maybe it would have been a right choice three weeks ago, but if it isn't right for you now, it's hardly a mistake. Simply detach yourself from what happened and move along. Such occurrences often teach a valuable lesson, if only that you needn't go that way again. So if you hear judgmental words like "failure" bouncing inside your head, examine them carefully before letting them come to rest.

Besides, our views of what's appropriate for us are bound to alter with time. In later life we often make choices based on their internal benefits to us instead of whether they represent success or failure in the eyes of society or our peer group. This can result in a fundamental shift in our motivation, with some fascinating results. For example, an energetic couple named Ted and Pat D. had for several years been trying out answers to the question of what might be appropriate for them when we first saw them on a crowded midtown Manhattan bus one bright summer afternoon. We couldn't help noticing that the two were poring over a book entitled *Beginning Japanese.* They laughed at our obvious surprise at this, acting as if such a thing were perfectly ordinary.

"*Hajimemashite,*" Ted began, greeting us politely as if we were in Tokyo. "What's so odd about studying Japanese?" he inquired, as if mastering a new language at age sixty-eight were like playing bingo.

"Isn't everybody doing it?" Pat joked, pulling her own copy of the grammar book out of her satchel. The two good-naturedly agreed to an interview later that evening—after class—to talk about how they'd both decided to tackle the Asian tongue. When we met again in the living room of their cozy apartment, they confessed that neither had harbored any lifelong desire to learn Japanese; it was an activity they'd stumbled upon through trial and error. Both also said a determination to stay busy and involved in new activities was instilled in childhood by parents who refused to put limits on themselves because of age.

"In my family, one does not retire," explained Pat, whose mother worked as a Wall Street stockbroker until age eighty-two. "I remember my father, a zipper manufacturer, having a long talk with one of his business associates the day before he died at eighty-three."

Ted's dad was also a role model. "He was a typesetter and printer who worked through age seventy-one, so as a kid I got used to the idea of seeing an older person going off to work every morning," he said. "So you see, just because Pat and I have decided not to keep working in paid positions doesn't mean we've decided not to keep on learning."

Ted retired a few years ago from his job as a high-school history teacher, and about the same time, Pat stepped down from her medical research post at a New York hospital. For this energetic twosome, work doesn't have to fit into a nine-to-five job. To them it means a deep involvement that's both stimulating and exciting. When their work lives ended, they realized quickly that they'd need something to fill the gap.

Both were convinced that they'd eventually find a satisfying and rewarding avocation that would hold their interest, but at the outset neither knew exactly what it might be. Since Ted and Pat had always maintained goal-oriented lifestyles, they were initially attracted to activities that offered some kind of concrete results. "I tried everything," sighed Pat, ticking off a laundry list of short-lived flings. "I tried painting. I tried baking. I tried gardening. I took piano lessons." Pat also felt obliged to sign up for an aerobics class, having heard so much about the importance of heart-strengthening exercise in later life. Her children and friends also thought it would be good for her. "I got hung up in the 'shoulds,'" she laughed. "Everybody said it was something I 'should' do, so that's the reason I did it." She cast a knowing glance at her husband, seated across the room. "I was so bored with aerobics that I simply couldn't go on with it," Pat admitted with an exasperated sigh. "Now don't get me wrong—I'm happy for anyone who takes it up and enjoys it, because I think it's good physical exercise. But it just wasn't the way I wanted to spend my time."

Ted found it somewhat easier to make the transition from a daily work schedule, although he also floundered for a while. "I did a little volunteer work in some retired teacher's clubs," he recalled. "I taught English as a second language to Puerto Ricans. We traveled for a while." Looking back, Ted said he doesn't regret any of these choices and that each experience was rewarding in its own way. He pointed out that he was forty-five before he obtained a teaching credential, having spent the previous two decades as a social worker assigned to the New York City welfare department. "I don't think I've made any 'wrong' choices during retirement. I learned what I could from each new thing I tried and moved on. So far, however, nothing has engaged me as much as Japanese."

The pair attend classes at a local community college three times each week, then study together at home for several hours a day. They have also become friends with a Japanese family, who coach them on proper pronunciation and usage. They were planning the first of what they anticipated would be many trips to Japan. Pat and Ted are eager to practice their skills among native speakers and have gained new insight into aging by reading about the traditional Japanese reverence for older people.

"We are learning not only the complex rules of grammar but also the ideograms in which Japanese is written," said Pat.

"Although it's difficult, every time we learn something, there's a real thrill."

"I've learned that if something is difficult or boring and you give up on it, that doesn't mean failure," concluded Pat. "You just try something else. And I've finally found 'my thing,' as the kids would say."

When you alter your personal definition of success and failure, you feel much more freedom to experiment. Your expectations change as you adopt a "playful" attitude. At the same time, the levels of fear and apprehension you once associated with risk taking can be reduced. You no longer operate on the assumption that, as one Late Bloomer put it, "I'm only as good as what I do and how well I do it."

We're reminded of Thomas Edison, who tried and discarded a thousand different designs before he finally came up with an electric light bulb that worked. When asked why he hadn't become discouraged and given up after so many "failures," Edison replied: "I didn't make a thousand mistakes. In the course of inventing the light bulb, I simply took a thousand steps."

It's all in the attitude, the perspective you bring to bear in a particular situation. Words like "mistake" and "failure" evoke feelings of inadequacy and a poor self-image, while phrases like "learning experience" or "growth steps" are positive and supportive. Like Edison, we're bound to recheck our bearings or correct our course as we go along. No big deal. It's part of the learning process.

The stakes in life have changed for many of us by the time we reach our later years, and we can enjoy being able to lighten up. In some—but not all—respects, we don't have to take our decision making as seriously as we once did. That's another distinct advantage of maturity.

It's also important to remember that, as at any other time in life, false starts will be part of our later years. We sometimes follow paths that lead in directions we eventually decide are inappropriate for us. These are simply side trips on the journey toward our ultimate destination: a personally rewarding and satisfying lifestyle that works for us in the here and now. And, when this approach seems no longer appropriate, we can be open to something else that enriches and engages us. Trying a sequence of new things is a process of self-discovery, not failure.

THE SECRET OF ACTION STEPS

The secret of this chapter is the importance of taking "action steps." Our definition of an action step is any conduct that moves an individual closer to his or her goal. Think of them as the systematic procedures you go through to get from "here" to "there." A step may be relatively passive, such as reading a book on a subject, or decidedly active, like engaging in vigorous physical exercise. The emphasis is on *doing*.

An action step represents our commitment to growth, change, and self-actualization. When we take such a step, we embrace the idea that it's never too late to enjoy a rich, full life. Action steps move us toward that goal.

The secret shared by Late Bloomers in this chapter is a determination to persevere and to experiment. Charlie, Helen, Jack, Ted, and Pat each learned to define and achieve their goals in different ways, yet they shared a common belief that those goals *could* ultimately be defined and achieved—a view that made all the difference.

Successful Late Bloomers are seldom thwarted, at least for long, by the disappointments they encounter inevitably in their exploration of new activities and interests. They don't orient themselves to the "either/or" model of success and failure. If something doesn't work out, they reflect on the experience, accept whatever lessons they can from it, and keep on moving. They feel good simply knowing they've stretched themselves and taken a new approach. Their measurement of success tends to be based on their own internal satisfaction, not the opinions of others. They may not know specifically what it is they're looking for, but they'll hang in there until they find it.

Late Bloomers recognize that we're not the same people at age sixty—or seventy, or whatever—as we were in our twenties and thirties. We change and grow in many ways throughout our lives, so past interests occasionally dim and some curiosities are satisfied. Conversely, some activities or pursuits we once dismissed as uninteresting may become attractive.

Listen to yourself critically when making blanket statements like, "I don't travel" or, "I'm not athletic" or, "I'm no good with languages." Is it possible that these declarations no longer ring true? Could your interests and aptitudes have changed over the years? If our encounters with Late Bloomers are any guide, the answer to both questions is an emphatic "Yes!" We therefore urge you to make an honest, up-to-date appraisal of the way you feel about activities you may have been rejecting out of hand for the past few decades. At the same time, you may want to reconsider your involvement in familiar pastimes that no longer provide the satisfaction and enrichment you're seeking.

HOW TO ACT ON THIS SECRET

When we at last commit to realizing a desire or achieving a goal, we are often filled with a fresh sense of determination and a boost of confidence. We somehow sense that we'll discover talents, interests, and skills we didn't know we had. We may feel recharged and invigorated, buoyed with self-confidence. Try to take full advantage of these newfound energies and abilities by taking action steps. Remember, these don't have to be complicated. They may, in fact, involve something as simple as composing a list on a piece of paper.

List making is something we all do. We make lists before going to the hardware store, setting out on a trip, or starting a busy day. We use this same organizing technique in preparing a favorite meal for family or friends, for example. We check our pantry and refrigerator to see what foods we need. And once we've assembled all the necessary ingredients, we make sure to use the correct proportions, follow the right sequence, and set the proper cooking temperatures to obtain the desired results.

Our mealtime preparations follow a sequence of basic action steps. They begin with a decision to get "more out of life" (a pleasant evening with people we like), a narrowing of that desire into a specific "goal" (a dinner party), and the completion of moves needed to reach that goal (selecting a date, calling guests, planning a menu, making a food list, going shopping, and so on).

Following a step-by-step procedure like this, whether it involves filing a tax return, going to a movie, or getting a car serviced, becomes almost effortless by the time we've reached our mature years. Yet, ironically, few among us actually sit down and think through a comparable plan of action for what is potentially the most exciting, enriching, and important journey of all: the one that carries us into the uncharted territory of later life.

Let's begin our organizational task by assuming that you've settled on at least one particular interest you'd like to explore. Suppose, for instance, you've become curious about the game of golf. A helpful beginning is to write down everything that you can think of which could conceivably get you closer to where you want to go, in this case a putting green or fairway. Some items on your action list will be very general and others quite specific.

Some general instructions to yourself might include: "Find out where nearest golf courses are," "Ask friends whether they play the game," "Check prices on equipment," and "See where lessons are offered."

Here are some specific notations: "Call Hillside Country Club and request their brochure," "Phone brother-in-law Larry and ask if he'll take me along on his weekly game," "Look at classified newspaper ads to see if anyone's selling used golf clubs," and "Ask doctor what the game's health risks or benefits are for me."

As in similar exercises we've already talked about, the idea is not necessarily to come up with a final, polished list the first time out but rather to get your mind focused in the appropriate direction. You can always return to eliminate some things, add others, and put question marks alongside those you're unsure about. Never mind how your list looks as you've first drafted it. Eventually, you'll want to be as specific and detailed as possible, but that can always come later.

Once you've brainstormed all the possible steps that could

lead you in the direction you've selected, set the checklist aside for a day or two while you go on about the ordinary business of your life. As other ideas occur to you or people make useful suggestions, jot them down on a piece of paper so that you won't forget them. Finally, after your subconscious has had enough time to mull over your ideas, it's time to sit down, update your original list, and start setting some priorities.

It's useful and more efficient to follow up on some things before others, so try to answer the most fundamental and far-reaching questions first. A series of phone calls may quickly reveal that the only golf course within twenty miles of your home is available exclusively to members of a fancy country club that you can't afford to join (which automatically poses a whole new set of choices). Your brother-in-law Larry and his pals may be happy to teach you the game's basics so that you can become more familiar with the pastime before investing in expensive private lessons or equipment. Or you may go out on the golf course a few times and discover you're utterly bored by it all, thus concluding that the game isn't for you.

If you decide that golf is an activity that's too expensive, inconvenient, or dull, it's obviously best to address those issues as soon as possible so that you can avoid wasting time and move in a more productive direction.

We tend to be more motivated if we feel a sense of accomplishment as we head toward our goals. That's why a checklist is often helpful, even if the only item we check off in the course of a day is something like "Buy a golf magazine and become more conversant with the game and its vocabulary." Crossing an accomplished task off a list is a way of patting ourselves on the back. And as we all know, praise from ourselves is the highest form of praise—*and* the most effective.

The secret is to keep moving forward—something our Late Bloomers have told us they needed to do in order to get wherever they wanted to go. They backed up their action steps with persistence, consistency, flexibility, and openness. They kept "an eye on the pie," whatever kind of pie that happened to be.

CHAPTER SIX

THE SECRET OF MANY HAPPY RETURNS

SOME OF US ARE LUCKY ENOUGH to find something we love to do early in life and then rediscover it joyfully much later on.

At the age of eighty, for example, Walter E. received his B.A. degree from Ohio State University in the Experimental Learning Program. He first attended college almost sixty years earlier and had long since abandoned his studies in order to take a job and support his family.

When she was a little girl, Louise S. begged her parents for dance lessons. But the family was struggling on a meager budget, so there was no money for such extravagances. In her late seventies, Louise's desire resurfaced, and she's now a member of a dance troupe of seniors that has achieved considerable recognition and even toured Sweden.

Then there's Art N., of San Francisco, who once caddied at a local country club and always hoped to become a professional golfer. Now that Art has stepped down from his position as a supermarket manager, he plays golf every single day and tutors private students on bettering their game.

We call this chapter "The Secret of Many Happy Returns" because the stories that follow tell of individuals who returned in their later years to an activity that was a first love or ambition. Their experiences underscore how, in our youth, many of us are shameless dreamers and incorrigible idealists. We picture ourselves as future movie stars, locomotive engineers, firefighters, nurses, or doctors. Then we go off to school, get married, and have children, with the attendant demands and responsibilities those events invariably entail. Often we wind up doing something for a living that we'd never considered when we were children, and in doing so we set aside our ideals and fantasies. But when we approach (or experience) our "retirement years," we finally have time to devote ourselves to the project, career, or avocation that we associate with our fondest memories.

Each of our Late Bloomers came to his or her current passion in an individual manner. The stimulus prodding them may have come through free-form writing or conversations with spouses and friends. The motivation that kept them going may have been as varied as the desire to receive a professional certificate or educational diploma, to reenter the job market, or simply to fill their days in a joyful and satisfying way. What they had in common was a willingness to pay attention when something struck a chord that put them back in resonance with the excitement and enthusiasm of youth.

Sometimes a new direction seems to surface unconsciously, as if out of nowhere. Such is the case of sixty-seven-year-old Bob P., who related his story over a brown-bag lunch in the cafeteria of a large Boston-area university, surrounded by fellow students young enough to be his grandchildren. "I was raised in Erie, Pennsylvania," Bob began, taking a break from the graduate school classes that fill his days. "After high school, I had two choices in front of me. I could either go to college or follow up on my successful audition at the Pasadena Playhouse and become an actor." It was the Great Depression, and the choice of journalism seemed the more practical one, so he decided to enroll in the Columbia School of Journalism. He became totally immersed in his new career and never gave acting a second thought. Although he enjoyed a night of theater once in a while, Bob was a hard-driving journalist with no spare time for hobbies. He spent forty satisfying years in his profession, working his way up from cub reporter to the editorship of a large metropolitan newspaper. Bob enjoyed great prestige in the job, shuttling from one important meeting to the next while constantly making tough decisions under relentless deadlines.

Then, quite unexpectedly, a big project of his collapsed, and Bob was offered a very attractive early retirement package. Without a clue as to what he'd do with himself, he reluctantly agreed to accept it. "My wife said, 'You've got to think of something to keep busy; you can't just sit at home all day.'" Bob rejected the obvious possibilities of writing or editing books and waited quietly for the answer to present itself. By becoming uncharacteristically detached and contemplative, he tried to empty his mind of distracting thoughts. He spent a good deal of time each day in a calm, detached state similar to meditation. For some unknown reason, Bob knew that if he were quiet the answer would come of its own accord.

"I decided to go back to acting almost on an impulse," said Bob, acknowledging the faith he placed in his own intuition. "I remembered—I don't know why—sitting on the porch of the house I was raised in and wondering about whether I was going to choose journalism or the playhouse. Suddenly I thought, *Why don't I make the other choice now?*" Even though Bob hadn't appeared on stage since high school, the choice seemed as natural as breathing. "Since we have only one life," he figured, "why not live a number of its possibilities instead of sticking to one?"

Through his self-reflective process, Bob had reached the conclusion that something essential had been missing from his daily routine as an objective, unflappable journalist. "When I worked for newspapers, I never lost my cool," Bob noted, his blue jeans, sneakers, and open-neck shirt a sharp contrast to the conservatively tailored suits and button-down collars he'd worn at the office. "I never got angry. I held my feelings inside. In order to become an actor, I had to break down the training of over four decades. In so doing, I've learned that I hardly knew what an impulse was. I had submerged my freedom to do things, to say things, to raise an eyebrow. Now I'm getting back that freedom to express my emotions."

Once he'd made his decision, Bob committed himself to becoming a pro. For him, this meant going back to graduate school, obtaining an advanced degree, and competing with hundreds of other actors for the handful of stage, movie, and TV jobs in his area. "I want to become so good that people will pay me to act," he emphasized. "That's still my standard."

Bob's days are long and taxing, beginning with an early morning workout (he's lost fifteen pounds) and continuing through classes, voice lessons, and nightly rehearsals, even on weekends. Fortunately, Bob enjoys good health, is financially secure, and has the loving support of his wife, Betty. "It's difficult for her because I'm away so much," he conceded, "but Betty's been great. We all need encouragement, and she's encouraged me a lot." Betty has grown in her own way from Bob's experience. After being inspired by one of her husband's courses, she even took singing lessons.

The transition from mild-mannered reporter to emotive actor has made enormous changes in Bob's life at an age when many of his peers are wondering if they have the time, strength, or inner resources to tackle something new. "I guess I have the courage of old age," Bob declared, defining this as the freedom and wisdom to follow his heart without the prior approval of an employer, family, peers, or the community at large. As Bob sees it, the drastic change in his lifestyle after age sixty-five has challenged him to grow in ways he knew instinctively would be positive. "Acting allows me to meet myself in a different way, and that's the most exciting part of it for me. It's almost a self-analysis situation and has made me wonder a lot about my previous life."

For Bob, returning to a first love seemed a natural means of maintaining the self-esteem and personal challenges he'd enjoyed at work. Yet he's also learned to trust his unconscious mind. Instead of rushing to make a decision about retirement, Bob created a tranquil mood that allowed his inner voice to emerge. This quiet approach may help you too. Of course, your way may be entirely different. There's no right or wrong path to self-discovery.

You may, for example, be as excited as ever about such early pleasures as collecting stamps, sewing needlepoint, swimming laps, or strumming the banjo. It's also okay if the passions of your youth have evolved into something new. One Illinois man we know followed a natural progression as his teenage interest in ham radios gave way to a later-life fascination with computers.

For Harriet Doerr, the discovery of a new and creative way of life came unexpectedly at age seventy-five, when her first novel was accepted by a major New York publisher. *Stones for Ibarra* won overnight acclaim for its author and led her to a successful writing career. "I liked to write when I was in grade school and high school," said Harriet, who spoke to us in the tiny, windowless corner where she begins each morning by putting pen to paper. "But I didn't seriously consider becoming a writer. I left college and got married instead. I suppose what is horribly and hideously called a 'housewife' is what I became." During forty-two subsequent years of married life, Harriet set aside a "back of the mind" curiosity about writing and devoted herself completely to being a good wife and mother.

Attempting to balance homemaking with writing, as many female authors have done, was never a consideration for Harriet. She's always viewed writing as an intensely personal activity that requires total silence and absolute concentration, not to be diluted with daily domestic routines. "I didn't see how I could possibly write if anyone else was in the house. If someone even walked upstairs, I think I would stop what I was doing."

Like many women of her generation, Doerr felt very strongly that her first responsibilities were to her family and that her own outside interests came second. For sixteen years the Doerrs lived in a small Mexican town where, as a keen observer of people, Harriet stored mental images she hoped to write about someday. Her husband eventually took a new job and moved the family back to California, where he died in 1972. It was only after her offspring had grown and she'd settled down by herself in Pasadena that Harriet found the time and solitude to reflect on her life in Mexico. After a few months of struggling to express herself by writing fiction, she felt a need to study creative writing in a formal setting. "If my husband had still been alive," Harriet speculated, sipping tea in the sprawling two-story house where she has spent many years alone, "it probably would not have occurred to me to go back to school. Picturing myself as an author was very remote."

Encouraged by her teachers and fellow students, Harriet gradually developed enough confidence at sixty-seven to write a full-length novel drawn from her vivid memories. After laboring painfully over every word and punctuation mark, Harriet bravely mailed the completed manuscript to a New York publisher, even though new authors are rarely considered without agent representation. Not knowing her age or background, Viking Press immediately accepted the book on its merits. *Stones for Ibarra* became a best-seller, and in 1988 CBS adapted it as a television movie starring Glenn Close. The author followed up in 1993 with another Mexico-based novel, *Consider This, Señora.*

Although her achievements are impressive by any measure, Harriet places the process of writing above the fruits of publication. "I had no idea that I'd succeed commercially," she emphasized. "I thought I was just spending my time in a way that I like very much. That was my only real goal."

Harriet is willing to take chances. She demonstrated this not only by returning to college in her later years and shuttling between home and campus on crowded freeways every day but also through the rigorous process of self-examination that her writing entails. "I would never have sent off *Stones for*

Ibarra if my teacher hadn't insisted," said Harriet, laughing at her own perfectionism, which yielded four years of near-constant revision. "I've already marked up the margins of one copy of the book with notations like 'Expand here.'"

The novelist mentions these ongoing corrections of a work that has already received prestigious awards in order to stress the importance of writing as a vehicle for self-discovery and renewal. "I truly think you must expose yourself to risk, or you're not really living," she said with conviction. "It's an emptiness, a diminishing of a person, not to see and feel as much as you can. I think facing sadness or tragedy—thinking about it, writing about it—makes one a complete person."

For Harriet Doerr, later-life success as a writer came as a complete surprise. She had approached writing cautiously, in much the same way that a diver checks a pool's temperature and depth before plunging in. And in order to write in a way that was meaningful to her, she had to overcome many fears. By actively choosing not to remain a prisoner of those fears, Harriet was able to follow her own path to a new world of creative satisfaction. Instead of letting stumbling blocks become insurmountable, she approached them as manageable challenges that would bring her closer to purposeful self-awareness.

As we grow older, there is usually less pressure on us to conform to the demands of family, employer, and society. We may conclude that the process involved in an activity is often more important to us than a finished product or specific achievement. Like an adventure-filled journey to a far-off destination, the process of getting there is frequently more rewarding than actually arriving.

Trying out unfamiliar activities or using rusty skills isn't easy. Remember how many times you fell off a bicycle before it was actually fun to ride? The European vacation when you embarrassed yourself by using high-school French on Parisians? The dinner party where your first soufflé collapsed? Each of these forays into the unknown may have seemed like failures at the time. Yet, as we've noted, events we label as failures or mistakes are often stepping-stones to wisdom. Maybe we learned from these experiences to put training wheels on our bike, or to enroll in a French course at the community college before we returned to Paris, or to double-check the oven temperature when trying a new recipe. Whatever the "wrong decision" was, we learned something important and made a wiser choice the next time.

It's more productive and life affirming to approach our own aging in the same optimistic spirit. Instead of seeing only wrinkles and thinning locks in the mirror, we can just as easily focus on aspects of our appearance that we genuinely like. Try telling yourself, *My smile is sincere and appealing* or whatever applies. Looking at these positives will result in your feeling more attractive, confident, and powerful. If we choose to view our aging from a fresh, upbeat point of view, the inevitable physical changes will become harbingers of the advantages available to us in our later years. We've got the time, desire, and energy to commit ourselves to what we really want to do. Growing older can be a plus, not a minus. Now is the time to concentrate on *you.*

Consider the creative approach to retirement taken by Ken R., a sixty-six-year-old retired salesman in Brooklyn Park, Minnesota. "I figure I play at home for myself, so I might as well play for others," the big fellow laughed, shrugging his broad shoulders as we sat with him in his living room. "I guess that's why folks call me "The Accordion Man.' "

For most of his life, however, Ken never played a musical instrument. He fooled around with the squeezebox as a young man but set the accordion aside after marriage and promptly forgot all about it. A tall, handsome man with a friendly smile and expansive manner, Ken was trained to be a grade-school teacher. He did a little substitute teaching early in his marriage, but that didn't pay enough to feed the four children who arrived in quick succession. So Ken switched to a more lucrative sales job and stayed with sales for the rest of his career, never giving thought to life after retirement. At sixty-five, Ken stepped down from his sales position, still not knowing what he'd do next. The first Monday after retiring, Ken's wife, Edith, walked up to him with a frown on her face. "I'm worried about your lack of hobbies," she told Ken, looking him straight in the eye. "What about that accordion you used to play when we were courting? Why don't you see if you can still play it?"

Edith's suggestion intrigued Ken. Since the original had been sold years before, he rented an accordion from a music shop and was pleasantly surprised to find he could still tap out a few bouncy polkas, along with such old favorites as "Three O'Clock in the Morning" and "Carolina Moon." When a friend spotted a used accordion at a garage sale, Ken rushed out to buy it. "It's a fun instrument," he explained, between snatches of "Golden Slippers" and "After the Ball." "It's not difficult to play at all."

But the best thing about the accordion was that it kept sociable Ken in touch with the outside world. Never one to play alone, he started performing for his three young grandchildren. The trio enjoyed his backyard performances so much that they invited all the neighborhood kids over to listen. A short time later, a man from the local senior citizens club knocked on Ken's front door. "He asked me to volunteer at day-care centers around the Twin Cities, playing and singing for all the little ones. So now I go out five or six times a month and play for them."

Ken is not a professional musician and has no desire to become one. He hasn't taken a lesson since high school, and his repertoire is limited. But audiences think his shows are fine just the way they are. "It's like I'm teaching the kids something. They clap their hands to the beat and sing along. Sometimes I think maybe they'll get inspired to pick up an instrument when they get a little bigger and start performing themselves. Besides, playing brings back my boyhood. At the same time, it's a new experience, because back then I seldom had an audience. It's added a dimension to my life that I really enjoy."

On the day of our visit, Ken appeared at a private nursery, surrounded by preschoolers. He also plays for older children at birthday parties and grade schools, as well as for seniors at nursing or convalescent homes. "The older folks hear the songs, and the tears start coming," Ken told us, his blue eyes shining behind thick spectacles. "It reminds them of when they'd go out dancing to those same old tunes. Helping them remember the old days makes me feel really good."

Ken's volunteer performances fill important needs in his life that used to be occupied by his sales job. Instead of the social and psychological rewards that came from dealing daily with people in the world of work, he now derives great satisfaction from appreciative listeners. Ken has created a situation outside employment that maintains his positive self-image as a likable, helpful public citizen.

Not all of us have the desire or ability to write a best-selling novel, attend drama school, or play a musical instrument, but everybody has some skill or talent they enjoy utilizing, for the pleasure it brings themselves or others. As Ken has shown, being an amateur can be just as rewarding as being a pro. His story brings to mind the word "serendipity," a useful term describing a seemingly random discovery that occurs when we need it most yet least expect it.

For some Late Bloomers, serendipitous events have made all the difference in their later years. These are people who've approached retirement with perhaps only a vague notion of the way they would be spending their free time. Then, suddenly, the answer presents itself gift-wrapped on their doorsteps. All of us can't count on that happening, but it's wise to keep our eyes open and scanning the horizon. For an illustration of the reason this is important, consider how a seemingly chance event changed the life of Carl Rakosi.

When he was only three weeks away from retirement as a San Francisco social worker, Carl received a gracious but entirely unexpected letter from an English poet whom he'd never met. It seems this young man had stumbled upon a cache of dusty magazines from the 1920s, publications in which poems written by Carl had appeared alongside those of the much-admired Ezra Pound. "The fellow who wrote me lived in London and wanted to know where he could find more of my poetry," Carl said, summarizing the fateful correspondence.

"I've scoured the libraries to no avail," the bewildered British fan informed Carl. "Why can't I find anything you published after 1930? I am very anxious to read your later work." Rakosi replied that there was no later work, for the simple reason that he hadn't written any poetry since 1931.

From the age of sixteen through his twenties, Carl, a native midwesterner, was a passionate and prolific poet whose compositions were highly regarded by critics and fellow poets alike. Literary journals eagerly awaited each new Rakosi composition, and enthusiastic audiences applauded the young poet's crowded public readings. Through four years of college, there was no doubt in Carl's mind that his career would be in some form of creative writing. But after college he stumbled into social work, Carl told us while sitting in the small apartment he shares with his ailing wife, Lee. "It was my first job, which I decided to take mostly because I'd discovered that I couldn't combine marriage, writing, and a profession." Immediately, Carl decided to stop using his pseudonym, Carl Rakosi, and use his given name, Calman Rawley, instead. This act distanced him from the literary reputation he'd developed and allowed him to create a separate new identity in social work.

"There were great tangible satisfactions in my new job," explained Carl, looking back on the four decades during which poems were the furthest thing from his mind. "I spent much of that time counseling, negotiating, and writing reports in the style of sociology, which of course is much different from poetry." But while the languages of the two disciplines differ, they both reflect on the human condition and incorporate the wisdom and insights of real-life experience. In retrospect, Carl thinks those similarities may have influenced his later decision to reclaim his lost identity as a poet.

"I feel very natural now in both worlds," he allowed. "But if it had not been for that letter from England, I wouldn't have thought I could get back into poetry. Knowing that somebody would take that much trouble to track me down and show such interest in my work gave me the boost I needed."

Over the next eighteen years, Carl reemerged in the literary world as what critics call "a poet's poet." He embraces the art form with an unrelenting passion, immersing himself in the writing, reading, teaching, and public presentation of poetry. Carl's many published works have received rave reviews, and he is frequently asked to speak at writing conferences. At age eighty-three, with his identity as Calman Rawley the social worker put firmly behind him, Carl Rakosi the poet is back. In retrospect, Carl realizes that he could easily have dismissed the complimentary letter he received from London. After all, he'd never heard of the Englishman and had long since abandoned his poetry. But because Carl was open to something new, he took the unexpected missive to heart.

All of us have had some experience with serendipity, although few are as lucky as Carl. But like him, we can listen carefully when someone compliments us or tells us he or she has been moved by something we've done. Do you dance or make music? Do you like to write poetry or stories? Have you an impulse to sing or act? Even though these talents may not bring you the kind of public acclaim some Late Bloomers are fortunate enough to enjoy, they may lead you in directions that are satisfying in and of themselves.

One of the frustrations of growing older occurs when we discover that some of the things we assumed would get easier seem as difficult as ever. Take the seemingly simple matter of learning, for example: the step-by-step process by which we are gradually able to drive a car, speak a foreign language, program a videocassette recorder, load a washing machine, prune an apple tree, or repair a dripping faucet.

It seems logical to assume that since we have been developing skills and acquiring information throughout our lives, the process of learning itself should become less difficult. Unfortunately, this isn't necessarily the case. Although it may be somewhat shortened, the learning process isn't any different in fundamental ways at age sixty-five than it is at sixteen. We all still share those overwhelming feelings of confusion and despair when at first an unfamiliar subject seems too difficult to master. As older people, we sometimes confuse this with a diminished ability to learn, probably because we've been falsely led to believe that "you can't teach an old dog new tricks."

The truth is that grasping something new always takes time. Learning to operate a computer, for example, places many of us in a completely alien environment. So fearful are we of making a mistake that we often feel too paralyzed to move. It is during this early phase of learning, when progress is painfully slow and rewards are minimal, that we are tempted to throw up our hands and walk away. While this urge may be strong, getting through this discouraging phase is essential if we are to reap the many benefits of learning.

Can you remember the excitement of finally getting the hang of something for the first time—like being able to change a tire, tune an engine, cook with a microwave oven, play a respectable game of bridge, return a serve back-handed in a set of tennis, put a crying baby to sleep, read a confusing road map? Maybe it was telling a good story that made people laugh, or having a complicated recipe come out just the way your mother's tasted. As we've learned from our Late Bloomers, the approach to learning that makes it fun, even ecstatic, is being kind to yourself, praising yourself whenever you've taken even the smallest positive step.

Learning opportunities come in both formal and informal

settings. If you enjoy formal study, you may want to pursue a college degree, get a high-school diploma, attend adult education classes, enroll in an Elderhostel seminar, hire a tutor, or take specialized training courses. Bob's theater studies and Harriet's writing instruction, for example, occurred in relatively structured settings. But we can learn from our daily experiences too. Ken's accordion playing and Carl's poetry writing take place outside traditional learning environments.

Eighty-five-year-old Mildred H. has decided to indulge in the rediscovered passion of simply learning for its own sake. Like Ken, her motivation is personal enrichment, not the external goal of a new career. She's an example of someone guided by an internal compass that has taken her, quite happily and purposefully, in many different directions. "I've been a jill-of-all-trades my whole life," Mildred explained, sitting in the sparsely furnished living room of the modest Arizona home she now shares with a middle-aged son. She reflected on her many jobs as a cashier, stenographer, beauty technician, office clerk, mail sorter, speech therapist, and secretary. "I'm simply curious about things, all kinds of things. I guess that explains why I do what I do."

Although Mildred always experienced an intrinsic satisfaction in taking on new occupations, she often felt frustrated by the demands of work. Her family's financial needs were such that she couldn't afford to quit working and finish college. No sooner had she acquired the skills needed for one job than a relocation by her husband or a layoff by her employer would force her to start over somewhere else.

As she approached her midsixties, with her children finally on their own, Mildred anticipated a comfortable and active life of leisure with her husband in a well-maintained life-care retirement village near Cleveland. The couple had looked forward to what they expected would be their final move into an all-expenses-paid community where long-term care was guaranteed.

The first years were good ones, filled with part-time jobs, overseas travel, and visits to the grandchildren in Arizona. Then, after a lingering illness that required three debilitating years of hospitalization, Mildred's husband died. After considerable reflection, the new widow arrived at the conclusion that what she'd like to do most was go back to college. So, about a year after her husband's death, Mildred and her recently divorced son moved into a suburban Phoenix house adjacent to the state university. "I'm a bookworm," she said, gesturing toward a floor-to-ceiling library that even contains the first book she ever read. "From an early age I've wanted to go to school and take liberal arts courses, just for the sheer joy of learning. Not to earn a degree or get a job, but simply for my own enjoyment."

Under an arrangement that is now common at many colleges and universities, Mildred was welcomed as an unclassified student free to take virtually any class she desired, without earning any units toward a degree. She pays only a small enrollment fee and audits most courses so that she doesn't have to turn in papers or take tests. Mildred has become what some people call a "perpetual student." She goes to class for the sheer pleasure of learning and sees no reason to stop.

"I live in a two-bedroom place within walking distance of the university," Mildred said. "Since my joints are awfully swollen, being near campus is very important to me." As a result of her painful arthritis, it is sometimes hard for her simply to get out of bed in the morning. But the desire to get to class is a powerful motivator that works wonders. During our visit, Mildred's son was installing a bedroom doorway and ramp that would give her wheelchair access out of their home. Even though she can still walk around, Mildred anticipates eventually being wheelchair bound and is determined not to let that keep her from the joys of education. "My goal is to keep myself mentally alive," Mildred emphasized. "I notice many people go back to school and enroll in subjects they're already proficient in. That may be fine for them, but the challenge for me is to tackle something I know little or nothing about."

In the past, Mildred faced obstacles whenever she tried to pursue her goal of lifelong education. Today her health problems impose burdens. Yet Mildred prefers to look at each of these situations not as a barrier but as a challenge. She assesses them realistically and solves them in the firm belief that they'll never prevent her from doing what she wants to do most. It's amazing how quickly solutions materialize when you know what you want and are determined to get it.

THE SECRET OF MANY HAPPY RETURNS

"Human beings need the freedom to invent and reinvent themselves a number of times throughout their lives," declares Dr. Robert Butler, an early advocate of active aging. This freedom to reinvent ourselves is what allows us all to discover and rediscover the wonderful capabilities of our minds, bodies, and spirits—at any age. As the storytellers in this chapter have shown, the most satisfying discoveries often lie ahead of us, even though they may be anchored in the past. This is the secret of "many happy returns."

Opening ourselves up to the loves and passions of our youth—whether they involve hobbies, travel, the arts, athletics, family, nature, work, or something else—may help these seeds germinate, establish roots, and bear fruit. The realization of a lifelong dream can be a source of tremendous satisfaction and fulfillment. We encourage you to consider all such possibilities.

In order to better accomplish this, remember that helpful "life messages" are heading our way all the time, although too often we neither recognize nor heed them. If we respond automatically to life's myriad possibilities with such rote statements as "I *can't* do that" or, "I have *no* talent for such a thing," we shut the door on opportunity before it's even opened. It's possible to prepare ourselves for new, untried activities simply by being accessible and responsive. In fact, it is often when we learn to trust that the answers to our questions lie within and around us that the universe presents them. As a sage pointed out a thousand years ago: "When the student is ready, the teacher appears."

Each of the Late Bloomers in this chapter differs dramatically in the approach taken to later-life fulfillment. Harriet's greatest rewards from writing are internal, while Ken's musicianship means little to him unless people are smiling and applauding appreciatively. Bob is discovering long-hidden aspects of his own personality through acting, while Carl is reveling in a much-loved activity that long lay dormant. Mildred relishes the pure pleasure of learning and the luxury of being a dilettante.

Your choices, of course, will be specifically yours. We know a "retired" manicurist who works "on location" in various retirement communities three days a week simply because she likes this lifelong career of hers too much to stop. Another friend volunteers regularly for a nonprofit religious organization because he loves giving of himself to the less fortunate in his community.

All Late Bloomers have one thing in common, however. They've given themselves permission to stretch and grow during their later years by following their confident hearts and curious minds. They've adopted an open-minded attitude that allows positive change not only to happen but to flourish. Many of them also used practical and effective techniques for reflection and self-discovery—including the composition and review of "passion lists"—to listen to themselves closely and, through this process, to help determine their direction.

You need not make any final decisions as you explore the secret of many happy returns. Be playful and curious. Keep in mind that growth and change continue until we die. Not only are we never too old to try new things, but the passage of time and accumulation of experience often help us make wiser and more appropriate choices than we did at thirty. Enjoy!

HOW TO ACT ON THIS SECRET

As Bob P. demonstrated at the beginning of this chapter, accomplishing a goal is much easier when you listen carefully to your "inner voice," even if you've spent much of your life ignoring it. By inner voice we mean the internal conversation that some people call "self-talk." This is the voice that expresses your deepest and most heartfelt feelings and thoughts. It serves as a kind of moral compass on your journey of self-discovery.

Bob cleared his conscious mind so that underlying truths could surface and be acknowledged. Instinctively, he knew that sometimes it's self-defeating to actively "think" too much. Even though we grow up in a culture that encourages cerebral activity and applied logic, we don't always find an answer by thinking a problem through. Instead, the mind sometimes needs to become quiet, like a placid pool, so that the delicate ripples of original thoughts, intuitive feelings, and significant memories can rise to the surface. If we pay attention to what's hidden beneath the shallow reflections of the surface, we will often discover deeper truths.

Another effective course of action is to have a frank conversation with a trusted mate, relative, friend, or member of the clergy who knows you well enough to make some informed suggestions about activities that they believe might appeal to you during your retirement years. Sometimes it takes gentle prompting, from a longtime confidant, to draw our attention to a moribund talent or interest. Remember how Ken's wife reminded him about his accordion playing? Or how Carl's distant admirer revived his passion for poetry?

We suggest you listen to these reflective and contemplative feelings and thoughts, then commit to paper those that seem most significant. You may rediscover, for instance, that you've experienced some of your greatest joys in the kitchen, making meals and snacks that you know will bring pleasure. Or you may find that interacting with people in the world of work is something you dearly miss and want to re-create through a part-time job or entrepreneurial activity. Candid observations about what brought you pleasures and satisfactions in the past are an excellent way to focus on what you really want in the present and future.

As our Late Bloomers have shown, writing things down is an important step in finding a direction. Once you've jotted some hopes and dreams on paper—whether they involve buying a farm, becoming a lawyer, or publishing a book of poetry—you're a step closer to having them come true. If they're not recorded in some manner, those vague plans may evaporate faster than a puddle on a hot summer day. And we've found that the actual process of writing, whether or not you ever refer to that piece of paper again, speeds you along in getting where you want to go.

One approach that has proven particularly effective is keeping a personal journal for a week, jotting down every activity you can think of that has brought you great pleasure in the course of your life. Describe in your own words what you particularly liked about doing these things. For instance, did you once enjoy dancing on Saturday nights? Were you stimulated by visiting art museums? Did people praise your expertise at auto repair? Have you enjoyed working for political candidates? After doing this for several days, you'll have a substantial list of preferred activities and a feel for the pleasures they've brought you. Remember, nobody has to see any of this writing except you, since its twofold purpose is strictly personal: to test those good feelings all over again and to provide you with some promising ideas for the future.

Spend the following week making a second list of activities. These are things you've always wanted to try but have never gotten around to doing, unfulfilled desires that you still think might be fun to explore. They may be ideas you've carried around since 1925 or as recently as this morning. Do you want to fly in a balloon? Drive to Alaska? Draw a self-portrait? Volunteer at a children's hospital? Go back to school? Re-enter the job market?

This is no time to fall into trite phrases like "I can't do that!" or "I might have done it forty years ago, but I'm too old now." Many of us invoke these excuses because we fear change and disruption, figuring that it's better to hang on to familiar routines and habits than try some new endeavor that might bring rejection, disappointment, or so-called failure.

Beyond a natural fear of failure, there is also a tendency to feel that it is somehow "inappropriate" for an older person to go back to a youthful passion or tackle something new. Society has adopted a mind-set suggesting that *youth* is the only appropriate time for exploring seemingly frivolous whims. Conventional wisdom holds that only our *formative* years should be devoted to training, apprenticeship, and learning.

But youth seldom encompasses the wisdom and vision earned over a lifetime of experience. As we grow older, we tend to discount the opinions of others and pay more attention to our inner needs and desires. It's not easy to overcome ingrained fears and change your mind's "I can't" chant to an "I can" mantra, but remember how a mere change in intention from negative to positive is a powerful tool in obtaining what you really want out of life.

Look back on this day and try to visualize every experience that stands out. Later on, as you go about your routines, observe your activities and feelings carefully. Are you proud of framing a new picture? Did a magazine article you read about a comedian make you smile? Were you surprised at how easily you resolved a minor property dispute between two of your neighbors?

Each of these seemingly mundane highlights may point you in a new direction. We can find clues to late blooming everywhere, if we only pay attention: by looking at and listening to our activities of the present as well as our dreams of the future and satisfactions from the past.

CHAPTER SEVEN

THE SECRET OF WORK

WHAT IS YOUR VISION OF "THE GOOD LIFE" in later years? For many of us, it is the freedom to do as we please with our time and energy, whether that means work or leisure or anything in between. Such freedom is made possible by having sufficient financial resources and health coverage to feel safe and secure. With our living expenses covered, we may feel more comfortable volunteering in our communities, visiting with our families, or traveling the world. We may also want to keep working, either for the income or the personal satisfactions beyond money—or both. Fortunately, there are a greater variety of work-related options for us now than ever before.

Still, a job search at any age is challenging. If you're a midlife or older worker, the process can feel especially daunting if the kind of work you're seeking is different from what you've done before. How do you choose a career path that meets your life goals? How do you approach employers who may be envisioning candidates who are younger? How do you wind down or ramp up a new career? How do you get the specialized training or higher education to do a different type of work? The answers to such questions are embodied in the actions of many Late Bloomers we've been privileged to meet.

Maureen K. is a prime example of how a graying but energetic individual can indulge in the many pleasures of leisure activities while still enjoying the equally compelling benefits of employment. At sixty-nine, Maureen accepted a five-day-a-week job that represented an entirely new career for her.

"I'm a lunchtime hostess at a restaurant near my home," she explains, with obvious excitement in her pleasant voice. "I come in around ten o'clock and leave at two or two-thirty, depending on how busy we are."

Maureen spent many years as an interior decorator, building a business that gave her tremendous satisfaction as well as financial success. During her early sixties she met and married her present husband, an older gentleman who had already retired to enjoy a life of full-time leisure and community service. Maureen decided to retire herself in order to spend more time with him. Not long afterwards, however, one of her sons became a business entrepreneur and opened two restaurants not far from the couple's residence. She was recruited—willingly—to do the interior design for both dining establishments.

"After my son's restaurants were done, I retired a second time," says Maureen, flashing an impish grin. "But I soon realized I was really missing something in my life. You see, I love being with people. I missed the sociability of working with others on a regular basis." She pointed out that the Wisconsin town she and her husband live in is fairly small, with limited options for meeting new folks. Many of her women friends like to meet for lunch and play cards regularly, but that does-n't hold much appeal for Maureen, who thrives on meeting new people and being part of a service-oriented enterprise.

This self-described "people person" set out looking for a job that was part time, since she still enjoyed many leisure activities with her husband. "I also wanted to work only during daylight hours," Maureen said, "because I don't drive at night."

First she considered employment as a business reception-ist, since this promised a daily flow of new and interesting people. Then one day she noticed a "HELP WANTED" sign for a hostess in the window of a local restaurant that specialized in lunchtime fare.

"I applied, but was afraid the manager would reject me because of my age," confesses Maureen. "And what's more, I'd never done this sort of work before."

Maureen was pleasantly surprised when the manager not only hired her, but also agreed to take the time to train her in the job's specific skills. The restaurant is known for its friend-ly, attentive service. For example, Maureen was required to learn every detail about the restaurant's rotating menu items. "You had to know it by heart," Maureen recalls, "and that was-n't easy. This kind of memorization went a lot faster when I was younger. But eventually I did just fine." She now can respond quickly and accurately when customers who may have food allergies, for example, want to know precisely what ingredients are in a soup or salad.

"Do I need the money I earn from this?" Maureen asks rhetorically. "No, not really. It's nice, but that's not the main motivation for my working. Being around all sorts of people and interacting with them is what counts."

Not everyone is fortunate enough to have the choice of

whether to work or not. Increasingly, however, there are new and creative ways to make the best of such necessities. The need to work in our mid to late years can be part of a quest, not a crisis.

Jan H. is a seventy-seven-year-old Midwesterner who, like a growing number of Americans, expects to "outlive" the money she has set aside for her retirement. Although diligent about saving and investing her money, rising costs threaten to undermine her best intentions. "I work for a lot of reasons," she confides in an interview conducted at her comfortable home office, "and an important one is the income. I need to have dollars coming in."

Life hasn't always turned out the way Jan expected. After getting married at an early age, she didn't think she would need to have a job after she graduated from college. "I thought I'd be a wife, raise kids, be a great hostess, and get involved in some volunteer activities," she recalls. "Eventually my husband and I would have an empty nest, he'd retire, and we'd go hand in hand into retirement really enjoying ourselves."

Instead, Jan's husband left her when she was forty. She's had fifteen jobs in the thirty-seven years since. Although she remarried, Jan's second husband died without leaving much of an estate. Her life as a single woman has included some profound career changes. Originally a municipal employee in a large city—including a stint as deputy mayor—Jan later began working in nonprofit youth programs as a researcher and administrator. Eventually she relocated to Chicago, but returned to her hometown after three years because she missed the family members and friends who greatly enriched her life. This meant that at age sixty-two she had to hit the streets to look for a job.

"While I was unemployed," Jan remembers, "I realized that I just loved going to school and learning things. So, at sixty-three, I entered graduate school in a Ph.D. program in Work, Community, and Family Education. Six years later I had my doctorate." During her years as a graduate student, Jan got by on savings and student employment, but it wasn't until she received her new degree that she started the non-profit organization that she now directs. The work engages her quick mind, draws on her newly developed skills, serves her community, and provides a decent income.

"The money from my 401(k) accounts will be gone in another three years," says Jan. "I still have some savings, and get a small pension from the city. I get Social Security checks, of course, but, even so, I need to earn at least $20,000 a year to get by. Meaningful work is my passion, so my job is not simply about monetary rewards. I'm like many people who will probably be employed for the rest of our lives in such work that physical health allows. That's our reality, and we need to accept it."

In the last few years Jan has cut down on her hours in order to devote more time to volunteer work and leisure pursuits. In addition, she consults with youth education and other nonprofit groups. Overall, life feels balanced for her. Jan cites pianist Arthur Rubenstein as the "par excellence" Late Bloomer: "He died at ninety-three after playing a concert the night before. Rubenstein practiced each day and continued to derive great satisfaction and pleasure from his performances. As he aged, he used compensatory strategies such as playing the slow passages slower so that the fast ones would seem faster. He's my role model."

As someone whose need to continue working has led to

satisfying career changes, Jan has plenty of good company. Carol S. is a sixty-three-year-old whose life over the past ten years has been a roller coaster. Carol was in her early fifties when her businessman husband died of a massive heart attack during a trip to China. She was left very little money. This setback, followed by a period of full-time caregiving for her terminally ill mother, led Carol to reinvent herself in Arizona as a gerontologist, a career for which she had earned a degree prior to widowhood. She soon relocated to Los Angeles, relying on that city's larger population to support her work as a planner of retirement programs.

"A few years later, I put all my savings into organizing a big national conference that I expected would become the first in a series of annual events," says Carol. "Although it targeted the aging Baby Boomer, the conference was 'mixed generational' and included older people as living examples that countered prejudices about aging. I had recruited prominent speakers from all over the country to speak about work, maintaining physical health, exploring spirituality, and other aspects of positive aging."

Carol's groundbreaking conference never happened. It was scheduled for the week of September 11, 2001. Even if she had not cancelled it following the tragic events of that day, most speakers and attendees would not have been able to participate as commercial air travel was suspended for much of that week. Because of the amount of nonrefundable money she had invested in the project, Carol lost virtually all of her personal savings. Undeterred, she went to work as a retirement counseling expert on contract to a large agency.

"When I learned that I was only getting thirty percent of what the company took in from my counseling assignments,

I decided to make a change," says Carol. Two clients who stuck with her provided enough money for Carol to get along. She then borrowed money from her two grown children and went back to school to receive certification as a corporate leadership coach. By age sixty, this Late Bloomer was in a new profession, drawing on her related experience as a gerontologist and corporate consultant.

"I love my new work," enthuses Carol, who is prospering and almost completely out of debt. "It's a different population than the one I used to work with, but they genuinely appreciate my life experience and skills." She often is hired by companies that are downsizing and that offer her contracted expertise to departing employees as a severance benefit. Her clients are geographically located nearby and pay handsomely. Carol now envisions the likelihood of earning an excellent income in her later years, while building a consultancy that itself will accrue considerable value. She has followed new dreams and enjoyed much pleasure from the world of work at a time when many people might expect her to be slowing down.

Perhaps surprisingly, many of us do want or need some kind of job in late life even though we enjoy financial security and a comfortable lifestyle. We find that continued employment meets deeply felt inner needs that have nothing to do with dollars.

Robert M., for example, had a long and successful career as a trial attorney. At sixty-five he reluctantly closed his law practice in order to better manage caregiving for his ailing wife and frail, ninety-year-old mother-in-law. Once he had attended to these obligations, Robert realized that he needed a little time away from his responsibilities at home. After engaging some caregiver assistance, he accepted a part-time position at a local college teaching law classes three days a week. This kept him involved in his field of expertise and brought in a small but regular income.

"It isn't the money that keeps me in the classroom," explains Robert, now eighty, "it's the stimulation and joy I feel from engaging with the nimble minds of future lawyers. After class I like to hang out with some of the school's staff and talk about professional issues. I'm teaching, yes, but I also continue to learn a great deal."

Over the past fifteen years Robert has cut down his workload to one day a week. He now offers a class in negotiating skills that is attended by students younger than his grandkids. "Age doesn't matter when it comes to work," Robert says. "One can always contribute something to other people. And, of course, you can always gain new knowledge."

Just as Robert has managed to create a flexible work situation that serves him well, you can, too—whether your compelling needs are for stimulation, money, fringe benefits, community service, or simply the pleasure of continuing on in your chosen field.

Here is another example of a creative approach to late-life work by a Late Bloomer who depends on the money her employment brings in.

Beth A., sixty-three, was divorced during her forties and married again nine years later to Daniel, a man seventeen years her senior. At the time of their wedding Beth was still employed full time as an editor for a major publisher. Her new husband had already retired from his career as a high school teacher. Instead of pursuing paid work, Daniel volunteered a couple of days each week at a local hospital and spent many of his remaining unstructured hours reading and going to a health club. He envisioned Beth joining him on fishing trips and other leisure activities.

"I knew Daniel wanted me around, and fishing together was a real priority for us," says Beth. "So I decided to quit my job and set myself up as a freelance editor working out of an office in our home." Thanks to her extensive experience and solid reputation, Beth now is engaged in the interesting and challenging editing projects she most enjoys. The transition has been as smooth as a polished sentence.

"I guess this is my retirement career," Beth says with a smile, adding that her freelancing provides the couple with the best of both worlds: work and play. "We do need my income, along with Daniel's pension and Social Security checks, to support our chosen lifestyle. My financial compensation is adequate, and my time is my own to plan around, so I really don't see any reason not to continue working."

Not everybody, of course, can claim the professional experience or teaching ability that can lead to part-time employment like Robert's and Beth's, or the academic bent that sent Jan and Carol back to school. But many unexpected opportunities are out there if you just look for them.

Mike O.'s story illustrates what determination plus serendipity can lead to. Now sixty-nine, Mike officially retired at age fifty-seven from a brewery in the Midwest where he had been employed as a supervisor since his discharge from the U.S. Army during his early twenties. "Once you got hired [at the brewery] and passed probation," Mike says, "it was a great job—one of the best places in town to work. The company was like a big family, and I enjoyed being part of it."

Mike accepted an early-retirement package, an

increasingly common incentive among large corporations, and immediately looked forward to a life free of the responsibilities of a forty-hour-a-week job. But this did not mean he stopped working.

Soon after leaving the brewery, Mike launched a small enterprise that installs and maintains real estate advertising signs for local real estate agents. "It turned out to be a better business than I thought it would," Mike says, pointing out that his inventory grew within a few years from fifty to more than two thousand signposts. His company makes a tidy profit for Mike without demanding much of his time. Even more fulfilling is Mike's part-time paid work as a "helper" for a bus service that shuttles children who are disabled or confined to wheelchairs. Mike assists the kids in getting on and off the bus, often attending to specialized needs as requested by the children's mothers and fathers. These parents are invariably devoted to their offspring, whose care they do not easily turn over to outsiders. The fact that they have learned to trust Mike to look after their kids while being transferred to and from school or appointments is a tribute to his kindness and devotion.

"You can't believe how much satisfaction I get from doing this," Mike told us, with a quiver of emotion in his voice. "I almost feel like I'm a grandpa to these kids, even though I have several grandchildren and even a few great-grandchildren of my own. What can I say? I just love being around these folks and their children; they're really the greatest people."

Mike lost an eye to cancer a few years back; otherwise, he might still be driving a school bus, the part-time job he held while working full-time at the brewery. "Because of legal restrictions, they can't let me drive a vehicle with passengers," he notes, "but I'm doing the next best thing. It's great being a helper on the handicapped shuttle partly because the job is so flexible. If I wish, I can take time off in summer, go to soccer games with my grandkids, or take trips to Florida in the winter."

Mike concedes that such diversions get him out of the house and away from the TV set, but when pressed he also pointed out that he grew up on a Minnesota farm in a family of fourteen children. "As a result, I have a strong work ethic," he says. "I love having responsibilities and staying busy. It simply feels good to help other people."

For thousands of retirees like Mike, a job is not simply filler for unstructured time. It is a constructive way to maintain a full, balanced, and satisfying way of life. This reality comes as no surprise to those who study retirement professionally.

Jan H., the seventy-seven-year-old whose story we shared earlier, is a public advocate for positive aging. She says the notion of an "idle" and financially underwritten retirement is relatively new. In the past, many men and women stayed employed or otherwise active as long as they could, regardless of age. "The stereotyped picture [of retiring to live on a pension and Social Security] only dates back to the 1940s," she says. "Social Security didn't start paying out until the end of the 1930s, so prior to that there really wasn't this expectation of a leisure-based retirement."

Jan observes that the average life span was considerably shorter a half-century ago, particularly for males. "So if men got to sixty-five and started receiving their pension and Social Security," she says, "they weren't likely to live very long. I believe retirement relying on that model [of financial support] will be virtually gone for most people by 2010."

Many Baby Boomers—the tens of millions born in the post-war era between 1945 and 1964—are now in their sixties and find themselves in a position where, as Jan suggests, it is not feasible for them to retire in the traditional sense. While they may be able to choose the enjoyment of expanded leisure to some extent, these Boomers are including work in the mix, often out of necessity. They are, to coin a phrase, the generation of "new old" Americans. Fortunately, they may choose from an unprecedented array of options that were rare or even nonexistent when their parents and grandparents turned sixty.

Patricia L., for instance, is a lifelong Maine resident who insists she "cannot afford" to stop working. At sixty-one, she is eligible for a retirement pension and other benefits from the state agency that has employed her as a medical social worker. "My employer actually is encouraging me to retire," says Patricia, "and I would really like to. But I cannot meet my living expenses without this regular income."

Mortgage payments and property taxes take big bites out of Patricia's paychecks, as does the cost of caring for her eighty-four-year-old mother, who has Alzheimer's disease and lives in an assisted-care facility. In addition, Patricia, a widow who has held a paying job since high school, helps support her daughter, Katy, who recently earned a college degree and sometimes has trouble making ends meet.

"I wish I had the time and money that would allow me to be sunbathing on a beach in Mexico," says Patricia, "rather than working every day. But at the rate things are going, I won't be able to quit my job for several years."

Patricia is like many others in their fifties and sixties who feel, as she puts it, "that the rug was pulled out from underneath us." They grew up in an era during which families with only one wage earner could easily earn enough to pay for a house, car, medical expenses, and other basic needs. "Somewhere along the line," Patricia says, "the cost of living for many of us rose to a point where even two full-time incomes weren't enough to pay all the bills, let alone save for retirement."

Patricia's decision to rent her four-bedroom house to a younger sister and her family is helping. Although Patricia still owns the home, she has consolidated her belongings into a single bedroom and a few closets. This has reduced her housing expenses enough that she has been able to shift to a flexible, part-time work schedule and can now take extended trips without putting her job in jeopardy. Her boyfriend, Rich, sixty-two, also works part time and shares his rural home with a rent-paying housemate.

"Rich and I can take trips together, and if I need to spend more time with my mom, I can do that easily," says Patricia, who makes weekly visits to her mother, confined to a facility over a hundred miles away. "I've even started spending two months each winter at a little village on the Pacific coast of Mexico. Now that I work shorter hours and take extended time off, I like my job a whole lot more. I'm looking at my responsibilities with fresh eyes and I'm actually having fun at work again."

Patricia exemplifies not only the financial bind that many contemporary seniors find themselves in, pressured as they are by fast rising costs for housing and health care, but also a shift in leisure-time preferences. Studies suggest that most of us are not opposed to continuing to work in our later years as long as that employment offers flexibility while delivering psychological and emotional rewards.

Older people now tend to be more healthy, self-sufficient, and mobile than previous generations, with a genuine desire (and sometimes a compelling need) to keep earning income, fulfilling new career goals, volunteering in their communities, or pursuing educational opportunities.

A May 2004 report entitled "Baby Boomers Envision Retirement II," which was prepared by the Roper polling group for AARP, identified changing expectations for the 77.5 million Americans born between the end of World War II and 1964. For example, forty-six percent of the 1,200 Baby Boomers surveyed said their retirement outlook had changed for the better in the previous five years, and sixty-nine percent described themselves as "very" or "fairly" optimistic about their own retirement years. Nearly four out of five Boomers said they plan to work in some capacity during retirement, partly for needed income and partly for the sake of enjoyment or interest in a particular type of work. About half said they expect to devote more time to community service and volunteering, while most of those who currently volunteer plan to devote more time to such activities in retirement. The Roper study found thirty-five percent had lost a job at one time or another, and an equal percentage had been responsible for the care of a parent. Seventeen percent claimed to have a better job now than five years earlier, and twenty-four percent reported that their financial situation had improved due to such milestones as paying off a mortgage or having their kids move out of their residence.

When asked to describe in an open-ended manner the meaning of retirement, the top responses included "relaxation, free time, and fun" (thirty-two percent), "having enough money or financial security" (thirty-one percent), "travel and vacations" (thirteen percent), and "not working" (seven percent).

About eight in ten Boomers said they expected to work in some capacity during retirement. Of these, fifteen percent planned to start their own businesses, while seven percent wanted to work full time at something other than their current occupation. Some forty-one percent of Boomer men and thirty-three percent of women said they will not want to stop working in retirement.

For some, this expectation of continuing employment stems from the need to help other family members. The survey found that eighteen percent of those questioned expected to provide financially for an aging parent or in-law during retirement, and seventeen percent expected to provide some financial support for their own children. Fifty-eight percent said they considered themselves to be in very good or excellent health. Yet twenty-seven percent have survived a major illness and fifty-eight percent did not expect their current employer to cover their health insurance needs into retirement. Forty-three percent did not expect Medicare to cover their health care needs in retirement.

"A substantial percentage [of today's retirees] do need income," agrees Jan H., the consultant on aging issues. "This picture is shifting dramatically. Many people do have a pension, but others need to have money coming in because they're living longer, need to cover health costs, are caregivers, or have been widowed and therefore lack resources they once had."

One tangible result of the current trend toward a later and more individualized retirement lifestyle—and an ongoing need for cash flow—is that companies are becoming more supportive of mature workers. They manifest this support in a variety of ways: by providing flexible hours, offering telecommuting options, and extending benefits designed to appeal specifically to Boomers. The latter include the chance to take time off to visit grandkids, go on vacation with retired spouses, or be consulted on areas of special expertise. Such employers have begun to recognize and appreciate the long-time experience, well-honed skills, and committed work habits of older employees. Members of this generation will be needed to fill shortages in key fields during coming decades as the younger labor pool shrinks—and the employers of America know it.

John C., now sixty-four, received a degree in computer science from a Southern California university during the 1960s, long before most colleges had a clue about the future importance of information technology. Although jobs in the field were difficult to find during that era, John parlayed his skills into a series of positions that eventually landed him a top job managing the computer systems of a major university in San Francisco. He loved working in his field and put off formal retirement as long as possible. Finally, faced with debilitating health problems and the gentle prodding of a wife who wanted to spend more time with him, our friend accepted a generous pension and benefits package and stepped down.

"The funny thing is," John told us, "my former employer has never really let me go. And that's just fine with me."

It seems that John's expertise is simply too valuable and too difficult to replicate. The university now contracts with him for special sophisticated projects that require his depth of knowledge, while, at the same time, accommodating his competing leisure-time interests.

"I am into all kinds of other things now," says John, "like walking my dog, remodeling our home, and being part of a men's group. My wife and I go to the theater together a lot, and we enjoy hosting dinner parties. She still works full time." The couple has slowed down enough to buy and furnish a second home in the Sierra Nevada, where they take long breaks with family and friends. The pair has become more involved in spiritual matters, family get-togethers, and community projects, which they find extremely satisfying.

"I still like having a hand in the work I've done for forty-five years," says John, "but it's not about the money. The extra money I earn goes to various volunteer agencies I support and the hobbies I indulge in. At this point, I can't imagine life without my tether to a job that helps me feel needed and important."

John's comments jibe with findings of a 2006 survey undertaken by San Francisco-based Civic Ventures in cooperation with Princeton Survey Research Associates and the MetLife Foundation. Pollsters asked one thousand Americans between the ages of fifty and seventy what type of work they aspired to undertake during their mature years. About half expressed interest in employment that either helped improve the quality of life in their communities, connected them to a life passion, involved a purpose bigger than themselves, or brought them together with other people.

Monique A. Dearth, president of Incite Strategies, an Atlanta-based human resources consulting firm, agrees that many employees over fifty now have different priorities on the job than older workers of the past. They generally are not striving to develop a high profile career, she says, "but rather they want to leverage past experience, feel valued in an organization, and contribute at a meaningful level."

We interviewed several Baby Boomers looking for a different kind of retirement than their parents experienced. Geoffrey K., a fifty-seven-year-old Santa Fe fine art painter and business administrator, is convinced that his later years do not have to be as restricted as they were for his mother, Elizabeth, an attorney who died in Philadelphia at age 76.

"My mom stayed at great expense in a retirement residence that was beautifully appointed but not very soulful," Geoffrey said. "The substance of life there was around such activities as bridge, golf, and bingo. Those are fine for individuals who enjoy them, and many certainly do, but none of these pastimes really interested Elizabeth. The residents were kept out of harm's way, yet from my perspective they also were rather understimulated and isolated from the outside world."

The experience "weakened my mom," Geoffrey told us, "and not just in a physical sense. Seeing that situation, I began to think, 'There has to be another approach to retirement that works better for me.'"

One way Geoffrey seeks to guide his own later years is by remaining active with various nonprofit service organizations and his spiritual community. He believes that helping others is a way to manifest his religious values and is rewarding for all involved. He allows that this approach is not for everyone; some may be happier with a physically active orientation.

"Overall, I find myself becoming more playful and lighthearted as I've aged," Geoffrey said. "Mine is a 'live and let live' philosophy. Personally, I am less interested in a country club retirement than one where I can be more engaged with those of similar interests. But I see so many options now for my generation that are very positive. I wish my mother had lived to see this day arrive."

Phyllis Moen, a sociologist at the University of Minnesota, believes our society is seeing the creation of a new "midcourse" life stage that institutions have not yet recognized. "Just as we have seen the social construction of adolescence as a way station from childhood to adulthood during the first half of the twentieth century," Moen wrote in her book, *Career Mystique,* "there is now emerging a life stage between the years of career building and old age." Examples of those in midcourse mode are people roughly from forty-five to seventy-five who choose either to scale back or switch careers, or even leave the workforce entirely. Many are healthy, wealthy and wise, ready to bring plenty of talents and experiences to whatever direction they follow.

For forty-seven-year-old David B., the desire to reset his equilibrium came in midlife. After earning a prestigious M.B.A. from the University of Chicago—"my ticket to ride," he calls it—the low-key Midwesterner expected to "go through success after success until becoming president of a multinational company. My goal was to become a high-powered developer. It didn't work out that way."

Just when he thought all was right in his world, David's employer laid him off during a massive downsizing that led to the exit of numerous workers. This came as a shock to David, since he had recently received a raise and added responsibilities. David was happily married with two young children at the time. Yet instead of jumping back in "the game," this Baby Boomer decided to take time off and reconsider what he really wanted from work.

"There's a period between twenty-five and forty-five

where you have your kids and you realize some important things about yourself," David told us, flashing a winsome smile. "During your first twenty years you learn what society expects of you. For the next twenty you try to fulfill that. And for another two decades you struggle with the realization that those expectations no longer fit you. Finally, for the last twenty years, if you're lucky, you get to say, 'What the heck, I'm just going to do what I really want to do.'"

David paused a moment. "I'm fast-forwarding all that and trying to find out what I really want to do a lot earlier than many folks I know."

Before we met him, David, with a friend, had recently started a nonprofit organization called SHiFT to provide guidance and support for people undergoing transitional experiences similar to the one David went through. They've discovered that there are hundreds of people in their community eager to realign their lives and work in order to better reflect evolving values and passions. "Society is changing so fast that institutions aren't keeping up with what people really need," David explained. "There are many individuals out there who, like me, want to find their true vocation and not settle for what they can get by with."

David's group is a valuable model for ways we can redefine the role of work. SHiFT sponsored a weekly discussion series at a local coffee shop where attendees could describe their own concerns and hear articulate speakers versed in various aspects of retirement. When as many as eighty people showed up for such talks, SHiFT expanded its offerings to include a website, mentorship program, resource referral service, affinity groups, and workshops designed to help people "who are not willing to settle for their present work lives."

In short, David created a new calling for himself as a catalyst for both mid- and late-life course correction. "Change is hard," he said. "It often makes us feel anxious and uncertain about the future; but it frequently is also very positive. Change can create more fulfillment and vibrancy. Our society is moving toward more purposeful employment because that's what so many of us are looking for now."

Indeed, the evolution of work as part of a balanced, rewarding lifestyle for Late Bloomers reflects bigger changes afoot on our planet. The shifting nature of employment is certainly due in part to the globalization of society—through shrinkage wrought by the Internet, world trade, and air travel—but it also reflects our collective acceptance of realities unimaginable only a decade or two ago. It's not unusual for a big corporation to swallow a smaller one, laying off hundreds of workers in the process. Though we may not like such downsizing, we're resilient enough to pick ourselves up and explore other options. If a company goes completely out of business or defaults on its pension plan, it opens the door for very challenging experiences as individuals are forced unexpectedly to redesign their retirement plans. Such shifts have become more common in today's fast-changing world, yet they also sow the seeds for healthy growth and future blooming. For example, thousands of employees and entrepreneurs now rely on home computers, cell phones, and overnight courier services to earn a fine income from the privacy of their homes.

Social observers agree that expanded choices for Baby Boomers are beginning to change the prevailing negative attitudes of the past, when "older people" were perceived as obsolete or deliberately excluded from the realms in which younger individuals lived.

"The aging of Boomers provides a rich opportunity to change our society," Theodore Roszak, author of *The Making of a Counter Culture* and *America the Wise,* told us in an interview. "As Americans get older, their evolving attitudes will help reshape social priorities." The human race now has a higher percentage of aged citizens than ever before, Roszak pointed out, and this ratio will only increase in coming years. When those over age fifty become a majority, older people "will no longer seem strange and they will certainly not be marginal: they will be in charge." And that includes the world of work.

THE SECRET OF WORK

The secret of work involves determining what kind of employment, if any, suits us in our later years. We are using a broad definition of work here—one that includes nonpaid volunteer duties as well as compensated part-time, short-term, or contract employment. One of the wonderful things about living in the current era is that the more traditional paradigm of an eight-to-five weekday position has become only one of many work options available, including some flexible enough to fit into any kind of schedule.

As the storytellers in this chapter have demonstrated, work can be the source of many rewards. Employment may generate much-needed income, of course, but it also can provide a greater sense of value to ourselves, to others, and to our chosen field of endeavor. As human beings, we all need to feel that our lives are worthwhile and our time is well spent. The work ethic we grew up with recognizes the fundamental human impulse to serve ourselves, loved ones, and

157

communities through purposeful activity. This healthy ethic and life-affirming impulse doesn't disappear magically when we reach a certain age.

At its heart, the secret of work is about looking at employment in a new way. After years—in many cases, decades—of using employment as a means to very pragmatic ends, our fresh eyes can see its other functions as a route to late-life satisfactions. We encourage you to consider all options.

In order to better achieve these satisfactions, try to reflect on what work has brought you besides the obvious rewards of money, marketable skills, and fringe benefits. For most of us, the workplace also has been an arena in which we have socialized and formed friendships, including some that may have led to romance or even marriage. A job brings intellectual stimulation, too, and the satisfaction from gaining knowledge, applying ideas, and displaying talents or aptitudes. Employment can bring travel, adventure, and recognition. It is also where we may have garnered praise, affected the lives of others, and successfully met personal challenges.

In an era of constant corporate merging and downsizing, coupled with quickly shifting technologies, our jobs may end in the wink of an eye. Or, as we age, we may be given little or no choice about when we are phased out of a position. The secret of work is not to see these eventualities as an ending, but as a beginning—a chance to reinvent ourselves in the world of employment, and to bloom with the many satisfactions that work can bring.

Bill Pinsoff of the Family Institute at Northwestern University told the *New York Times* in a 2007 interview that late-life exploration offers many people a chance to reshape their imprint on the world. "Retirement represents an opportunity for spiritual or psychological rebirth or renaissance," said Pinsoff. "In many cases, people engage in activities that have been long postponed. People who have devoted their lives to making money now have the opportunity to work for what they believe in."

HOW TO ACT ON THIS SECRET

In order to act on this secret, we suggest you first examine closely the role work plays in your life and how that relationship may have changed over time—and how you anticipate it may change in the future. In the preceding pages, we have presented examples of individuals whose needs and desires regarding work are substantially different from one another and have evolved during life's inevitable transitions. Some of the Late Bloomers we have met are fortunate to enjoy financial security and good health insurance, with enough income, investments, and savings to live comfortably. For these folks, having paid work is an active choice rather than the necessity it represents for others. We also know many Late Bloomers who, regardless of financial circumstance, seek employment to fulfill other needs: for social interaction, service to their communities, personal growth, sharing of expertise, a sense of purpose, or eagerness to stay engaged in their chosen field. Many people, we have discovered, have no intention of retiring, in the traditional sense, because they simply enjoy what they do, whether or not they get paid.

Four out of five Baby Boomers say they plan to work in later life. Fifteen percent of these say they hope to start their own businesses. Uncertainty about the solvency of Social

159

Security and Medicare no doubt plays a role in this expectation, but values are another factor. One of the key characteristics of this group, which represents the largest sustained population gain in U.S. history, is their diversity in relation to hopes, dreams, and expectations. Baby Boomers want to do things their own way.

What way is that? As with several other action steps described earlier in this book, an excellent prelude to manifesting "the secret of work" is to do a realistic appraisal of your attitudes and needs viz a viz employment. (Each of these action steps, by the way, applies equally to Late Bloomers of all ages.) It is important to gain a realistic understanding of how gainful employment or volunteer work fits into the bigger picture of your life as a whole. If you have a spouse or partner, this might best be done by sitting down for a heart-to-heart talk. You may wish to include in this conversation other family members, such as sons or daughters. Best friends, counselors, and spiritual advisors can provide helpful feedback, too. In addition, writing down your ideas might provide clarity on what you need and want from employment in the present and future.

A valuable next step, once you have narrowed down some possibilities about your own late-life work, is to gather specifics about what opportunities are available. If your emphasis is on service to your community, for example, find out if there is a volunteer coordination center of some type in your area. If you don't find one listed in your local phone directory, inquire through the local chamber of commerce, visitors' center, church auxiliary, library, or city hall. Lists and descriptions of organizations needing volunteers are widely available.

Those seeking paid employment have even more options in gathering information. Besides the traditional employment agencies and newspaper classified ads we grew up with, today's jobseekers can hunt for opportunities online via computer and circulate their résumés electronically. For those whose skills and interests lend themselves to working at home, growing numbers of employers are happy to oblige. Thousands of Americans now earn excellent part- and full-time incomes from offices in dens or spare bedrooms. Late Bloomers with an entrepreneurial bent also have an almost an infinite number of opportunities available using the assets of a computer and Internet connection. If you feel your high-tech skills need some brushing up, find out what classes are available through your community's adult education or continuing education classes. These are often offered free or at low cost to older residents through colleges or municipal parks and recreation departments.

The object of these exercises is to help you conduct an inventory of your needs and attitudes as they relate to work, using feedback from those you trust as a sounding board for evaluating visions and decisions that will influence your daily routines over the months and years to come. As you do this, clarity will emerge about what seems appropriate for your course of action. Part of this process, remember, involves realignment as you go along. No matter what your age, you can always change or update your intentions as you accrue information and experience.

CHAPTER EIGHT

THE SECRET OF NEW ROOTS

Elwood Chapman, the author of *Comfort Zones* and several other books on later-life planning, jokingly refers to retirement as "the dreaded R-word," since the term carries so many negative connotations. We've all been told that once we've reached a certain age we're "over the hill." But Chapman insists that retirement doesn't bring an end to personal growth and change. He points out that our preoccupations between ages fifty-five and seventy are often very different from those *after* seventy.

It's a fallacy, for example, to think that a lifestyle that's appropriate for an active, married sixty-eight-year-old will automatically be suitable for a sedentary, widowed seventy-nine-year-old. As the average life span has lengthened, we can be reasonably sure that we'll spend as many as a third of our days in that amorphous stretch of time known as retirement. Yet the venerable ninety-five-year-old is *chronologically* as far apart from the just-retired sixty-five-year-old as the five-year-old kindergartner is from the career-minded thirty-five-year-old. So much for generalizations about senior citizens!

Despite these crucial distinctions, only a generation ago the housing and lifestyle options of older Americans were painfully limited. A newly retired person usually chose between staying in the traditional family home, sharing quarters with a son or daughter, moving into a smaller house or apartment, or entering an institution like a boarding home or convalescent hospital. Few other choices seemed available, and friends often discouraged more innovative alternatives.

In large part, this narrow range of choices accurately reflected society's limited outlook on the way its aging members should live. The prevailing expectation was that an older person would simply find a quiet, out-of-the-way place to wait patiently for sickness and death to arrive. Within the last decade, fortunately, much has changed for the better. Following are some real-life examples.

When he was in his early fifties, Peter D. decided to take early retirement from his position in the airline industry. He and his wife, Julia, sold their Boston residence and built a brand-new, rambling "dream house" in a small southern California town. The couple spent ten happy years in their adopted home. When Peter died at sixty-two, Julia decided to sell the house and take a one-bedroom condominium in a nearby retirement complex that caters to "mature adults." Although she'd once dismissed such communities as "the human equivalent of the old elephants' boneyard," Julia was pleasantly surprised to discover a warm, friendly place where she leads an active and independent life among like-minded seniors.

By the time she reached fifty-five, Betty L. had divorced

her husband and packed her last child off to college. Rattling around a big empty house in White Plains, New York, no longer appealed to Betty, who longed to write and paint in a tranquil setting. After contemplating many possible changes in her lifestyle, Betty sold most of her belongings and moved into a small apartment in the cosmopolitan city of San Miguel de Allende, Mexico. Over the next twenty years she became fluent in Spanish, wrote and painted to her heart's content, and married a fellow American expatriate named Murray. Now the two of them are planning to move back to the United States in order to be closer to modern medical facilities and spend more time with friends and family. Because both crave such cultural amenities as live music and theater, Betty and Murray are checking out college towns in the Northwest. They're ready for a trade-off: giving up their distinctive lifestyle in a foreign country in exchange for access to sophisticated medical care, familiar pleasures, and loved ones.

When Effie B.'s husband, Louis, died of Alzheimer's disease a few years ago, she believed most of her major decisions were behind her, although she felt a bit overwhelmed by their rambling four-bedroom home on the outskirts of Houston. Still, after owning a home for a half century, Effie doesn't relish the thought of becoming a renter, and she's very attached to the greenery of her well-landscaped yard. "I don't even think about going into senior housing or a retirement home," said Effie, who's in fine physical shape at age eighty-two. "And fancy resort-type developments cater to a lifestyle I'm not interested in. So for the time being I'm going to stay put. My house is full of happy memories."

Edgar T. spent most of his professional life teaching college economics in the Pacific northwest. His goal was to develop a "transition career" as a consultant. This would gradually ease him into retirement, drawing on his considerable experience in business strategy and financial planning. After publishing several books and magazine articles, Edgar has developed an enjoyable sideline as a public speaker and teaches a series of popular seminars. A heart attack has persuaded Edgar to cut back on some of these activities, and he and his wife, Fran, now manage a four-unit apartment building overlooking the Florida beachfront. Their rental income is enough to allow Edgar to continue comfortably with his teaching and consulting.

The common thread that links these Late Bloomers is their flexible attitude toward the prospect of putting down new roots in their later years. Their stories show that while it's impossible to predict every phase of retirement, determining *what* you want and planning how to get it can help post-retirement dreams turn into reality.

"Twenty years ago it was not uncommon for Granny to live in a three-generation household," observes Charles Longino Jr., an expert on aging at the University of Miami. "Now she lives by herself, drives her own car, talks to her friends on the phone, takes care of her own business, and wants to do so for as long as she can."

Chapman, in his seventies at the time of our interview, goes a step further in his analysis. Chapman views the retirement years as "the second life," years that are subsequently broken down into five distinct phases: the busy transition period (when we're often confronted by more changes than we've experienced since young adulthood); the spontaneous and unexpected "serendipity" of discovering joyous new activities; the "sweet, golden" pleasures of nostalgia; the quiet reverie of inward reflection or spirituality; and finally the "sunset time," in which individuals are most intent on putting their affairs in order and basking in the satisfactions of a life well lived.

Chapman believes we go through definite stages of personal growth in retirement just as we do during earlier periods of development, such as childhood and adolescence. During this period of continuing maturity, our lifestyle and housing needs are based on many changeable factors that, in turn, can shift dramatically from one year to the next. What feels right at sixty-five may chafe at seventy-five, or even sooner. Our values and attitudes evolve as we age. A way of life we're happy and content with when we're working and raising a family may no longer be fulfilling, satisfying, or even appropriate when the house is empty, the job is complete, or the loved ones have passed on. As we navigate our "second" life—that vast and uncharted domain of the "dreaded R-word"—we can anticipate that our needs, desires, and lifestyle will change as well.

Questions about lifestyle—what our physical and psychological needs are at a particular time, which amenities we do or don't require, why we prefer a certain environment—are as important an ingredient in the retirement recipe as are questions about money, geography, and health. Retirees are as different as any other segment of the general population, with as varied interests, dreams, needs, and expectations. In fact, gerontological research has documented that as we get older we generally become more individuated. We become more secure and more comfortable with simply being who we are. And just as we may look for a studio apartment when we're young, single, constrained by a limited budget, and living away from home for the first time—or a place in the suburbs when we've married, had kids, and bought a minivan—our needs don't remain static during the later phases of life. It's wise to get yourself into a flexible state of mind and know that along the way there will be changes as well as growth and rewards.

Many books and publications present the diverse post-retirement housing options now available: everything from living in an Israeli kibbutz to an intergenerational group home (a modern version of the once-common three-generational household). We urge you to tap these information resources in addition to reflecting on the personal experiences of such Late Bloomers as Min H., who lives in a Minneapolis high-rise residential complex for the elderly.

Min says there isn't enough room along the walls of her small apartment to display all the certificates, plaques, and awards she's received for her volunteer work in the Twin Cities. They honor a woman who's been campaigning for social reform since, at age fourteen, she took a miserable, low-paying factory job to help promote passage of much-needed child labor laws. Min is an activist who once had sixteen garbage men over for tea in order to solicit their advice on how to make the city prettier. She also organized a Maid's Club because she felt Minnesota homemakers, herself included, were exploiting their household servants. Then there was the time she welcomed forty-eight women into her home in order to gift wrap eighteen thousand Christmas presents for the mentally ill. Or the summer she plied a group of wary but hungry physicians with hundreds of homemade blintzes as part of a successful campaign to establish the first free eye and diabetes clinic in her area.

"I love living," Min told us, as we shared some of her famous fresh blintzes in her cheery dining room. "And to me, living means being helpful and useful." Min is five-feet-two and has sparkling brown eyes. Her smile seems to reach out and hug you. A first-time visitor seldom realizes at first that Min is confined to a wheelchair. As a result of this circumstance, she seldom goes beyond the boundaries of the complete-care, government-subsidized housing development she now calls home.

"I moved here because after my husband died it became difficult for me to get around on my own," explained Min, who suffers from a severe form of arthritis. "I've never had a great deal of money, and here my rent is only a small percentage of the Social Security check that I live on."

Min attributes her nonstop volunteerism to her late mother, who instilled in her only child the selfless notion that "we are not placed on this earth simply to live for ourselves. Everyone benefits when we work on behalf of others."

In between charitable endeavors, Min raised two daughters and two sons in a large house that's not far from her present apartment. Her surviving children (one son died a few years ago) and nine grandchildren are regular visitors, often bringing her groceries and taking her to medical appointments.

Despite Min's limited mobility, there's been no letup in her activity over the last couple of years. She serves on the food and hospitality committees at her residence, which houses some 150 seniors over age sixty-five. Fluent in Yiddish, Min is able to translate on behalf of several non-English-speaking neighbors. She volunteers her skills as a grief counselor to those who are coping with the death of loved ones and has received national recognition for her ongoing letter-writing campaigns on behalf of mental health and diabetes associations. As if this weren't enough, she's organized a monthly lecture series that take place in a downstairs auditorium.

"Because I'm in a wheelchair, I usually ask people to come to my apartment for meetings," Min told us. "Every Monday morning, for instance, a group of us get together in my living room to make safety banners that are used to educate school children. We give away over a thousand of these each month to classrooms all over the country."

Min downplays the significance of her volunteer work, pointing out that she doesn't enjoy cards, isn't athletic, and has never held a paid job. She recalls that when she got married, women weren't expected to have careers of their own. "So I put all my extra energy into looking for ways to help people," Min explained, as if no other clarification were necessary. "If you're used to doing certain things, I don't see any need to change just because you've gotten older or moved to a new living situation."

Min got rid of most of her possessions when she sold the family home two years ago, and although she misses some of her former neighbors, she has managed to adapt easily to her new surroundings. "Yes, this place is smaller, and I feel somewhat more limited than before. But I'm still doing the kinds of things that I enjoy the most," she said. "In fact, I've discovered there are some real advantages in living in a retirement setting like this one. There's no yard to worry about, for one thing, and I'm among people I have a lot in common with."

As part of her housing stipend, Min takes twenty-five free meals a month in her building's communal dining room. "I've always thought that true hospitality was eating with somebody," she told us, "and every day I can find friends to share conversation over a meal. It makes a lot of difference to me to be able to do that."

Even though she no longer travels far, Min finds that the constant flow of people in and out of her apartment building—residents, social workers, doctors, family members, and others—gives her more than enough stimulation. "People are not going to say that Min died of boredom," she laughed. "I never feel confined or isolated here. Living this way is a delight."

Min's story illustrates how a productive, constructive, and life-affirming attitude can be applied in what, for most of us, might look like a "throw in the towel" situation. After all, what would *you* do if, after a busy, active life, you suddenly found yourself living alone on a small fixed income in a tiny apartment and confined to a wheelchair by a painful chronic condition? Making this adjustment would sap the energy and enthusiasm of many people, but not Min. She's shown how much difference a positive point of view can make.

Similar issues—and choices—face the more than forty million Americans aged sixty or older, about three-quarters of whom no longer work full time and most of whose children have formed households of their own. And while a majority of those approaching retirement need not face the sort of issues Min is confronting, most of us will at some point have to decide how and where we want to live, depending on factors like money, relationships, and health. In making these decisions, we may conclude that we don't want to move at all or that we want to experiment with not one but *several* different lifestyles.

Perhaps, for example, we'd be happiest retrofitting the house or obtaining a reverse mortgage (sometimes called a home equity line of credit) that provides a monthly income while we're living in our own home. Maybe we'd prefer turning the upstairs into a rental unit or finding one or more roommates to lower our expenses and provide companionship. Others are "down-sizing" their housing to reflect evolving needs.

Several years ago Jim D. and his wife, Nancy, bought a modern condominium in a resort-style Florida community that caters to active seniors. The couple's decision to sell their spacious home in Connecticut was dictated, in part, by the fact that Nancy had tired of cooking and Jim had lost enthusiasm for mowing lawns. For these and other reasons, Nancy and Jim were interested in a complex that gave them the option of eating their meals in a group dining room and one that took care of all gardening chores. Because he is diabetic, Jim also wanted a facility that took his special nutritional needs into account and was close to a medical center, should he need treatment. "None of the other places we looked at, which met our criteria, would accept pets," Jim told us, explaining what influenced the couple's final decision. "So it was our dog who really picked this place."

Unfortunately, Jim's wife spent only a few months in their new condo before she died of a heart attack. Nancy had been his loving companion for more than thirty years, and Jim still misses her very much. Nevertheless, he has no plans to move and has developed a late-blooming lifestyle that conforms with his recently adopted community. "I've met many wonderful people," said Jim, a sixty-eight-year-old retired insurance executive with a gregarious personality and engaging manner. "This place feels like home. I have a car, so I can always get away to see old pals from work or visit family in New England. The complex has a very good security system, so I never worry when I leave the condo empty for long periods of time."

For Jim and Nancy, who were eager to sell their home and most of its contents, moving to a smaller place in a carefully planned community made a lot of sense. They could still enjoy their privacy and intimate companionship without feeling tied down. Now, as a widower, Jim finds himself sustained by the social interaction afforded by a community dining room, clubhouse, pool, and on-site classes on topics like world politics. He's joined an ongoing Friday-night get-together and tries not to miss the dinner dances held every Saturday evening. In addition, Jim volunteers three afternoons a week at a local hospital. "I visit people without families who are confined to intensive care," he explained. "I try to cheer up kids who aren't feeling well and organize birthday parties for long-term patients—pretty much whatever needs to be done."

Jim's has adopted an outlook on life that allows him to pursue new leisure activities, including golf and tennis, and to enjoy the company of retired peers from all over the country. Jim is fortunate. He has demonstrated the ability to thrive in a situation that he neither anticipated nor planned. He has forged a new lifestyle, without the companionship or support of his late wife, in an unfamiliar place. He has courageously turned potentially negative setbacks into positive challenges. Jim is blessed with inner resources that imbue him with a spirit of curiosity and adventure. He knows how he wants to live, and he continues to actively reinforce his positive, life-affirming outlook.

We can't stress enough how important it is to first decide how you might want to spend the upcoming years, then to investigate the various options and actions that will best support that lifestyle, given your particular circumstances. Be reminded that even when you've done all your homework, the unexpected can (and frequently does) intervene. Remember how Mildred, the eighty-five-year-old "perpetual student" who lives with her divorced son in Arizona, decided to leave a comfortable retirement community in Ohio after her husband died. And remember how Henry, the high-ranking executive, expected to become a high-powered consultant for his former employer, but was ignored instead.

A living situation that's fine for neighbors, cousins, and folks you read about in books may not be right for you. What will work is an attitude that leaves you open to the multiple options available. These range from staying right where you are, perhaps with the help of a reverse mortgage or retrofitted residence, to the possibility of having intergenerational housemates, trying group living, moving in with family members, or choosing among a variety of retirement residences and communities. Research, imagination, and invention may bring you exactly what you're looking for. This is the time to be creative!

Consider the example of Florence W., a Late Bloomer who now lives in a small apartment near her son and daughter. "I had a five-room house, and it got to be too much for me to handle by myself," said the seventy-year-old South Dakota widow. Florence thought about moving in with one of her children before concluding that she really cherished her independence and privacy; it was just the snow shoveling, grass trimming, and house cleaning that had become burdensome. "I told my kids one day, 'This is it! I'm going to find a place to live where I don't have to do so much work just to maintain things,'" Florence explained. "They told me, 'If you're sure about this, Mom, we'll help you look.'"

Her middle-aged son, Rudy, drove Florence around her neighborhood until they found a quiet apartment building that offered all the amenities she was looking for. It's on several major bus routes—Florence no longer drives—and it provides excellent security. The complex is home to many friendly seniors who share her interests in knitting, reading, and visiting with family. "I still love gardening," Florence noted, "and I have a big balcony where I can care for all my favorite plants."

For Florence, the decision to give away most of a house full of belongings (she kept her favorite pieces of furniture) and walk away from a comfortable family home without regret was surprisingly easy. "Material things matter less to me now than they used to," she explained. "I left almost everything in the house and let my kids decide what to do with it."

Florence doesn't dwell on the past and has fashioned a new way of life that she considers even more rewarding than the one she left behind. "I think of the people in my new building as a sort of extended family. Many of them are around my age, but we have younger people too. They've given me a fresh perspective on life."

Florence has rediscovered how much she enjoys the energy and enthusiasm of teens and young adults. Because her apartment is close to a university, a number of students live within the complex. She has become friends with several of them, and they often stop by to swap stories and ask for advice. There are also two single parents in the building, a twenty-year-old woman and a twenty-nine-year-old man, and Florence frequently baby-sits for them. Florence's former neighborhood consisted mainly of people around her own age, so a whole new world has opened up for her in her new surroundings. "I feel very alive here and very much appreciated," she concluded.

Florence stumbled unexpectedly upon something that many older people tell us is one of the most important secrets of late blooming: access to the youthful, positive energy of people of different ages and backgrounds. Gray Panther founder Maggie Kuhn once told us how rich her life became after she began renting extra rooms in her house to young women. "Look at it this way," she said. "I've got a huge place that's all paid for, with more dishes, linen, and furniture than I could ever hope to use on my own. They've got CDs, guitars, and idealism—but very little money. We both come out ahead on the deal!"

The notion of renting a spare bedroom to a college student or young working person has caught on among seniors. In a growing number of communities, intergenerational houses and apartment complexes have matched the complementary needs and interests of young and old. We know one former nurse with a spacious room in a three-story Victorian home near a university who's been welcomed into an intergenerational women's consciousness-raising group. Another acquaintance, a retired sporting goods retailer in his midsixties, introduced two of his young roommates to wilderness camping and enticed a third to join him regularly on early morning fishing trips. Many seniors have also found practical benefits in such arrangements. As part of his or her rent, a young boarder might mow the lawn, fetch groceries, and run errands. Whatever cash is part of the deal can supplement a fixed income, pay a mortgage, or cover the cost of home repairs.

Meeting their needs through group housing has become the goal of many Late Bloomers, and the creative possibilities are endless. Because institutions tend to lag behind social changes, you may still have to do a bit of legwork to track down some of these innovative opportunities.

David Wolfe, an author and consultant on marketing to older consumers, says possessions often become less important as we get older—something that makes it easier for some folks to sell a big house and move into something smaller. "Past middle age," Wolfe points out, "people become less interested in things and more interested in interpersonal relationships, philosophical introspection, and the conscious seeking out or contemplation of the joys of 'just being.'" By Wolfe's definition, a "just being" experience may consist of a pleasant social encounter, the enjoyment of a beautiful sunset, hearing music that recalls a pleasant memory, or sailing on a tranquil lake. "Being" can also mean "being all you are," he adds, by realizing your untapped potential and looking into previously unexplored activities. That is why so many older people pursue a new career or hobby, create a dynamic social life, help the less fortunate, enjoy the enrichment of travel, interact frequently with family members, or expand later-life learning. Sometimes what fulfills them most is a set of experiences that combines several such pursuits.

An example of intergenerational compatibility is the encounter with a young admirer that made Walter S. resume his love affair with the camera. Once considered the top portrait photographer in Milwaukee, Walter wasn't sure if he'd ever set up his lights and tripod again after taking up residence in a nursing home. "Photography isn't something that takes a lot of physical effort," Walter acknowledged, "but it took more strength than I could muster."

A severe, painful form of spinal arthritis had virtually paralyzed Walter by the time he reached his late fifties, forcing him to close his photo studio and sell off most of its contents to pay for his health care. After several weeks of hospitalization, Walter's doctors said there was nothing more they could prescribe for him except bed rest. Because mounting medical expenses had exhausted his savings, Walter couldn't afford to receive private care at home and, at age fifty-nine, he reluctantly moved into a nursing home. "For three months I couldn't walk," he recalled, "and didn't much want to. I was sulky and kept to myself. It was as if the roof had caved in on my life."

Walter's depression dragged on for many weeks. He barely had the strength or motivation to get in and out of his wheelchair, and it was only after much prodding from the nursing staff that he finally started using a walker. "What really changed things for me was meeting Susan," Walter told us.

Susan is a local painter in her late twenties who met Walter two years ago through a fortuitous series of events. As a volunteer for a Jewish community organization, she was director of a project aimed at increasing the involvement of nursing home patients in the arts. While conducting videotaped interviews at Walter's facility, Susan learned of his extensive background in photography.

"One of the staff administrators told me that this shy man had run the city's finest portrait studio," Susan explained when we sought her out. "I started talking to other photographers and businessmen who'd worked with Walter and was shown some of his work. I was truly amazed by the great sensitivity and humanity reflected in his photos."

Susan returned to Walter's facility, intent on the idea of getting this fellow artist to start taking and developing pictures again. "She suggested we team up and put together a show based on portraits of people in my nursing home," he said. "At first I thought she was kidding. Then I had to be convinced I could actually do what she wanted, since I hadn't even touched a camera in three years. But in the end we managed to bring it off."

Walter's enthusiasm for the show began to increase after the results of his first few photo sessions drew much praise and encouragement. The local newspaper ran some of the pictures, and congratulations poured in from fellow residents. Walter and Susan began visiting similar facilities in the Milwaukee area, and soon they had put together a substantial portfolio. "The *Faces of Aging* exhibit was a terrific success," Walter told us, his blue eyes sparkling with pride. "I was amazed by the response."

As Walter's self-esteem improved, so did his health. Although he's now strong and mobile enough to get his own apartment, Walter no longer wants to spend his energy on that kind of independent living. He enjoys what the nursing home offers and, in the course of preparing for the photo show, got to know his fellow residents in an entirely new way. Walter says he feels great respect for them and would miss them terribly if he moved.

Of course, not everyone can continue a satisfying and creative career like portrait photography in a nursing home, the way Walter has, but this Late Bloomer advises other retirees to "keep their eyes on the pie," whatever their circumstances happen to be.

"I used to think that when I got to this age I'd be very dignified, very pontifical, very straight laced," said Walter. "But now that I'm here I don't act very differently. I feel the same inside as when I was young, and my emotions aren't much different. I may *look* older, but I certainly don't *feel* it."

During the time he's spent in a nursing home, Walter hasn't always felt happy and young at heart. For many long and lonely months he felt absolutely numb. What changed was Walter's attitude—and the conviction, inspired by Susan, that challenges could be tackled head on. Sometimes it's hard to feel that inspiration when we're all alone, which is one reason many seniors are wise in seeking living situations that put them in touch with interesting individuals and stimulating groups of people. Such regular contact can soothe the soul, quicken the mind, and nourish the spirit.

Not everybody wants to stay around like-minded people when they retire, however. Some would just as soon avoid individuals who had similar professions or lifestyles. For instance, a retired Manhattan brain surgeon who lives in North Carolina never mentions his profession because he wants his friends to treat him "like a good ol' boy," not somebody who went to college for twelve years, has an international reputation, and is listed in *Who's Who*.

Other seniors are restless when retirement rolls around. They shop for places to live the same way some people look for shoes, hoping for the perfect fit. And if they don't find exactly what they want, some of these Late Bloomers take advantage of the fact that they don't have to stay in one place. They may split their time in two locations, wintering in a balmy climate and spending summers in the northern latitudes. This way they can develop two sets of friends, enjoy two kinds of homes, and pursue two distinct lifestyles.

Still other folks never let grass grow under their feet. They adopt the vagabond lifestyle of the perpetual traveler. Their mode of transportation may range from a streamlined motor home to a fully equipped Airstream trailer, from a round-the-world plane ticket to a Eurail train pass. They may take a bus, rent a car, join a tour group, or try other creative combinations that suit their fancy. Many older people see the world from such unusual vistas as the Peace Corps (former president Jimmy Carter's mother, Lillian, began a two-year stint in rural India at age sixty-six) or atop the deck of a tramp freighter. Their options, like yours, are expanding every day.

THE SECRET OF NEW ROOTS

The secret of "new roots" is finding out where and how we want to live in our later years. It may mean staying put and living pretty much the same way we always have, or moving someplace else and changing our lifestyle. But it definitely means taking time to consider other options.

Few decisions in life are as far reaching as the one that concerns where and how we live. This single choice goes a long way in determining who our friends and neighbors are, how much time we spend with our families, what our leisure options are, and the kinds of work that are available to us. Thus one of retirement's biggest challenges is sitting down and figuring out what kind of life we wish to lead in our later years. The central underlying question is "What will contribute to an enjoyable life?"

Each of this chapter's Late Bloomers espouse an attitude that fosters successful adjustment to change, to new roots. At first glance, some of their life situations may seem formidable, even depressing. But these individuals manage to prevail within the limitations of their circumstances and surroundings. Many insist that they're happier now than ever.

These Late Bloomer stories remind us that as we mature, an unlimited number of lifestyle and housing choices are available to us. And there are just as many individual responses to these choices, each influencing how we adjust to changes in later life. Late Bloomers have learned how to plan with the head, the heart, and the spirit, as well as the atlas, the moving van, and the checkbook. Their focus has broadened to include—even celebrate—their own attitudes and values. They realize that while such practical matters as health, family, and finances are key considerations in retirement planning, they aren't the only ones. It's all a matter of attitude and choice.

Keep in mind that a Late Bloomer can look only so far ahead. Although you may make an appropriate choice for your active years, your needs, family situation, financial resources, and health will inevitably change as you continue to age. At seventy-five or eighty-five, the place where you put down new roots may no longer be appropriate. In fact, it may be the first of several. Since we're living longer, it's important to remain flexible throughout our retirement years!

HOW TO ACT ON THIS SECRET

In order to act on the secret of new roots, think of our physical dwelling as a kind of stage set in which we're going to act out our individual lifestyles. In real life, as in the theater, it's much easier to make a personal scenario "work" when our home base is nourishing and appropriate, our community and environment are agreeable, and the setting for our changing lifestyle is supportive.

"Also, if you want to get the most out of your retirement, you've got to do some homework first," Leah Dobkin, a housing specialist with the American Association of Retired Persons, told the *Los Angeles Times*. "People who don't do some advance planning often wind up being sorry."

We must determine at the outset, for example, what choices are realistically within our reach, depending on factors like health and money. At the same time, we must ask ourselves what kinds of lifestyles, values, and amenities are most important to us at this time of our lives. We also need to consider the trade-offs that are part of any decision, since any choice about where and how to live will contain some inherent limitations and advantages.

Drawing up a list of action steps and priorities is an excellent way to move toward your heart's desire. Remember how Barbara and Bernie, the New York snowbirds who bought a condo in Florida, brainstormed together and wrote down their favorite activities? Although they had already decided where they wanted to live, the same approach can be effective in carefully evaluating the housing needs and lifestyle adjustments of our later years. List making forces us to think carefully about what is and isn't important to us. If nothing else, it should help clarify whether you want to stay put or live somewhere else.

Your list should be highlighted by what matters most to you in the place that you live, whether it's low fixed costs, proximity to family, mild climate, access to medical care, or other factors. As you write down possible options, make a separate column for "pros" and "cons." You'll probably eliminate some possibilities quickly as you discover trade-offs that seem unacceptable.

In drawing up your list of "option preferences," it may be most important to you (or your spouse) that you stay close to lifelong friends or your religious institution. Depending on your needs and desires, anticipating these feelings can influence your decision making. What's of primary importance here is looking closely at your personal situation, not at what somebody else did or what you assume to be appropriate choices. And for many people, key retirement decisions wind up being people oriented. In fact, according to studies, a desire to be close to relatives is the single most important contributing factor in the decision by retiring Americans to make a geographic move.

"A lot of people retire just because they want to spend more time with their family and friends," reminds Leah Dobkin. "You can't do that when they're all thousands of miles away." Given the fact that many of our children—and friends—move away from home, this means a lot of retirees must make tough decisions about pulling up roots.

Whatever the circumstances, for many of us such a decision has practical as well as emotional ramifications. Perhaps we feel safer knowing our children or grandchildren will be around to look in on us or take care of any emergencies that come up. There's often a sense of security simply in knowing that the family is close at hand, or that we have family members to help us relocate in case maintaining a household becomes too onerous.

Ask yourself whether it's the wisest choice to live close to your children and grandchildren. Although many of us are attracted to that kind of proximity, it can sometimes put a strain on relationships. And being near the family may automatically foreclose some other options. There may be few senior services or cultural amenities where your children live, for instance, or the area's public transportation and health facilities may be limited.

Some retirees place a higher priority on becoming part of an "active-adult" retirement community, located some distance from their family and friends. Others opt for a life of travel, or split their time in various locations. Some may want to be near favorite recreation sites, such as golf courses, hiking trails, and fishing streams. Still others decide to remain exactly where they are, perhaps figuring that "if it ain't broke, don't fix it."

If moving is an attractive option, test your feelings about a new place by visiting it several times and talking to long-time residents who are in your age group. If possible, check it out during different seasons of the year. Most communities look their best in summer and early fall, but winter and early spring can be another story. A different climate may also be too much of a transition. You'd be surprised how many people from other parts of the country never get used to the desert southwest or subtropical Florida, no matter how appealing the advertising makes them look. If you've visited there and are still interested, consider renting temporary quarters for several weeks or months. This way you'll meet neighbors and get a well-rounded view of what it's like to live there.

If planned retirement communities intrigue you, investigate them carefully. You may find that some are geared exclusively toward serving healthy and active older residents, with little or nothing in the way of "assisted living" or on-site medical facilities. This could pose a problem if you need comprehensive health care or have a chronic or deteriorating condition. And while some people are comforted by having details handled by a builder or manager, others are annoyed by regulations that accompany life in such a complex. These may range from rules about what color your walls can be painted to the length of time your grandchildren can visit. Sometimes people discover that they're paying for a lot of extras they thought they'd use but never do. It's vital for you to assess which amenities are real advantages to you personally rather than to the community at large. Finally, consider the fact that many retirement communities are located some distance from metropolitan areas—which means that to enjoy urban amenities you may have to rely on a private vehicle, car pool, or public transportation.

A thorough search will reveal that there are now retirement communities to fit nearly all lifestyles and pocketbooks. Many accommodate the inevitable changes that occur throughout aging, providing the kind of flexibility that encourages many Late Bloomers to blossom. To obtain free information about retirement communities and services in a particular region, you can contact local agencies that serve seniors or even local chambers of commerce. Take your time and do your research. Be assured that, as in all of life, external circumstances and internal changes will yield new perspectives, so try to build in flexibility.

Making a choice about where to put down new roots—or whether to uproot yourself at all—is something that demands careful consideration. Once you've made that choice, the doors to other opportunities will open or close. And while your decision is certainly not irrevocable, it's usually easier to plan an appropriate lifestyle during retirement's transition phase than to reverse your course later on. Good luck!

CHAPTER NINE

THE SECRET OF INTIMACY

"Song birds cannot sing in isolation," writes Elise Maclay in *Green Winter*, her book of poems about aging. "No bird can. Neither can any human being."

Human life is enriched enormously by intimate emotional interaction, whether a person is three years old or ninety-three. Every one of us needs someone with whom we can share our joys and sorrows, challenges and surprises, triumphs and disappointments. Daily exchanges with acquaintances, friends, spouses, and other loved ones are the currency of life. To a large extent, the caring and closeness provided by such contact are what living is all about.

But intimacy doesn't come gift wrapped in our later years. We can't claim it at a senior discount. Considerable effort— frequently more effort than we used when we were younger— is needed to maintain past relationships and, especially, to start and sustain new ones.

A major contributor to this later-life reality is the "empty nest" syndrome. Once our children have grown up and left home, we no longer meet other parents through a son's Boy Scout troop or a daughter's baby-sitting job. Nor are we invited to attend parents' night at their school or a Friday night football game with other moms and dads.

If we've retired from work, there aren't any jokes around the watercooler or gossipy coffee breaks in the employee lounge. Retirement means an end to trade shows and business conventions as well as commuting with neighbors and co-workers in a bus or car pool.

Following retirement, it's also possible that our favorite neighbors and colleagues have moved and our children have relocated far away. Yes, we may talk to these friends and children on the phone or see them during holidays or vacations, but that's hardly the same as sharing the routines of everyday life. Other loved ones too, as time goes by, are lost to debilitating diseases, accidents, or death. Life is about people and, as we get older, they tend to disappear.

"It's the hardest thing to get used to," conceded a sixty-seven-year-old retired military officer interviewed in a Missouri retirement community. "There are so many deaths. At the same time, having people around who care about me makes all the difference in how I feel."

This chapter seeks neither to belabor the inevitability of such losses nor to offer specific schemes for filling the painful voids that result. Its message is that *if* interaction with other people becomes a priority, you *will* find a way to bring that into your life. You can accomplish this in many ways. Some seniors who work part time, for example, tell us that holding a job isn't so much about earning extra money as it is keeping in regular contact with other people. We have older friends who are "trial watchers" in courtrooms because it puts them in touch with real life. We know other folks who are hooked on RV travel because they love the "people connections" they make in campgrounds.

Shifting gears as one ages isn't a predictable or easy process, especially if you find yourself alone in a "Noah's ark" world, where everything appears to be designed with couples in mind. If you're on your own, it takes energy and imagination to adjust social patterns with friends, co-workers, and loved ones. If you haven't been on a date in thirty or forty years, things will be a little scary, no matter how experienced you are in tackling other challenges. If a recently departed spouse was also your best friend and confidant, it will feel awkward to seek new companions with whom you can share your most intimate thoughts. Taking such risks, however, often brings many rewards and much enrichment as well as unexpected satisfactions.

We've met a number of folks over fifty-five who share living quarters with a new roommate, spouse, lover, or best friend. Others have formed meaningful friendships with teenagers and young children, for whom they serve as mentors or surrogate grandparents.

Sometimes these later-life relationships can teach us important lessons in compatibility, as was the case with our friend Samuel T., who is the first to admit that he and his roommate, Larry J., "are worlds apart." Sam is outgoing and social, spending many evenings playing cribbage and backgammon or talking on the telephone with his pals. Although a mild heart attack has slowed this eighty-four-year-old down, he's still rather impatient and short-tempered. Sam is also very organized and methodical, even while working in the kitchen. "No microwave meals for me," declares Sam proudly. "I cook a four-course dinner nearly every night."

Larry, on the other hand, describes himself accurately as "introverted and shy." He loves to read and hates to cook. The random piles and careless clutter in Larry's bedroom make Sam roll his eyes and cluck his tongue. Larry prefers one-to-one conversations or, better yet, the silent company of his own thoughts.

"It may sound funny, but I feel lucky to have Larry as a roommate," said Sam, when we visited the condo they share on Long Island. "He's a nice man." In short, Sam continued, Larry is a wonderful, gentle companion. "And after I lost my wife of fifty-three years, companionship is what I missed most."

Larry feels much the same way, having been widowed five years ago at age sixty-seven. "Nights were tough after my wife died," said Larry. "I felt depressed and lonely. I'd look around, and no one was there."

Despite Larry's natural reticence and Sam's gruff exterior, the similarity of their experience has drawn the pair into many heart-to-heart conversations about their feelings. "It's never been easy for me to talk about my emotions," Sam allowed, "and I know Larry would say the same thing. But opening up with each other has brought us a lot closer."

The two men were matched through a local nonprofit agency designed to help older people with their housing needs, one of many such organizations around the country. Because Sam's heart problems have caused him to turn in his driver's license, Larry does most of the shopping and other household errands. He also makes sure his roommate gets to his doctor's appointments on time and waits patiently to drive Sam home. "We do our own thing," concluded Larry. "And at the same time, we really appreciate and rely on each other."

Sam and Larry, like many men of their generation, have had difficulty forming intimate relationships. When they were growing up, a man was taught to be strong and aloof, to hold his feelings in check. Showing emotion was considered a sign of weakness and reaching out to others an admission of defeat. Talking about being lonely, especially with another man, simply wasn't done.

Thankfully, times have changed, and men are now allowed to express a wider range of emotions, including lone-liness. We know that nothing—not gender, money, power, education, talent, or beauty—exempts us from the need for intimacy. Loneliness is felt by infants, growing children, young people, adults in the prime of life, and, finally, those who are older. Aging often increases the pain because we have less energy to cope with it—and because the demographic odds can work against us. Women live longer, so as they get older they outnumber men.

If John or Joan is gone, his or her shoes may indeed remain unfilled. Yet this loss need not mean life must be devoid of intimacy. There are many action steps you can take to make sure that intimacy is part of your life. Having some kind of emotional closeness in your life requires that you take responsibility for seeking out and forming relationships, whether they are romantic attachments or platonic friend-ships with individuals of either gender. It's up to you to make whatever "people contacts" will help replace what's missing. This requires both commitment and action.

"We adapt, with enormous difficulty, to the altered

circumstances of our lives," writes Judith Viorst in her book *Necessary Losses.* As a survival strategy, says Viorst, we modify "our behavior, our expectations, our self-definitions" after a death, divorce, or other trauma. Even the mourning process "can lead to creative change."

Our late-blooming friends Bill M. and Cecile K. illustrate this principle in the decisions they've made in recent years. Both have endured great sadness, anger, and loss, yet managed to let go of their pain to embrace the joys of the present and a future together. Bill was in tears as he told us how much he loved his first wife, who died after sixty-two years of marriage. Then an edge crept into his voice as he told us how angry she made him by dying. "I was really mad at her for abandoning me," explained Bill, who turned eighty-three a few weeks before our interview. "I was angry with all women. I didn't have anything to do with them for quite a while." His range of feelings is something many older people share. The undercurrent of rage, which might seem illogical at first, is actually fairly common among widowers.

A few months after the funeral, Bill quietly sold his home and moved into a retirement community in Anaheim, California, where he kept pretty much to himself. Later that year Bill met Cecile, a bright-eyed eighty-year-old widow and another recent arrival in the neighborhood. She was nervous about meeting new people, but Bill quickly broke the ice. "He was a real kidder," recalled Cecile, who found herself sharing a table with Bill in the community dining room. "So I decided to take his words with a grain of salt. But as I got to know him, I found there was a real gentleman underneath." Because their apartments were both on the third floor of the retirement residence, it was easy for the two to get better acquainted.

"At first I felt guilty about seeing her," confessed Bill, a handsome man who is over six feet tall. "I still held the image of my first wife in my mind." Yet there was something special about Cecile that captured Bill's attention. He found himself sitting with her frequently at the meal table and asking her along on an occasional group activity.

"Bill seemed to be good natured and always upbeat," said Cecile, "but I could tell there was a side of him that he wasn't opening up to me. Since I wasn't necessarily looking for a romance, I let him proceed at his own pace."

A few weeks later, Bill found himself seated in a crowded bus next to Cecile, who looked splendid in a new spring outfit. "I turned to her and asked, 'Cecile, may I hold your hand?' She turned to me and said, 'Why yes, I'd love it.' " When they both stood up, they felt as if they were walking on air. So much for the idea that you have to be young to fall in love. Later that summer the couple was married in a private ceremony. In attendance were Cecile's son and daughter and Bill's twin girls. All residents were invited to a reception held that same weekend in the retirement community's auditorium.

Like Bill, Cecile came into their relationship after a long and satisfying relationship. She, too, knew firsthand about sadness and loss. Her resilience in love is testimony to her wisdom in years. "We both had enjoyable marriages, and now I think we know what life is all about," Cecile said. "I believe the reason Bill and I are so good together is because we were happily married before." Like her new husband, Cecile never dreamed that anyone could fill the void left by the death of her first spouse. "Bill and I have learned the true value of living," she concluded. "We each want someone to share the happiness as well as the sadness."

Cecile and Bill are living proof that you're never too old for romance and that the loss of a loved one doesn't necessarily mean you can't find intimacy again. Their experience runs counter to the stereotype of older people as passionless, nonsexual beings.

That most healthy older people can enjoy physical lovemaking throughout later life is documented by the research of the Masters and Johnson team, among others. A sixty-five-year-old acquaintance named Vivian M., for instance, insists it was "sexual attraction" that first brought seventy-three-year-old Carey S. to her attention. Vivian, a New York psychologist, now shares bed and board with this former student, who had enrolled in a seminar she taught on self-relaxation techniques. "Long before I met Vivian," Carey chimed in, "I was taught all this [sexuality] would end at age fifty or sixty. I can tell you from firsthand experience that the best may be yet to come."

The two are quick to add that they have a deep and caring relationship that goes beyond the physical. "We're partners not only at home but at the office too," Vivian explained. One year after they began living together, the two started a Washington, D.C., business as practitioners of "healing therapy." They use an innovative approach that combines Eastern traditions, such as meditation and yoga, with therapeutic techniques and nutritional regimens developed in the West.

"A lot of people might think twice about opening a practice like this at eighty," said Carey, his healthy good looks radiant beneath a sparse crop of white hair and a wrinkled brow. "We both believe very strongly in the life-enhancing aspects of personal growth and empowerment. We tell our clients that we have more than 145 years of combined experience!"

Carey, a former educational administrator, is relatively new to the self-help field, while Vivian has taught and written widely on psychology for many years. Despite this career difference and the eight-year gap in their ages, Vivian and Carey say they have a great deal in common, including long-standing involvement in the peace movement, a keen interest in teaching, and the hobby of restoring early American furniture. "I really enjoy Carey's mind," adds Vivian, with a flirtatious, loving wink. "He was the best student I've ever had."

Although their mutual attraction is strong, both feel it's important to have time to themselves and with other friends they know independently from each other. Each has a separate study area, and they respect the need to sometimes take long walks in solitude. "After four years," Carey concluded, "we seem to have found the right balance between togetherness and separateness. It's something I don't think we could ever have achieved when we were younger."

These Late Bloomers have found happiness in a loving relationship that didn't even begin until both were receiving Social Security checks. For various reasons, including financial and health-insurance technicalities, they've decided that, rather than getting married, they would just live together. We realize that setting up housekeeping outside the institution of marriage may seem improper to many people, especially those who've grown up under a traditional set of social mores. Yet for an increasing number of later-life mates, it's an alternative that works well to provide intimate caring, sharing, and companionship. Within the parameters of a more formal long-term marriage, there's also plenty of room for the life-affirming growth and healthy separateness that Vivian and Carey describe.

The ability to keep a partnership flexible after decades of togetherness is something some couples demonstrate with great enthusiasm, tenderness, and skill. Actors Hume Cronyn and the late Jessica Tandy were married to each other for nearly all of their adult lives and learned to cope with their differences. "We've been marvelous partners for over fifty years," Hume began, when we met the two in the spacious New York apartment where they'd lived part time from the 1930s until Jessica's death in 1994. "Our kids even seem a little intimidated, thinking they'll never be able to duplicate that kind of longevity in their own relationships!"

Like Vivian and Carey, Hume and Jessica shared not only a domestic domain but professional lives as well. They acted together in numerous stage plays and several movies. Yet both also succeeded independently. In Hollywood, Hume Cronyn is best known for his acclaimed performances in the films of Alfred Hitchcock and the more recent *Cocoon* movies. Jessica Tandy won the 1989 "best actress" Oscar for her starring role in *Driving Miss Daisy*. As we talked, the couple volunteered the secret of their enduring marital commitment in an industry rife with divorce.

"It's not the moments of mutual ecstasy that hold you together," Hume ventured, "but the mutual crises you've survived. . . . The things that stick in your mind are the times that were tough and that you got through somehow. And when you held out a hand, there was another hand there to grasp it."

Jessica nodded as her husband spoke. "Difficulties can strengthen your relationship," she said. "It's absolutely essential in one's marriage to be able to laugh together, even at painful things. It's absolutely *essential!*"

These aren't the truths of fast-lane celebrities. The couple's interaction reflected the mutual respect and acknowledgment of differences that nourish and sustain all long-term relationships. "When you have somebody to share the problems and the joys with," Hume said, "the problems are cut in half and the joys are doubled. There's always someone there to support you in the clutches."

Another technique worked to the benefit of these long-married partners, who at the time of our interview were in their seventies. Hume and Jessica maintained physical space of their own that each withdrew to when time alone was important. "If I'm struggling with something," Hume explained, "I may want to go to some secret place within myself and not discuss the problem with anyone. And Jess lets me literally go off on my own, which is one of the reasons she's been able to put up with me for so long." Sometimes they even slept in separate bedrooms, reuniting the next morning with fresh affection and commitment.

"I think there's nothing wrong with having a jolly good cry sometimes," Jessica emphasized, "and one needs to be left alone to do that. Other people will try to make it all better for you, but it's something you just have to go through. If you've suffered a loss, you have to grieve. Only then can you feel whole once more."

Jessica and Hume forged a partnership that remained flexible and alive. Their love affair evolved and flourished through a half century of changing needs and desires, soaring successes, and crashing failures. A long marriage endured, prospered, and prevailed as a result of mutual respect and support.

For many of us, the full life to which we aspire will include getting married, no matter how tumultuous and aggravating the arrangement sometimes feels. Through marriage, observes author William Attwood in *Making It through Middle Age*, "you come to appreciate the value of companionship, consideration, and continuity." Yet because of circumstances beyond our control, mutually supportive relationships may often occur outside marriage and romance.

"I have a 'best girlfriend' whom I love doing things with," seventy-two-year-old Malvina told us. "I can talk with her about anything. We run errands together and take walks in the park. We're real pals!" After moving into a retirement community following the death of her husband, this Late Bloomer recalled that "it was easy to find people who were friendly but much harder to find true friends." She succeeded by asking her neighbors if they needed anything at the market before setting out on her weekly shopping. "One woman told me that in the two years she'd lived there nobody had ever asked her that question," Malvina said. "And that person, Joyce, is now my best friend."

Many people pride themselves on their ability to remain independent and self-sufficient in their later years, perhaps not recognizing the natural interdependence of all human beings. They may find it humiliating or embarrassing to ask for help or show any need that might be interpreted as a weakness, especially if this extends beyond spouse and family. Sometimes it's difficult to find the right balance between reaching out and holding back. Yet many Late Bloomers are doing just that.

Russian-born Natasha S., for example, has lost two husbands in her sixty-nine years. She's also raised three children, who've since scattered across the country and started families of their own. Natasha now enjoys a living situation that could be described as a cross between a congregate-care facility and a board-and-care home. "It's called a housing cooperative," the retired Toronto salesclerk explained. "I'm one of fourteen renters in an apartment complex that [for a modest monthly fee] provides my utilities, upkeep, and an evening meal every night." The complex has a common lounge and kitchen area, where residents frequently get together to eat and socialize. Natasha also spends a part of most sunny afternoons sitting in the communal courtyard, knitting sweaters or reading inspirational literature.

"The residents live like a family and have a lot of say in the way the place is run," Natasha told us over a cup of hot tea. "Most of the time we do pretty much as we please." She likes the warm camaraderie that's developed within her "mini-neighborhood" and the way neighbors keep an eye on each other. "Most of the people who live here realize how lucky they are," she noted. "We're never really alone." Natasha has discovered that one can maintain a separate household with an independent lifestyle and still not be lonely. She's found the balance of companionship and freedom that she began looking for after her second husband died.

Late Bloomers might find this "nourishment" of human contact in a housing complex such as Natasha's, a long and satisfying marriage like Hume and Jessica's, a "live-in" situation like the one Vivian and Carey have, or a roommate arrangement similar to Sam and Larry's. Yet to enjoy any of these situations, we'll probably need to go out and look, to take some risks, and to expend some effort. To be fair, it's also possible that the intimate companion we're seeking is close at hand.

Roland F. and Sue F. are a brother and sister who genuinely *like* being together. They enjoy reasonably good health and share a modest two-bedroom house in a small Kansas town, where they pool their Social Security funds and look after each other.

Roland is a sixty-nine-year-old widower, and his sister, sixty-four, divorced her husband some time ago. Their marriages yielded several children, now grown and raising families of their own. Although most of their respective sons and daughters live nearby, Roland and Sue prefer to maintain their independence and, as the latter puts it, "not be a millstone to anybody." They moved in together awhile back and have managed to create a situation that has not only pragmatic advantages but many fringe benefits as well.

"I've always enjoyed my brother's company," Sue told us, "and now we've developed a new aspect of our relationship that is really delightful. I've discovered all over again what a great sense of humor Roland has and how much we have in common."

"We've gotten reacquainted," Roland agreed, "and have made a nice place for ourselves in a comfortable old house. Our grandkids and great-grandkids love to visit, and they get lots of attention whenever they come."

Besides enjoying the requisite cookies and lemonade, the visiting youngsters are an appreciative audience for the unique brother-and-sister comedy team Roland and Sue created three years ago. Called New Tricks, it's the product of an unusual hobby the siblings share: the re-creation of vaudeville theater. Sue told us they perform mostly in nursing homes and senior centers, with no ambition for fame or fortune. The troupe's name comes from that hoary cliché, You can't teach an old dog new tricks. "We've proved the naysayers wrong," laughed Roland. "Sue and I learn new routines all the time."

The pair have no professional experience in drama, but during early childhood, when traveling carnivals and variety shows were common in the Midwest, both showed a natural aptitude for composing lyrics. "We've always loved to sing," said Roland, who is blessed with a smooth baritone voice.

The inspiration for New Tricks came over supper one night, when Roland and Sue discovered they knew the words to the songs on some vintage records they hadn't listened to in years. They've interspersed stories and jokes in their repertoire—including quite a few that poke gentle fun at aging—plus several vaudeville-era skits. Reviews for New Tricks have been so positive that the duo perform at least once each week.

Roland and Sue make late blooming sound easy. But, when pressed, they concede that living together successfully required lots of adjustments. Making compromises and exercising restraint, Roland insisted, is a prerequisite after years of "doing your own thing."

Conceiving and creating a new lifestyle with a family member is one way of finding companionship, but it's certainly not the only way. There are almost as many creative living arrangements as there are people, as we discovered during a visit to two innovative Late Bloomers who live in the Pacific northwest.

By sheer coincidence, they are both named Pauline. At eighty-two, Pauline K. is the younger of the two. Her best friend, roommate, and co-worker is Pauline G., age eighty-six.

"We met each other in Jamaica," explained Pauline K., a brown-eyed redhead.

"Both of us were in the Peace Corps," added her companion, Pauline G., who's gray haired and two inches shorter.

We visited the two Paulines in Seattle, where they've

become something of an institution, ministering voluntarily to the city's disadvantaged and homeless. The women spend as many as forty hours a week conducting home visits with people who need help applying for food stamps or taking care of utility bills. They visit nursing home residents who are lonely and without families. The Paulines are also familiar figures at centers for those with disabilities and at hospitals, where they deliver homemade cookies and help patients fill out Medicare forms. Through the auspices of the Red Cross, they are outspoken advocates for the poor.

"Some people think the Paulines are a religious order, like the Paulists or Catholic Workers," chuckled an administrator who works with the women, who are not affiliated with any particular organization. "I see them together so often that even I sometimes lose track of which Pauline is which."

Living and working together is not all they do. Until some health problems arose, the Paulines took overseas trips together at least once a year. They've traveled to South America, the Middle East, Australia, and Alaska. "I've been so lucky to live with her because she is kinder and more thoughtful than I am," Pauline K. said of her companion. "I think she's made me a better person."

Pauline G., in turn, feels "the greatest thing my friend has given me is just being an extrovert, when I'm the opposite. Having grown up with seven brothers, I learned about how far you can go and when you'd better keep quiet."

Because they have done so much work in their community, the Paulines say they appreciate each other more now than if they'd met twenty years ago, when both were involved in unrelated careers of their own. By sharing so many challenges, their friendship becomes stronger and more satisfying with each passing year. "We love each other," Pauline K. told us. "It's as simple and as profound as that."

THE SECRET OF INTIMACY

Our conclusion is that life is people, and people are life. In order to remain healthy and happy, all of us need to give and receive affection, appreciation, acceptance, and friendship on a regular basis. Having someone with whom we can share our ins and outs, highs and lows, is a precious treasure. As the song says, "Love makes the world go 'round!"

As humans, we all need emotional intimacy: some form of consistent, heartfelt interaction and sharing. This is a truth, too often kept secret, that knows no boundaries and encompasses all nationalities, cultures, ethnicities, religions, genders, and age groups.

Accepting, understanding, and fulfilling this fundamental need helps us create a life that embraces and celebrates the wonderfully infinite diversity of people. In order to accomplish this, we must first gain insight into our personal requirements for intimacy, which vary from one person to the next, and then take responsibility for designing a lifestyle that meets these needs.

As they grow older, Late Bloomers often learn the secret of intimacy by accepting and reaching out to new people in the course of everyday life. They celebrate the possibilities that each person represents. Some individuals are people with whom they can walk, play cards, wash their laundry, swap stories, attend plays, drink coffee, go to the movies, or even make love. Whatever their particular circumstance in life,

Late Bloomers manage to build mutually beneficial and rewarding relationships that offer high-quality experiences in loving, playing, and working with their fellow human beings.

A bold determination, optimistic attitude, and energetic spirit can be reflected in the ways we respond to our own aging. This applies to our marriages, friendships, and other types of intimate relationships as much as it does our hobbies, travel, work, religion, and other aspects of a full, rich life. It isn't enough to fill our days and nights with external activity if we feel lonely and empty inside. For many, this may mean taking direct, overt action to provide ourselves with the level of intimacy we want and need. It may mean taking some risks that, at least at first, are scary and anxiety-producing.

At this point you may be saying to yourself something like *I've always lived a certain way, a way that doesn't demand much risk taking. I'm comfortable with my lifestyle and have no intention of changing.* Yet within two, five, or ten years your life may be very different. In fact, if the authors' experiences are any guide, it probably *will* be. And the more prepared you are to respond positively to these kinds of changes, the better off you'll be.

We'll leave you with another pertinent stanza from the poetry of Elise Maclay. "Old Lovers" is about a man and woman who fall in love late in their lives. If, as you read this excerpt from the poem, you substitute two men, two women, two cousins, two siblings, two neighbors, or two friends for the poem's two "old lovers," you'll find that Maclay's message can be applied to any of us.

Today I saw an advertisement
In a magazine, a picture of two people,
Old,
Hurrying to meet at a fountain in a park.
I couldn't stop looking,
Misty-eyed at the sweetness of it.
Oh, I know the people in the photograph
Are probably paid models,
But I also know that somewhere
Two people
Dowdy to the world
But beautiful to each other
Are finding each other
And finding the world new

HOW TO ACT ON THIS SECRET

Although intimacy is a very personal and private matter, many practical and public steps can foster its development during our later years. The first is to take some time to determine what kind of intimacy we really want and need at each stage of the game. As we've seen in this chapter, an intimate companion can run the gamut from a traditional marriage partner to a close friend or even an exercise buddy. The choice is up to you.

So sit back and flex your imagination. On the stage of your mind, mentally create the world you wish to inhabit. Transport yourself, in your mind's eye at first, into situations where companions, friends, neighbors, lovers, and family members are a more important part of your life. Brainstorming and writing things down are other effective techniques for accessing the secret of intimacy. Once you've fantasized and strategized, plan and initiate changes in your life that will bring you into contact with the kind of people you most want to be with.

For many of us, the priority in later life is not necessarily on finding a mate. You may have a spouse to whom you're happily married, yet you may want other friendships. If you're widowed or divorced, you may have had your fill of domestic life, at least for the present, and wish to maintain an unmarried status. Perhaps you're looking for a companion who might eventually become a housemate or best friend.

Late Bloomers use many worthwhile, proven strategies for developing new friendships. A good first step is to ask those you already know what they do to meet people. Relatives, neighbors, co-workers, fellow churchgoers, and current friends may have some excellent suggestions.

You may be surprised to find that within the circle of people you already know are individuals with whom you share many interests—friends of friends, for instance. Once you get to know them, these folks might even become better friends than those who introduced you. Taking advantage of this situation is a matter of opening your eyes to the opportunities that surround you.

Suitable companions can also be found through chance encounters in daily life: the result of casual conversations in post office lines, for example, or recipe swaps in the grocer's produce department. Another good way to meet like-minded people is through volunteer work with a church, school, political campaign, or community organization. You also can donate your time and talents to a hospital, religious auxiliary, library, museum, service club, senior center, or nonprofit agency. Each volunteer assignment will put you in regular contact with people who share your concerns and values. In many communities, the chamber of commerce and main library keep track of many worthwhile organizations that are looking for help. Take a close look in your local newspaper for such listings, which often appear in regularly published "community calendar" or "datebook" features. Public service announcements on local TV and radio are a good resource too.

Other ways of meeting like-minded people include recreational travel, gardening clubs, art tours, exercise groups (like the early morning "mall walkers"), part-time employment, and continuing education. Opportunities for education can be found in most communities through a college, Elderhostel, private instructor, or university extension.

If you're serious about finding a new mate, or simply a playmate, we have good news: dating services and personal ads have become respectable! Even mainstream newspapers and magazines now frequently run advertisements placed by individuals who are looking for varying levels of intimate companionship, from platonic friendship to marriage. Many publications have a separate category for persons fifty and older and, to protect the anonymity and privacy of participants, offer a box number for the initial contact. The cost of such introductions is nominal, and you can choose either to respond to existing ads or place your own—or do both.

If you decide to participate in this kind of service, we urge you to be honest about your age and interests. Face-to-face introductions should be innocuous: meeting over a cup of coffee in a restaurant during daylight hours, for example. This way there's an opportunity either to comfortably and safely end the encounter or to arrange another meeting.

Many of the same publications that offer personals also feature display ads for professional dating services, which try to link individuals by matching personality, age, and interest profiles. These firms charge a fee, sometimes rather hefty, for screening and processing applicants. You might think these companies cater only to the young, but this is no longer the case. In fact, a growing number specialize in introducing only older singles. If you enlist such a firm, you'll be asked to provide information about yourself and your ideal mate; a photo or videotape is also placed on file. If another client is attractive to you—and vice versa—a date is arranged discreetly. The rest is up to you!

Another approach is to attend "singles" events, like dances and mixers, that are sponsored by churches, synagogues, clubs, or other organizations. If you participate, you'll have the advantage of meeting someone who already shares your interests and/or religion. Many of these occasions are also senior oriented.

Similarly, enrolling in an adult education, Elderhostel seminar, or community college class will put you in touch with potential new mates or friends with whom you automatically have something in common. Check newspaper listings and college catalogs to find out what's available in your area. Taking classes that teach special skills, such as using a computer or cooking Asian food, are great ways to meet new people with whom you implicitly have something to talk about.

Whatever level of intimacy you're seeking, the options and opportunities are already out there. The challenge is to use your imagination and take the initiative to explore them fully. Whatever the ultimate outcome, you're certain to be rewarded!

CHAPTER TEN

THE SECRET OF HEALTH

YOUR HEALTH IS A MAJOR INFLUENCE on the way you plan and live during your retirement. This simple statement may come as no great surprise until you start thinking about its subtle implications. As long as you're in good health, almost any lifestyle and goal seem attainable. But if you're like most of us, you have at least one or two personal health issues that affect the choices you're able to make in later life.

Are you a diabetic? Have you had a bout with cancer? Do you have high blood pressure? Do you smoke cigarettes? Do you suffer from allergies or arthritis? Are you overweight? Has your vision, hearing, or sense of balance deteriorated?

The answers to these health questions may pose limitations that can be dealt with in what the medical community refers to as a "personal wellness program." Such a program is designed to maintain or even improve your well-being by taking into account your particular physical situation, habits, interests, or disabilities.

Developing such a program requires commitment and participation. Finding and maintaining a way of life that fosters fitness is primarily *your* responsibility. If you haven't done so, we suggest you develop an individualized plan for a health-promoting lifestyle that involves sufficient exercise, an appropriate diet, life-affirming habits, and appropriate preventive health care.

Let's be clear from the outset that this isn't a chapter on how to plan your daily exercise schedule or menu. We won't outline specific techniques for staying healthy; plenty of excellent books, videotapes, and other materials can help you with that. Your personal physician also can be of assistance, and he or she can answer your questions about diet, exercise, and lifestyle.

This chapter deals instead with the subject of health through the examples set by our Late Bloomer role models. Some enjoy good or even first-rate health and have committed themselves to whatever it takes to stay that way. Sixty-six-year-old Martha S., for example, walks briskly for an hour each morning with her next-door neighbor Jenny, who is a spry seventy. Harvey P. has switched at age seventy-two from meat to a largely vegetarian diet. And Eileen J., sixty-nine, reads the newspaper and listens to classical music while she rides her stationary bicycle at 6:00 A.M.

These individuals, like millions of older Americans, have found that being fit makes a big difference not only in their physical well-being but in their stamina, alertness, and ability to enjoy life.

"You need to have respect for the body as well as the mind," emphasized Ralph K., a seventy-one-year-old retired civil service worker who has the tanned, ruddy cheeks of someone who spends a lot of time out-of-doors. He and his wife, Betty, sixty-five, have, after some very traumatic moments together, discovered the many later-life rewards of physical fitness. "Truthfully," Betty told us, "Ralph's heart attack saved his life. And maybe mine too."

When her husband retired seven years earlier, neither Betty nor Ralph considered themselves to be in poor health. "We were both overweight," she admits, "but we always considered ourselves fairly active and reasonably fit. Our health was something we just didn't think about very much. Like most people, we took it for granted." Actually, both were (and still are) eager participants in the Senior Olympics, a non-profit organization of amateur athletes over the age of fifty-five that is dedicated to "doing your physical best with the health you have." The group is composed of thousands of ordinary people who like getting together in a friendly environment to demonstrate and test their skills. Unlike those "other" Olympians, whose activity is marked by fierce competition, these senior athletes challenge themselves more than they do each other.

"We started participating in the statewide Senior Olympics," Ralph told us, emphasizing that the organization caters to older athletes of every ability. This explains why he was winning medals right up to the day he keeled over in a drugstore with a mild heart attack. "Luckily, the pharmacist knew CPR," he continued. "I made it to the hospital in time, but my doctor insisted I had to take better care of myself in the future. I'd heard it all before, of course, but this time I really listened."

With Betty's enthusiastic support, Ralph changed his eating habits, cutting back on fats, red meat, salt, and sugar.

Together, they began a daily routine of fast-paced walking, covering four miles every morning in about an hour. Over the next few months he dropped forty-two pounds, and Betty lost forty.

"It was important to me that I join my husband's walking and dieting program," Betty emphasized. "I knew he'd appreciate my support and that the changes would help me too."

With his physician's okay, Ralph signed up again for the Senior Olympics. As his health improved, he trained in basketball and horseshoe tossing. Betty qualified in the latter event, plus racewalking, archery, shot put, and the high jump. The two now spend part of each year traveling to regional meets, with a goal of taking part in the Senior Olympic national competition held every four years. "Our greatest satisfaction comes not from winning the gold but from doing our personal best," said Ralph, who defines the latter phrase as "the best your individual talents or physical limitations allow." Now, after several years of conditioning, he takes great pride in his appearance and stamina.

With his newfound energy and confidence, Ralph feels challenged to start doing things he's always wanted to try but has never gotten around to. He's started painting and drawing, and he takes introductory Spanish classes at the local community college.

"By getting back into shape," added Betty, "we learned we could do much more than we'd ever thought possible. I know it sounds corny, but the most important thing is to get off your backside and do something, anything. You can't just sit there: it isn't healthy." Besides achieving her own impressive athletic status, Betty has become a voracious reader and is now well versed in the history of archery. She's encouraged

Ralph to start displaying his paintings, and several art galleries have expressed interest in showing them. She and Ralph agree that their improved physical functioning has much to do with their heightened intellectual curiosity and creative energy.

A life of taking trips, meeting people, attending classes, developing new hobbies, and improving health has brought Ralph and Betty enormous satisfaction. Not everyone wants to compete in organized athletic events like the Senior Olympics as they do, but every older person can benefit from regular physical activity that matches his or her needs and abilities. This couple's experience also shows how easy it is to fool yourself into believing you're healthier than you are. Until the heart attack, Ralph and Betty ignored the fact that they were overweight, eating too many rich foods, and not getting enough exercise.

Poor health habits keep your energy level low and dampen your enthusiasm for life. As they became more fit, Ralph and Betty felt more self-esteem and hopefulness. This allowed them to take full advantage of the virtually endless opportunities available to them.

"The goal is not to excel against others but to excel against yourself," reiterated the late George Sheehan, a physician and author who started jogging regularly at age forty-five. "The struggle is for the prize that is our total self: body, mind, and spirit."

Study after study confirms that taking good care of oneself reduces susceptibility to disease, slows the loss of abilities, and improves overall body function. Even after a heart attack, cancer, or stroke, diligent attention to eating habits and exercise, however modified or limited, can make an enormous difference on many levels.

Scientists have shown that the healthy heart of a seventy-year-old, even one who has suffered a heart attack, can function at 90 percent or more of the capacity of a teenager. We know of many instances in which the health of Late Bloomers has improved dramatically after long bouts with a disease or disability, as an apparent result of attention to diet, exercise, lifestyle, and preventive medical care.

Yet it would be overly simplistic—and inaccurate—to suggest that an improved diet and exercise program will make all of one's physical problems disappear. As we get older, some of us develop chronic conditions that we must learn to live with. Some people see these disabilities as limitations, while others view them as challenges that can be turned, in at least some respect, to their advantage.

Spirited octogenarian Maggie Kuhn, for example, became well known in her later years as an articulate, energetic champion of the rights of older Americans. Often described as "feisty" and "forceful," Maggie is in person a surprisingly slight and fragile-looking featherweight, barely five feet tall. Unless they'd been told beforehand, few would peg her as the founder of the Gray Panthers, a coalition of thousands of senior advocates committed to positive social change. Even fewer would suspect what an ordeal it is for her to rise every morning. "I suffer from severe arthritis," revealed the then eighty-two-year-old activist, soon after we arrived for an interview in her Philadelphia home. "Getting out of bed is a very difficult proposition for me."

As her disease progressed, Maggie had to figure out how to make starting her busy day easier. As anyone with arthritis knows, there's no scenario more tempting on a cold, damp morning than huddling beneath the covers and waiting for the sun's warm embrace. But no matter how inviting that option seems, someone with a schedule as demanding as Maggie Kuhn's eventually has to get up and take care of obligations.

"This is why I bring my adorable cats to bed with me every night and deliberately shut the door," said Maggie, flashing a big smile. Because she intentionally locks the two cats inside her bedroom with her, they begin clamoring for release every morning about 6:00. If she ignores them and continues to snooze, the cats become even more rambunctious, demanding to be fed as soon as the sun peeks over the horizon.

That does it for Maggie. "No matter how much I dread getting up, I still manage to put on a robe and go into the kitchen to get them something to eat," she said. "After the cats are fed, I crawl back into bed for a while to let my stiff joints warm up. Then I draw a hot bath and take a nice soak. This is the only way I'm able to keep the throbbing pain of my arthritis under control." After her soothing bubble bath and a nutritious breakfast, Maggie plunges into the whirlwind of activity that awaits her next door at the Gray Panther headquarters. Her days are spent answering letters, taking phone calls, coordinating legislative campaigns, and preparing for her many speaking engagements and talk-show appearances.

"I would never have predicted that I'd have such a rewarding 'old age,'" Maggie told us during our conversation. She wasn't well known until she was in her late sixties, and the Gray Panther organization didn't even exist until Maggie and four colleagues began protesting mandatory retirement laws after being forced to leave their government jobs at age sixty-five.

"There is a kind of exuberance in being this age," Maggie

concluded, her voice brimming with gusto. "You can raise hell and say exactly what you feel. I made a vow on my eightieth birthday to do something outrageous at least once a week, and so far I've lived up to it. I don't let anything stop me."

Maggie made gradual adjustments in her life to deal successfully with advancing arthritis. Instead of letting the condition control her activity, she let her beloved cats solve one of the biggest problems imposed by her illness. Many of us use similar "tricks" or "bribes" to get ourselves to do something we don't feel like doing. Maybe you've promised yourself a favorite food, a night at the movies, or a phone call to a special friend as a way of rewarding yourself for finishing a difficult or unpleasant task. In Maggie's case, a comforting bubble bath is compensation for braving the chilly morning air.

A more dramatic example of the disruptive effects of a chronic health condition involves May Sarton, who at age seventy-four suffered a mild stroke, from which she partially recovered. The acclaimed novelist and poet later developed a heart condition that proved difficult to treat. Nevertheless, May prefers to continue living alone in her rambling old house on the rugged Maine coast.

May's health problems began after she'd already produced more than forty volumes of writing. She has elected not only to continue her literary work but to describe on paper her experience of the stroke and the profound personal growth that followed. "Life at this time is lived at its most aware and intense," she wrote in a piece that described her slow, agonizing recovery. "I have learned, above all, the power to endure and be renewed."

During our interview, May explained that her long road back to reasonably good health had yielded much time for introspection and reflection. "At first I found that if I walked ten paces I was exhausted," she said. "Later, if I talked ten minutes I was exhausted. And when you can't do your work, you face long periods of solitude. Solitude is being with yourself and learning to enjoy the richness of self. . . . Anyone who writes knows that it's a labor requiring an enormous amount of psychic energy. Solitude provides and protects that energy." During this quiet time, May learned "that to close the door on pain is to miss the chance for growth. Nothing that happens to us, even the most terrible sickness, is unusable."

Climbing the wooden stairs to her study, where she sits and writes for several hours each morning, became May Sarton's foremost goal. Although this simple act was very draining at first, she was determined to keep at it. Gradually she built up her strength, and after several months she was able to resume a modified version of what had previously been a daily routine: "For me, writing is the only valid medicine I have against the flu, old age, depression, and so on. So that is what I do every day."

Like many people who've lived through similar traumas, May has a heightened appreciation of the gift of time. She's much more selective about her social calendar and personal appearances, preferring mostly to visit with her dearest friends and to work in her backyard garden.

May has a sense of contentment now, a feeling that she's at a comfortable place in her journey through life. While her stroke and heart condition have slowed May down physically, necessitating a two-hour nap each afternoon, her appreciation of the creative spirit has been enhanced, and she feels a fresh sense of excitement about work to come.

Not all of us have the iron will (or celebrity status) of a

May Sarton or a Maggie Kuhn to help us through the adversities of our later years. Yet even "ordinary" folks sometimes find that challenging health conditions *build* strength rather than sap it. Here's the story of a Late Bloomer who tapped inner resources he never knew he had before his disability occurred.

Jerry L., a retired Indiana-based traveling vacuum-cleaner salesman and ex-smoker (three packs a day), was undergoing a routine chest X ray when he suffered a severe stroke. Looking back on the experience during our interview a few years later, he said he felt very fortunate to have been in a hospital at the time. "I'd had tunnel vision all morning," he recalled, "which I now know is a warning sign of a stroke. During the scanning procedure, I lost all feeling on my right side. Then, as a nurse led me to an examining table, I collapsed and was completely unable to speak."

As he recounted the incident in his bright and cheery living room, Jerry was so overcome by these painful memories that he began choking back sobs, and tears streamed down his face. "All I could do was sit on that examining table and cry. I knew what was happening, and there was nothing I could do about it. I couldn't talk, I couldn't move. I felt so utterly helpless."

For the next several weeks, Jerry could communicate only by blinking his eyes or gesturing with his left hand. The right side of his body remained numb, and he was unable to walk. "I'll never forget the morning I woke up and could move my right pinkie for the first time," Jerry said. "It took all my concentration to wiggle that little finger half an inch, yet it was wonderful to feel again, to have pain. You could stick me with a pin and, hallelujah, it *hurt*! That's the day I knew I'd make it."

Jerry's recovery was slow, but within a month his ability

to feel returned to his entire right side. Instead of numbness, he began to feel excruciating pain—but that disappeared over a few weeks. His power of speech also improved, and he began uttering single words, followed by simple expressions and short sentences. With daily therapy and constant encouragement from his wife, Dorothy, Jerry's muscles finally grew strong enough to allow him to stand unassisted. Eventually, after an awesome effort, Jerry was able to walk again.

"There are people who are so damaged by a stroke that they can't recover as much as I did," he noted, cautioning those in similar circumstances not to expect too much. "However, I think there are many who could come back at least in part if they had something to strive for. Whether you're angry or depressed, the determination has to be there."

In Jerry's case, the conviction that he could and would recover came from an almost obsessive desire to play music again. "I *had* to have music in my life," he said, explaining that he'd played the saxophone and clarinet virtually every day since childhood. "But because I no longer had the strength or muscle control for those instruments, I knew I'd have to give them up. So I decided I would take up keyboards. And I knew I was going to play them, even if I had to use my elbows."

At first Jerry felt victorious if he could merely coordinate his hands well enough to form a simple chord on the electronic organ Dorothy had purchased while he was in the hospital. But with several weeks of practice, he managed to tap out an entire song. "I sat at that keyboard every day and played for as long as I could play, regardless of how I felt," said Jerry.

Because of irreversible damage from the stroke, Jerry was forced to learn music virtually from scratch. It was as if he had to totally reroute his thoughts in order to get his muscles to do what he wanted. Luckily, his sense of rhythm and pitch had survived intact, so Jerry could concentrate on developing his physical coordination. "After a stroke, you've got to dedicate yourself mentally to a goal like this one for twenty-four hours a day in order to make it work," he told us. "I think if I hadn't, my hands would still be crippled."

Not only does Jerry practice his keyboards each morning, he also leads an eight-piece band two nights a week. Its members perform at a local night club, and on weekend afternoons, they are often invited to entertain at weddings and parties. "On Thursday evenings I do a solo act at a restaurant," said the sixty-eight-year-old. "I play straight through from four o'clock to eight without getting up. And you know something? The manager tells me business has doubled since I started."

Jerry is quick to praise Dorothy for her unfailing support throughout his ordeal. She prepared his meals, relayed messages to the family, and made sure he followed all of his doctor's instructions. "At the time, I thought she was being mean to me," he recalled. "I'd ask her to pick something off the floor, and she'd order me to do it myself. She wouldn't let me be a helpless victim, and that was an important part of my recovery."

Jerry's partial recovery from his stroke illustrates the merit of a gutsy response to a guarded prognosis. He refused to accept his initially debilitating condition as a boundary within which he'd have to function. Jerry fought as hard as was physically possible to bring his abilities back. His example shows how participation in your own recovery, through an attitude of determination and commitment, can be a key factor in its final outcome.

Another Late Bloomer who in her own special way fought back against physical misfortune with courage and determination is seventy-nine-year-old Jean C., who operates a private Vermont campground with her husband Earle. "About fifteen years ago I learned I had cancer," Jean explained, as we sipped lemonade with her and Earle on their front porch. "I decided to handle it in a holistic way. I'm not saying this is what everybody should do or that I might not have fared better with conventional chemotherapy or radiation treatments, but it's what I chose."

Carefully following the guidelines set forth by a campground visitor who happened to be a physician, Jean's holistic regime calls for a low-calorie macrobiotic diet that relies heavily on unrefined whole grains, alternating with periods of complete fasting. She practices deep-breathing exercises, takes daily walks, and uses both yoga and meditation to minimize stress. "My husband has been very intuitive and supportive," Jean pointed out. "In these last few years we've truly appreciated each other in some important new ways."

Jean and Earle moved to Vermont following Earle's retirement as a soil conservationist. "We never started the campground to make money," Earle said, adding quickly that the project was a dream that took them thirty years to realize. Their primary reward for running the retreat has always been the pleasure the pair derives from meeting and interacting with an unusually diverse and stimulating spectrum of people. Both insist that "very special things happen" at the campground. Many of their several dozen summer guests have become like members of the family, returning year after year.

"The two of us have grown tremendously from the many wonderful individuals we've gotten to know," Jean said. "There is so much love exchanged here, so much enthusiasm and appreciation." The one-hundred-acre retreat that Jean and Earle operate seems to be a mecca for interesting guests, from pipefitters to politicians, biologists to bankers. "Just when we think we've gotten everything we can get out of running our little campground," added Earle, "along comes somebody new who is brimming with joy and filled with provocative ideas."

Jean said she derives great satisfaction from these encounters, and her struggle with cancer has helped her appreciate the rewards of her lifestyle more fully. "In an odd way, I'm grateful for the disease," she confided. "It's given me so much to think about." This courageous Late Bloomer has also returned to painting, an activity she abandoned more than fifty years ago because she couldn't face the frustration and self-doubt that welled up as she faced a blank canvas. "When I was painting before, I was afraid of looking deep within," Jean explained. "I've learned that it isn't fear that makes you a failure, it's fear of failure that's the problem."

Jean now accepts the important role that sharing has played in her long, rich life. For many years, she shared her talents as a painter by teaching art. Now she shares her love of people by running a restful retreat with Earle. "Cancer has taught me that there is no limit to what we can do," Jean concluded, "and that you have to appreciate yourself before you can really appreciate other people."

The stories of these Late Bloomers illustrate the strong connection between mind, body, and spirit. In each situation, the attitude and response of the individual toward his or her physical condition had an enormous influence on the quality of his or her life.

Many among us have been taught to accept the idea that only properly trained and credentialed medical authorities know best how to deal with our diseases and disabilities. This isn't always the case, however. According to Dr. Steven Fox, director of Wellspring Gerontological Services in suburban Chicago, "only 4 percent of physicians have ever taken any geriatric courses to understand the *older* body and system." The result is that doctors sometimes misinterpret symptoms described by older people and downplay the importance of making lifestyle changes or taking preventive measures to enhance health.

During his eight-year tenure as the U.S. surgeon general, Dr. C. Everett Koop pointed out that "disease is not a part of aging. In the older body most all natural functions continue, but even if there is a decline in the system output it is still enough to support the body in a disease-free condition."

Dr. Koop, himself over sixty-five when appointed to the post of surgeon general by then president Ronald Reagan, blames his fellow doctors for "overdiagnosing" older patients and urges physicians to put much more emphasis on basic things each of their patients can do, like quitting smoking, reducing or eliminating alcoholic beverages, and losing weight, to take charge of their own health.

Developing a strong sense of responsibility for her own wellness is precisely what seventy-year-old Harriett F. has done in her small corner of the universe: a multilevel house she shares with her husband, Keith, on a broad, tree-lined boulevard in Atlanta.

"I still feel as if I were twenty-one inside, even though I don't look it," Harriett began, as we talked over coffee on the top floor of her restored Victorian home, which serves as Harriett's office. All around us were papers, photos, and brochures associated with her one-woman advertising agency, which she's operated by herself for more than three decades. Although Harriett's health is otherwise excellent, for most of her life she has had a profound hearing loss. "I've depended on a hearing aid since my early twenties," she explained. "Without it, I couldn't do half of what I do." Harriett can hear nothing with one ear and has a 50 percent loss in the other. She had six operations to correct the problem before her doctors gave up and advised her to adjust to what would become a lifelong disability. "I almost had a nervous breakdown when they told me that," Harriett said. "But I'm not a quitter. You have to accept something like this and keep on living."

One of Harriett's business clients is a hearing-aid manufacturer, who agreed to let her handle the company's ad campaign when Harriett pointed out she'd been a faithful customer for many years. "Talking about hearing aids gets me up on one of my soapboxes," she declared. "If your eyesight goes bad, nobody thinks twice about getting glasses. But somehow, if we don't hear as well as we used to, nobody wants to talk about it. If they do, folks are afraid they'll be treated as if they're over the hill." If they don't use such devices, she warns, the hearing-impaired tend to withdraw unnecessarily from social interaction.

As you can guess by now, Harriett has refused to let her hearing loss get in the way of anything she wanted to do. "I started out as a commercial artist," she recalled, "but I decided to take things a step further by going out on my own. I wanted to have more control. When you go to a downtown ad agency for service, you may get a rank beginner in a branch office. When you come to me, you get the boss!"

Besides running a very creative and rewarding commercial enterprise out of her home, Harriett takes care of her ninety-four-year-old mother and watches after a grandson each weekday afternoon from the end of school until the boy's mother returns from work. Harriett is active in many community organizations, plays bridge regularly, and has organized a newspaper's public service campaign designed to convince the hard of hearing that "the longer they wait to get a hearing aid, the more difficult it will be to adjust."

A self-described "overgrown tomboy," Harriett loves the outdoors. She and Keith celebrated her seventieth birthday by taking a canoe trip through the Okefenokee Swamp. Next year they plan to cross-country ski for the first time. "For me, successful aging means staying involved and keeping in touch with my friends and family," said Harriett. "I don't think I'll ever get lonesome." Leading a life full of activity and accomplishment is Harriett's way of nurturing herself. Although she's never unaware of her hearing loss, she has not allowed it to exert undue influence over the choices she's made.

It may be tempting to dismiss Harriett's example on the grounds that she accepted her disability early enough to make whatever adjustments were necessary. Yet consider the story of another individual whose passions persisted in his later years even as his physical abilities eroded dramatically.

Hollywood legend John Huston loved making movies so much that his enthusiasm for his work never ebbed, even after emphysema confined him to a wheelchair. Shortly before his death from the debilitating disease in 1987, at age eighty, the director was still barking orders to cast and crew at a Rhode Island film location. Huston was by then so short of breath that he kept an oxygen tank constantly at arm's reach and a nurse within hailing distance. Yet his physical infirmities failed to prevent him from completing the movie on time and personally supervising its editing.

"I don't think of myself as a young man or an old man," Huston had told us a few years earlier, as he relaxed between projects on the veranda of his whitewashed home in the lush Mexican jungle near Puerta Vallarta. "You don't look at the changes that take place in a plant in those terms. You don't say, 'This is a middle-aged flower.' No, a flower is born, it lives, and it dies; the process is all one. And people are really no different."

Having early discovered the joys of acting, writing, and directing, Huston simply never considered living any differently as he got older. "Aging flesh has its own beauty," Huston observed, looking back on an adventure-filled life that immersed him at various times in painting, hunting, boxing, travel, and architecture, as well as movies. "I suggest that those who fear aging take a look at some Rembrandts. They will discover that old can be beautiful too."

Beauty lies in the eye of the beholder. When some of us look in the mirror, we are discouraged by what we see. Although we may feel youthful and healthy *inside,* our *outward* appearance doesn't exactly fill us with confidence.

Beyond the tangible benefits we've described, for some Late Bloomers it's just as important to *look* slim, trim, and toned as it is to have a body that's organically healthy. They are the first to admit that their own psychological self-image is tied closely to their physical appearance. They see a direct relationship between *feeling* youthful and looking youthful, and vice versa.

The impact of this trend is all around us. Health clubs and gyms are attracting more and more older people, as are the providers of face lifts, liposuction, breast augmentation, and so on. Millions of people go to great lengths to get their bodies in exactly the shapes that they covet. Many Late Bloomers have discovered that taking better care of themselves (without surgical shortcuts) brings about positive changes that go beyond vanity.

Jane M., for example, introduced herself to us through the mail by sending a snapshot taken during the aerobics class she teaches in a small Oregon city. At age seventy-four, this gray-haired retiree's turquoise leotard showed off a flat abdomen and shapely torso that could easily belong to one of her thirteen grandchildren. Later, when we went to visit, unsolicited testimonials from her satisfied alumni confirmed Jane's abilities. "I work out with her every day," said Toni, a twenty-two-year-old secretary whom we caught up with after observing Jane's thirty-minute exercise routine at a YMCA gymnasium. "She even schedules an aerobics class on Christmas Day!"

After bouncing off the trampoline, Jane explained to us that she's been exercising most of her life and, at one of the Y's fitness classes she was taking, had outlasted all of her fellow students. "So I figured that as long as I was coming here every day anyhow, I might as well teach!"

This trim and petite woman, moving swiftly and gracefully, delivered her optimistic message about aging as if she were a coach giving a halftime pep talk. "Don't give up," she stressed. "Don't make yourself feel old. Be optimistic, and keep on trying."

A retired businessperson who spent thirty years in retailing, Jane didn't begin her daily fitness regimen until her mid-sixties, after selling a profitable clothing boutique and deciding she needed a new, productive way to spend her spare time. Ironically, this "aerobic grandmother" has found even more business opportunities opening to her since she starting teaching her popular workout class. These include standing offers to write a "mature fitness" book and host an exercise videotape for seniors. "I like the way I look," said Jane. "It makes me feel good. And when I feel good, I'm ready to take on any challenge."

Jane told us that one of her early role models was exercise guru Jack LaLanne, who had a daily calisthenics TV program she first tuned in years ago. "He was an inspiration to me," Jane confessed. "He got me into shape and kept me that way."

In a separate interview with LaLanne, we were surprised to learn that long before his TV show made him a household name and changes in lifestyle pushed his fitness message into the mainstream, Jack LaLanne was dismissed as a kook. "I opened the country's very first health club in Oakland [California] in 1936," he told us, taking time out from one of the many speaking engagements that kept him hopping around the country far into his late seventies. "People thought I was crazy." LaLanne said he was inspired to start his fitness emporium after a delinquent childhood that he now blames on an inappropriate diet. "When I was a kid, I was a real 'sugarholic,' eating candy all the time. For that reason, I was a lousy student and in and out of trouble just about every day. I got failing grades and even dropped out of high school for six months."

During that fateful dropout phase, LaLanne happened to attend a lecture that changed his life. The topic was the relationship between diet and fitness, and the "health nut" at the podium (his name has long since been forgotten) challenged audience members to change their eating habits—or run the risk of contracting cancer, heart disease, and other life-threatening diseases. "I immediately cut out all white flour and white sugar from my diet," LaLanne recalled. "I became a strict vegetarian and started working out a couple of hours every day." More than sixty years later, LaLanne still gets up at 4:00 each morning to spend several hours exercising in the pool and gym adjacent to his Los Angeles–area home. "This is still my first priority," he said. "I know that vigorous exercise and a healthy body have a positive impact on the mind."

A man who practices what he preaches, Jack LaLanne celebrated his seventieth birthday by swimming a mile and a half through Long Beach Harbor while towing, at the end of a rope tied around his waist, seventy people in as many boats. "If you retire," LaLanne advised, "get something new to keep yourself busy. The worst thing you can do is just sit there."

THE SECRET OF HEALTH

Obviously, not many of us are going to be as physically active in our later years as are Jack LaLanne and Jane M. But their stories, along with others in this chapter, confirm the secret of health as an important aspect of becoming a Late Bloomer. Diligent attention to physical fitness can, and does, yield powerful results, even in nonphysical domains.

Our Late Bloomers describe the confidence, energy, and self-esteem they derive from their wellness as a kind of rejuvenating tonic or elixir that enhances the overall quality of life. Fitness is a powerful brand of self-administered medicine that's available to everyone, and it can literally add years to your life.

In a report to the public on disease prevention a few years ago, the American Medical Association pointed out that "Your health is primarily in *your* hands. What you do to your body—or for your body—is the *largest* determinant of whether you will need medical care [in the future]."

The prevailing but false assumption that the older we get the sicker we'll be is finally giving way to the realization that a positive and preventive approach to our health needs can slow, stop, and sometimes reverse physical ailments and disabling conditions in our later years. And when our bodies are put in tune, our minds and spirits follow. So it's never too late to make positive changes in your daily fitness routine. What's really dangerous is to do nothing and thus to let your body, along with your mind and spirit, continue to atrophy.

Comedian George Burns once observed, long after his sixty-fifth birthday, that "If I'd known I was going to live this long, I'd have taken better care of myself." Like Burns, when you turn sixty-five you may have thirty or more years left, so don't hesitate to get—and stay—in shape.

HOW TO ACT ON THIS SECRET

Thanks to some amazing advances in medicine and diagnostic testing, as well as changes in diet, exercise, and other positive lifestyle changes, the average American is living longer and staying healthier than ever before. What's more, with regular checkups, many problems can be detected in their earliest, most treatable stages. At the same time, doctors and other professionals are increasingly willing to prescribe exercise and diet as a preventive and protective health measure.

The best way to start preparing your personal wellness

program is to consult directly with your health care professional. Ask him or her for suggestions about exercise, diet, and lifestyle approaches that are appropriate for you. As a general rule, make it a point to see a doctor not only when you're sick or need medication but when you're feeling good; this way you can get proper guidance and support in creating a personalized wellness program.

Once you've received some professional input, start gathering information about physical activities that have been suggested. Try to select a form of exercise that you genuinely like, be it swimming, aerobics, walking, or whatever. Not everyone enjoys the same kind of exercise routine, and many people have physical limitations that make some activities inadvisable.

Remember that regular exercise is a discipline, a habit that has to be cultivated. Physical strength and ability take awhile to develop, especially if you're sedentary or out of shape—so be patient with yourself. Your physician, chiropractor, or physical therapist can help you learn how to stretch—an important prelude to any exercise session. They'll probably tell you that your feet and muscles may be weak in the beginning and, as a result, get sore easily. Ask about getting custom supports for your shoes to cushion your feet from the impact of certain movements.

It's often easier and more fun to work out with other people than on your own, especially if you haven't engaged in regular exercise for some time. The routine of a scheduled class and positive energy of like-minded participants can make all the difference. You'll find that there are low-cost (sometimes no-cost) fitness programs for people of every age and ability at your local YMCA or YWCA, community center, private or public fitness center, and community college. Many offer exercise sessions for those who use wheelchairs or walkers, or who have disabilities requiring a specially designed program.

If you like walking, an excellent form of exercise, you can join all sorts of groups whose members walk regularly at various hours and locations. Many indoor shopping malls open early in the morning to accommodate "mall walkers," who can avoid bad weather by striding through these warm, dry environments. If you prefer to walk in natural surroundings, you can get in touch with the Sierra Club or other groups that sponsor regular outings catering to a wide range of interests and abilities.

Stationary or outdoor bicycles are also popular forms of aerobic exercise, and many communities have outdoor bike paths that are safe and scenic. If you prefer to "ride" indoors, you can exercise on a stationary bike while watching your favorite TV show or reading a magazine or newspaper.

Ethnic folk dancing, square dancing, and other kinds of dancing, besides being great fun, are also excellent forms of exercise. In Sun City, Arizona, we encountered a group called The Dancing Grannies, composed of six tap-dancing women in their sixties and seventies. They rehearse five days a week for public performances, expanding their repertoire and increasing their proficiency. Each of the women says the experience has improved her self-image and brought her a leaner, stronger body. As a side benefit, The Dancing Grannies have become great friends and are much healthier than they were when they started out.

Whatever choice you make, it's important that you set a regular time for your exercise and stick to it. The key is discipline. Make a "fitness appointment" for yourself, as though you were going to baby-sit your grandchildren or have your hair done. When exercise becomes a habit, it's harder to stop.

While paying attention to the *outside* of your body, don't ignore what's *inside*. Consider taking some of the many classes offered by community colleges, senior centers, and other service agencies that deal with nutrition, vitamins, cooking, and shopping. Newspaper and magazine stories can keep you informed on the important revisions in expert thinking about what we should and should not consume. Your health and energy level can improve dramatically as a result of changes in your diet. We also suggest looking into the use of vitamin and mineral supplements.

You may also want to check out health clubs, fitness centers, or spas that are within your budget. Many of these facilities offer one-day or half-day treatments that include massage, herbal wraps, facials, mineral baths, and so on. Besides the considerable revitalizing health benefits of such indulgences, they represent a nice way to reward yourself for being regular with your exercise and careful with your diet.

The secret of health means feeling good about yourself by staying in the best shape possible and, in this way, respecting the vital body-mind-spirit connection. Physical fitness is its own reward.

CHAPTER ELEVEN

THE SECRET OF HUMOR

EVERYONE'S HEARD THE TRUISM THAT "laughter is the best medicine," but the late Norman Cousins actually lived it. At the relatively early age of fifty, the noted critic and *Saturday Review* editor was stricken with a crippling form of spinal arthritis that bears the difficult name of ankylosing spondylitis. Once hospitalized, Cousins was told there was no known cure for the disease and that it was impossible to predict how long he'd remain bedridden. His physician told him to get his affairs in order, and an attending doctor passed a note to another that said, "I'm afraid we may be losing Norman."

Under the shadow of that grim prognosis, Cousins fell into a deep depression. As he grew more and more depressed, his disease worsened. Doctors told their morose patient that he could use some cheering up. "So I called up my friend Alan Funt, producer of the old *Candid Camera* TV show," Cousins told us in a subsequent interview. "He shipped me copies of several episodes, and I also sent out for some old Marx

Brothers movies." A film projector was set up in the hospital room and a nurse ran it for him. When they were barely into the first reel, Cousins was laughing so hard that his sides ached and his eyes watered. "I discovered that ten minutes of genuine belly laughs had an anesthetic effect and would give me at least two hours of pain-free sleep," Cousins later wrote in *Anatomy of an Illness*, a best-selling book about his experience.

On the second day, Cousins watched more comedies, along with some vintage Laurel and Hardy clips. He laughed so loudly that patients down the hall complained about all the noise he was making. "But the more I laughed, the better I got," said Cousins.

Within a few weeks, Cousins left the hospital, which seemed to him unnecessarily gloomy and stressful. He checked into a nearby hotel, where he found he could "laugh twice as hard at half the price." When he wasn't viewing his favorite sitcoms, Cousins read about the relationship between laughter and sickness, and followed up on a related interest: the connection between stress and certain vitamins. With the consent of his physician, he began supplementing his laughing sessions with massive doses of vitamin C. These self-administered therapies, in addition to prescribed medical treatments, apparently contributed to Cousins's complete recovery.

At the time of our conversation, four years before his sudden death from a heart attack, the author was leading a full and active life that included frequent lectures to medical students on the subject of positive emotions and healing. "You can't 'ha ha' your way out of a serious illness," advised Cousins, who was seventy-one when we met in his office at the Medical School of the University of California at Los Angeles. "Laughter is no substitute for competent medical attention, and humor should be part of an overall treatment plan. I always emphasize that I never abandoned what my doctors prescribed." Cousins referred to laughter as "internal jogging," a kind of inner aerobics that gets the body's positive juices flowing. He cited scientific evidence suggesting that a deep, hearty laugh can improve lung respiration, oxygenate the blood, and promote the body's production of endorphins, natural painkillers that enhance our general sense of well-being.

Today the once-theoretical correlation between mood and health is accepted widely in the medical community, and many of the nation's most respectable hospitals employ some variation of Cousins's "humor therapy." Psychiatrist William Fry, who has for more than thirty years studied the physiological effects of laughter, estimates that three minutes of knee-slapping guffaws are equivalent in health benefits to about ten minutes of mechanical rowing. Measurable side effects include a temporary reduction in blood pressure, pulse rate, and muscle tension. "More important," said Cousins, "laughter can block the despair, panic, and depression that figure in the onset or intensification of disease." Without laughter, he said, we are often cut off from a whole range of life-affirming feelings, including faith, love, determination, and creativity. "A lot of us, it seems, are starved for joy."

The man who laughed his way back to robust health contended that "joyousness is as much a biological need as food is." Long after his recovery, Cousins continued to nourish himself with regular doses of funny movies and TV shows, along with plenty of practical jokes and wry stories. "I've never felt more engaged with life than I do now," said Cousins, who, at the time of our visit, was happily writing four books, teaching at UCLA, and playing both tennis and golf regularly. "Without question," he assured us, "I'm in my most productive phase ever."

What Cousins discovered was something each of us knows instinctively: the mind is a mysterious, powerful thing, and we seldom take full advantage of its potential. Just as we can learn to manipulate our thinking in order to see a glass of water as being either half empty or half full, so can we choose to focus on either the *benefits* of aging or its *disadvantages*. Our outlook can be dominated either by a fear of future unknowns and upsets or by excitement about undiscovered challenges and opportunities.

This insight brings to mind an anecdote about the late *Power of Positive Thinking* author Norman Vincent Peale, who remained on the lecture circuit into his midnineties. Peale had just finished delivering a motivational speech at a convention of the National Speakers Association. As the sharp-witted senior descended from the podium, a phalanx of dark-suited ushers rushed forward, intending to guide him gently back to his seat. "My gosh," Peale called out as they approached, "you all look like pallbearers coming to get me!" The crowded ballroom rocked with laughter. With that quick, casual remark, Peale displayed a vital ingredient of later-life humor: he showed that he refused to take his advanced age seriously, thus revealing a balanced perspective on a world in which our mortality is assured.

"The best laugh is always on yourself," reminds Dr. Clifford Kuhn, a practicing psychiatrist and researcher at the University of Louisville School of Medicine, who conducts humor-sensitivity sessions for patients with chronic diseases. "And for something to be truly funny," he adds, "it must have a grain of truth in it." Peale's spontaneous quip acknowledged the audience's unspoken awareness of reality, for at age ninety-two, he was closer to the end of his life than most of us. He died about three years later, still an active motivational speaker at age ninety-five.

Once comedian George Burns, making public appearances well into his nineties, was asked if a man his age could find happiness with a thirty-year-old woman. "No, not often," Burns deadpanned, clenching a cigar between his teeth. "Only once or twice a night."

Celebrities who are around for as long as George Burns and Norman Vincent Peale know the importance of peppering their remarks with clever and even risqué observations. Their one-liners can relax members of an audience who may not think growing older is particularly amusing. Such humor generates empathy—the feeling that "we're all in this together." Yet it isn't always easy for us to laugh at the truths of our later years. The painful reality is that by the time we're sixty, seventy, or older, our lives sometimes feel like an unending succession of losses: through illness, death, impairment of physical abilities, and so on. How is it possible to remain lighthearted in the face of mortality? When is it helpful and appropriate to laugh at our own misfortune?

To a great extent, we already know the answers to these questions. We've proven that, merely by surviving the trials and tribulations of daily life with our sanity more or less intact. As comic actor Carol Burnett has observed, "Humor is tragedy plus time." Some might argue that if you're over sixty and can still wake up with a smile, you already know the healing power of laughter.

"[Humor] is simply in the way we look at the world," suggested Robert Fulton, a sixty-five-year-old sociologist who founded the University of Minnesota's Center for the Study of Death, Dying, and Bereavement. "It's a matter of laughing *with* yourself, not *at* yourself." Fulton can't recall a time when he wasn't able to see at least some irony in every situation, no matter how unsettling. He tells the poignant story of the way his much-younger wife, after a long battle with cancer, died quietly at home in their bed as he sat clutching her hand. When she'd breathed her last, Fulton placed a bandanna over the top of his wife's head, which had gone completely bald during chemotherapy treatments. Sobbing and trembling with grief, he reached out his palm to close her lifeless eyes, still open and staring into space. "As I drew my hand away, one of her eyelids suddenly popped back open," Fulton remembered. "No peeking!" he exclaimed, before he could stop himself. Then, stunned that he had responded in a manner that seemed so inappropriate, Fulton quickly pulled his wife's eyelid shut again.

Reflecting later on this bizarre, spontaneous remark, Fulton realized that even though he was completely overcome with sadness, part of him had been able to find some levity in the situation. "I knew my wife would have understood my reaction," he added. "She had a way of always keeping things in their proper perspective."

Fulton believes this ability to laugh at ourselves and our dilemmas is essential if we are to successfully endure the slings and arrows of modern life. "You find your humanity this way," he said. "You acknowledge the world's seeming randomness, unpredictability, and downright absurdity."

Unlike Fulton, many of us take a fair amount of time before we can laugh at a particularly painful experience. We need to be gentle and consoling with ourselves after a loss. In time, however, laughter often proves to be a balm that soothes our wounds.

This is a truth that our friend Eve Blake came to understand more fully after her seventieth birthday. A writer with a long list of literary credits, she's written scores of TV scripts (including many episodes of *The Lone Ranger* series) and had articles published in *Collier's* and *The New Yorker*. Yet the source of her greatest satisfaction is a short book full of homespun humor and heartfelt advice that she wrote and self-published a few years ago.

"I did showbiz work for many years and got utterly sick of it," Eve recalled, as we relaxed on the deck of her home in the Hollywood hills, overlooking the blinking lights of Los Angeles. "I said to myself, *I'd like to do something worthwhile before I shuffle off this mortal coil.* It took me another eighteen months to figure out that what I wanted to do to make my mark was creative writing and public speaking."

A longtime democratic party activist who has kept abreast of local politics for many years, Eve first considered the suggestion that she run for public office. She speaks in the sort of deep, animated voice that commands instant attention. Although flattered by the positive feedback that greeted her tentative campaign feelers, Eve decided she'd be much happier putting together a collection of her own thoughts about aging, which she believes her peers approach much too pessimistically. "The title of my book, *Old Age Is Contagious but You Don't Have to Catch It*, simply came to me one day," Eve explained. "Everybody treats old age as if it were an infectious disease, but that doesn't mean you automatically have to come down with it."

Eve takes a joking approach to her subject: she warns older people against becoming "a misery to themselves and a damned nuisance to others," but her underlying message is very serious. "You have a choice in almost any situation you'll ever find yourself," said Eve, "and old age is no exception. You can be depressed and upset or optimistic and hopeful. It's all up to you. That's why keeping a sense of humor is so important as you get older, because most people seem to find more to feel gloomy about. It's as if the calendar gives them an excuse to feel sorry for themselves."

Our friend wrote *Old Age Is Contagious* after her infirm mother asked Eve to help her find a suitable nursing home, anticipating that she'd soon be unable to take care of herself. "Mom and I looked at various places," Eve recalled. "I was very much surprised by what we found." Appalled by the lethargy and boredom she observed in many institutions, Eve saw no justification for allowing older people to settle for less than they were capable and worthy of. "It's not that I disapprove of nursing homes," Eve stressed. "I must tell you that Mother and I found one that we were both very happy with. What bothers me is the idea that people in these situations are so often conditioned to accept a dull, listless existence as all they deserve."

Eve wanted to demonstrate that growing older doesn't have to be dull and dreary. She collected an assortment of humorous thoughts, quotations, and anecdotes about aging, then wove them into an inspirational speech. It wasn't long before she was invited to deliver her upbeat message to retirement centers, bridge clubs, and community groups. After each presentation, Eve was surrounded by admirers who asked if she'd written anything else on the subject. "Although I was tired of writing, I decided I'd better put something on paper, if for no other reason than to be able to respond to these constant requests."

The practical wisdom in Eve's book is drawn from a life that, like almost everyone's, has seen its share of tragedy. When Eve was fifty-two, her husband died suddenly of a heart ailment. Eve's own health began to falter a few years ago when a bad back threatened to confine her to bed. Chronic insomnia sometimes keeps her awake all night, but she doesn't let it get her down. "What little disability I have is not worth talking about," she insists. "Griping about 'poor me' is not calculated to win hearts. When I encounter self-pity face to face, it provokes in me a desperate desire for a quick getaway."

Eve's conclusion is that we must apply the same skills to learning humor that we've used throughout life to master anything new. "A sense of humor is like anything else: you have to work on it if you don't come by it naturally," she explained. "You have to think about it, develop it, and keep it honed by constant use. You do this by making light of your drawbacks or trying to see the funny aspect of something. Unfortunately, once they're past fifty, most people don't think about changing. They stick to the same old routines and think the same old ways. It takes a lot of work to take a different approach, but it really pays off."

Eve fosters flexibility in her own life by traveling the world as an inspirational speaker. This gives her the chance to meet interesting people and experience new ways of living in places like South Africa and New Zealand. The speaking engagements she sets up are deliberately scheduled in countries Eve is intrigued by, so that they can also be part of a memorable vacation.

"If there's one word of advice that I could offer in connection with retirement," Eve summed up, "that word would be 'don't.' In nine out of ten instances, you *don't* really have to retire in the stereotypic sense. If you leave one thing, move on to something else, whether or not you're getting paid for it. To be forever interested in the possibilities of one's future is a major youthful trait. In fact, it's basic to the life process."

A bright, easygoing approach can help get you through both relatively minor aggravations like tax returns, and major traumas like a life-threatening disease or the death of a loved one. Moreover, we've found that a lighthearted, open-minded perspective is useful in preretirement planning. One strategy for cultivating this is through regular contact with young people, such as your own grandchildren. Even if you don't happen to have grandchildren, or if they live too far away to visit easily, there are plenty of other strategies for achieving this goal.

We know a bachelor Late Bloomer who has chosen an unusual route to remain in touch with his childlike sense of wonder and to rub shoulders with young people. Through careful preretirement planning, he is able to surround himself with the energy and enthusiasm of creative individuals who are frequently sixty years his junior. Our friend Merle L. is an eighty-one-year-old San Franciscan who loves nothing more than a night of live theater. "I attend as many as a hundred plays a year," this cheery, diminutive octogenarian revealed during an intermission at the American College Theater Festival. "But I don't want to see theater in only one city because there is up-and-coming talent spread out all over the country, and I'm eager to experience as much of it as possible."

In order to accomplish this formidable task, Merle spends about nine months of each year traveling. In one recent season, he saw performances in eighteen American cities, as well as in Toronto, London, and Paris. He keeps his expenses down by staying with friends whenever possible and by using the senior discounts offered by hotel and airline companies.

"When I retired, I wanted to get the hell out of my ivory tower and move around," explained Merle, who for thirty-five years managed the theater box office of a major midwestern university's performing arts center. His job put him in daily contact with student actors, dancers, directors, and playwrights, many of whom remain his close friends long after graduation. "My whole adult life has been involved with the theater and with young people," he explained. "Since my shiny, bald head is very recognizable, I find that lots of former drama students come up to me wherever I go, asking, 'Do you remember me?' Most of the time I do, and often they invite me to stay at their homes or at least share a meal."

Because his finances are limited, Merle has to be careful about money. Yet each year he is able to embark on a long series of trips to major theater festivals and premieres as well as Broadway shows and resident repertory companies. He keeps his acquaintances updated with a semiannual newsletter that details his travels and offers thumbnail critiques of every performance he's seen. Merle maintains a post office box and single room in San Francisco, where he lives when he's not on the road.

"My budget for last year was around $50 a day for everything," he informed us proudly. "This includes rent, medicine, travel, and incidentals. I made thirty-five trips and put 92,000 miles on my senior discount pass, which allows me to fly wherever and whenever I want without having to buy high-priced tickets."

Merle, who's always lived on his own, decided to adopt his unorthodox lifestyle after a bout with cancer caused him to reevaluate what was most important to him. "I made up my mind that I was not going spend my later years sitting around," he recalled. "I've visited too many friends who sit around and watch each other to see which one is going to get sick next. I don't need that. It sounds trite, but being around young people keeps me young at heart." The students Merle got to know while working in the box office have become a kind of extended family for him. They welcome him into their lives, solicit his opinions, and invite him to cast parties. As they perform, Merle's actor friends are constantly beckoning him into the theater's magical world of comedy and tragedy, fantasy and adventure. "I'm having a great time," he told us, checked his watch, and then, as the house lights began to dim, hurried back to his fifth-row-center seat.

Merle and his fellow Late Bloomers know that cultivating a mirthful, accepting outlook as we get older isn't as simple as telling jokes at parties or watching funny movies. Some of us find precious few films amusing anymore, especially the teen-oriented pictures coming out of Hollywood, and many of us couldn't remember a joke if our lives depended on it. But where there's a will, there's always a way.

Lila G., for example, is a Late Bloomer in her midsixties who has found a way to balance the serious and lighter sides of life. Her blithe spirit is boosted by a great deal of firsthand experience with the healing power of laughter and is anchored firmly in a Depression-era childhood where the sober realities of poverty were mitigated with a smile and a song. Throughout her life, Lila has been uplifted and inspired by working with the less fortunate. She insists that her own burdens are eased when she manages to turn someone's frown into a smile.

A retired publicist who now speaks widely to medical professionals on the topic of humor, Lila told us how incensed she became when she first attended a support group for family and friends of patients with Alzheimer's disease. Their private comments about Alzheimer's victims seemed decidedly callous and uncaring. "It seemed like one put-down after another," said Lila, comparing the jokes she overheard to the kind of disparaging ethnic humor ordinarily relegated to nightclubs and bars. "I was really quite shocked." But the longer she listened, the more she realized that the Alzheimer's jokes were told in fondness, out of genuine love and affection, and their function was to release the tensions that had built up during the endless, tedious routine of caring for spouses or other family members. "In these personal situations, as well as in nursing homes and other long-term care facilities, humor is something that is usually lacking totally," she continued. "And yet nowhere is it more sorely needed."

Responding to this perceived need, Lila has made it her later-life mission to create a second career out of training front-line health professionals to make better use of laughter in patient therapies. She speaks at community centers and at women's groups, businessperson's service clubs, nursing groups, and physician's associations.

A firm advocate of Norman Cousins's patient-centered "laugh therapy," Lila draws on the people-oriented skills she developed during her many years in public relations, and on an inborn talent for cheering people up. "When you work so closely with people who aren't doing as well as you are, it takes your mind off your troubles," she said. "I've found that if you dwell on your own petty problems too much, you get caught up in a downward spiral."

Lila uses many imaginative tricks and techniques to keep up her own spirits. She carefully rations the amount of time she spends with "whiners and complainers," who seem hopelessly awash in their own negativity, and she always turns to the comics for a chuckle before scanning the headlines. After an especially difficult day, she treats herself to a movie that she's reasonably sure will make her smile. When she goes to work in the morning, Lila's goal is to reduce the level of tension that seems to have become an acceptable standard within the health care establishment. "The way I see it, we're always asking people to 'be grim and bear it.' Well, I think it makes more sense to 'grin and share it.'" Too often, however, she finds that adults, particularly those who are under stress, have lost their ability to play, so rigid is their concept of what constitutes "appropriate" grown-up behavior.

Many psychologists believe the latent child that dwells within us is frequently trapped by our unyielding determination to take life seriously. It's their opinion that a vital part of us remains childlike throughout life. This free-spirited aspect of our character is often squelched, though, because we're encouraged to act like sober, responsible grown-ups rather than playful, spontaneous children.

"Life is too important to be always taken seriously," Lila reminds audiences at the end of every lecture. A brash Brooklyn native who says she grew up in a "poor but happy" household during the lean 1930s, Lila finds "it's more difficult to reverse hardening of the *attitude* than hardening of the *arteries*." All of us can apply to our daily lives her strategies for loosening up. They are simply ways of reexamining routines that lull us into complacency.

"One very easy way to start is by changing all those 'little things' you never think about. You can reverse the way you put the toilet paper on its holder, for example, sit facing backwards in the bathtub, or eat chocolate ice cream for breakfast. Try going to the grocery store by a brand-new route, or watching a recommended TV series you've never seen—whatever it takes to get your mind out of the rut it's in."

To brighten the lives of downcast people she comes into contact with during the course of her work, Lila wears wacky jewelry, carries a sack stuffed with toys, and keeps an "emergency" cache of chocolate in her purse. Sometimes she wears clown makeup, puts on a silly hat, and blows soap bubbles. Lila always breaks the ice with a happy grin and finds that a favorite memory opens people up. "I like to ask the new folks I meet about the funniest thing that ever happened to them," she said. Some people draw a blank. When that happens, Lila tries a question designed to provoke uplifting mental images. "I'll ask what the smile of a baby looks like. Or, if the person is a woman, I may ask her to describe the prettiest dress she's ever worn."

Lila has found that merely watching a happy three-year-old at play can frequently put a person in touch with his or her own long-repressed "inner child." Interestingly, she's observed that these same innocent qualities often emerge spontaneously among Alzheimer's disease patients, who many times inspire playfulness among the weary, battle-scarred adults who care for them. "We all need to be able to get in touch with that sense of play," said Lila, describing with great relish situations where she has turned somber, white-robed physicians into crowds of giggling gray-haired kids by passing around hula hoops, face paint, jump ropes, and jacks. When she does this, Lila is careful not to demean or infantilize people, and she uses these games and toys only to break up inflexible routines. Invariably, the patients, family members, and health professionals she works with are more relaxed, stand up straighter, and sleep better after letting loose with some boisterous behavior and uncontrolled laughter.

"You don't need to be in a group or have a leader to get the same results in your own life," Lila concluded. "Stick a goofy cartoon on your refrigerator door, take a five-year-old to the zoo, call up a friend or old roommate and remember the silly things you used to do together. Whatever it takes to make you smile, it's worth it."

In response to the kinds of life-embracing truths celebrated by Lila G. and Norman Cousins, many hospitals and outpatient clinics are finding ways to make their patients happier. They've added comedy channels to their closed-circuit TV systems, for example. Some have asked clowns, comedians, and other professional merrymakers to stroll their corridors and prowl for anyone who needs cheering up. Most health care providers are now encouraging their physicians, nurses, and other staff members to use humor as a diversionary tool for keeping the minds of patients off pain and on recovery. Registered nurse Patty Wooten, for example, has lectured to more than seventy thousand health professionals about the healing power of humor and is the author of *Heart, Humor, and Healing*. "Any nurse who can provide the patient with a sense of hopefulness has the true gift of healing," says Wooten, who often dresses in a wacky clown costume in order to get her message across.

"It's essential for people to learn that, even in the midst of complete turmoil, they have this wonderful resource inside themselves called laughter," adds Dr. Steve Allen Jr., physician son of the well-known comedian. "Laughing, especially at yourself, is the most powerful stress-releaser we have." In an interview about the stress-management workshops he conducts around the country, Allen told *Mind-Body-Health Digest* magazine that humor not only reduces the body's negative reaction to stress, it helps prevent such stress from occurring in the first place. Too often, though, when adults try to inject humor into their day-to-day lives, they are criticized as silly or immature. "A Puritanical notion that pervades our culture suggests that playfulness, even in children, is the devil," Allen pointed out. "Just the opposite is true."

Through our conversations with Late Bloomers, we've reached much the same conclusion. It seems that our society conditions us to feel not only that there's something vaguely wrong with laughing often or having a lot of fun, but that easing our doubts, fears, and anxieties with "a jolly good time" is somehow not responsible adult behavior. It is far better, we are taught, to stoically and dispassionately endure our misfortunes rather than make jokes about them. We tend to admire people who are courageous and emotionless in the face of adversity, not those who crack jokes.

"Wipe that smile off your face," our teachers and parents commanded whenever they wanted us to act more grown up. "Get serious—this is no laughing matter," our bosses or colleagues assert when we make sport of a work-related problem. "When are you going to act your age?" we're asked throughout our lives, as if frivolity were the exclusive province of children. Life is so filled with admonitions *not* to laugh that by the time we reach our mature years many of us are very much out of practice. In fact, we may have reached the point where we don't really know how to make ourselves laugh even if (and when) we really want and need to.

"Many people believe that laughter is spontaneous," wrote Allen Klein in his book *The Healing Power of Humor*. "[They] feel that there is nothing they can do about making it happen. Well, it is spontaneous, but we can nevertheless set the stage for it to occur. We can encourage or discourage it, plan for it or ignore it, be open to it or closed." Once we open ourselves to seeing the humor around us, we'll suddenly find plenty to smile about. When he gets up in the morning and peers into the mirror, entertainer Burl Ives told us that he sees "a funny old coot" with a snowy beard and mischievous twinkle. The image sometimes strikes the folk singer as so hilarious that he doubles over with laughter.

Whether we're using it to take our minds off the numbingly ordinary or the excruciatingly painful, humor can be a wonderful tool for enhancing our healing. It is not always the facts of our circumstances that cause us so many difficulties, it's the way we relate to them. As a coping technique, humor can distance us from some of our pain and stress. While it doesn't make a problem vanish, it provides a new perspective that usually helps us deal with it. "If you can find humor in a thing," says comedian Bill Cosby, "you can survive it."

The late Gilda Radner was a television personality on *Saturday Night Live* who, like Cosby, built her reputation by making people laugh. She also used humor to sustain herself in a long and ultimately unsuccessful battle against a terminal illness. Before she died, at age forty-two, Radner willed herself to finish creating *It's Always Something*, a book and audiotape describing the tactics she'd used to make her painful experience more bearable.

"Once I learned I had cancer," Radner wrote, "I had to find a way to make it funny." By breaking down her experience of the disease into small, manageable components, Radner was able to inject each of them with humor. Her fanciful imagination transformed the cancer cells invading her ovaries into evil, black-uniformed invaders that would be shot down by the good, pink-cheeked cells sent in via chemotherapy. The comedian used the loss of her curly brown hair, a side effect of cancer treatment, as an opportunity to amuse her friends by donning wigs of the most outlandish style and color.

The same kind of approach changes the character of everyday challenges just as easily. Beatrice Wood, a ceramic sculptor who works daily in the studio adjacent to her rural California home, described how "dreadfully bored" she was after nine decades of preparing breakfast for herself every morning. "I'm always in such a hurry to get through it," she told us, "so I've turned it into a game. I try to make my breakfast with as few movements as possible, like a dance. When I do that, I get so interested in the movements that it becomes fun."

When we do things that encourage the release of this childlike spirit, the travails of everyday life seem to evaporate like the morning dew. Otherwise, the cumulative effect of these daily frustrations can really get us down. We've all had days when everything seems to go wrong. If we've already learned, like Beatrice Wood, how to turn potential drudgery like making breakfast into an amusement, then other messy details of life will seem less troublesome.

A little levity goes a long way. It's an easy medicine to swallow, and the immediate reward is a new and often healthier perspective. The alternative is often a rigid, resigned seriousness that paints the world as a doomed place without hope of redemption. If you've ever thrown up your hands in despair after reading the newspaper and watching the news on TV, you know exactly what we're talking about.

THE SECRET OF HUMOR

The secret of humor is the ability to laugh at one's self, the world, life, and even death. It is the adoption of a perspective that allows us to step back and avoid taking things too seriously. When we approach a situation with humor, we are easing our tensions and letting lightness into our lives. "You cannot prevent the birds of sorrow from flying over your head," says an old Chinese proverb, "but at least you can prevent them from making nests in your hair." In other words, you have the power not only to make the best of a bad situation but also to improve upon it.

Successful Late Bloomers use the secret of humor to keep the birds of sorrow from nesting in their hair. As they age, these people find that laughing and smiling make life not merely bearable but actually enjoyable. They recognize that a certain amount of pain, tragedy, and disaster is inevitable, but they deflect and dilute its impact with an optimistic attitude. They know life is more positive when it includes a healthy dose of levity, a wry sense of fun, and an appreciation of the absurd.

When we find a blessing disguised in something that upsets us, such aggravations no longer seem as large or overwhelming as they once did. A lighthearted approach expands our limited view of the world and allows us to see more than our own small problem. In this way, humor can be used effectively as a coping mechanism, a healing strategy, and an antidote to pain.

HOW TO ACT ON THIS SECRET

A sense of humor requires a lighthearted attitude and a flexible perspective. Naturally, this approach can be difficult when life seems grim and unpromising. It's hard to feel optimistic when you're ill or under stress, or when things are falling apart.

At one time or another, all of us have slipped into a dark depression where the light seems never to shine. The biggest challenge is to convince yourself that there *is* a bright side and a way out of the negative morass. How do you develop techniques to get back on track when life is so discouraging?

To succeed fully, the process takes some focused effort. As odd as it may sound, serious concentration will lighten things up. The power of suggestion also comes into play. Simply *remembering* to smile, for example, can make a great deal of difference. Even *forcing* a smile seems to have a physiological component that starts to bring back our equilibrium. A smile is an important beginning.

Try smiling at yourself when you rise in the morning, and see how your frame of mind is altered for the rest of a busy day. Next time you're sharing a long train or airplane ride with a stranger, see how a friendly greeting eases the tension of unfamiliarity. When you're stuck in a slow-moving line, try offering a small joke to deflate the collective sense of frustration.

This is not to say that smiling—or laughing, or joking, or even maintaining a good sense of humor—will solve all of our problems, but these techniques do seem to bolster a healthy perspective that integrates challenges into our lives in a positive, optimistic way.

As you go through your daily routines, therefore, make a point of noticing what buoys your spirit or makes you grin.

Perhaps you have a certain friend or relative who invariably makes you feel better when you talk to him or her. Maybe you know a waitress or store clerk whose sunny disposition is particularly infectious. Possibly someone with whom you exercise, go to church, or take classes is blessed with good humor and a positive outlook on life. Keep a mental list—better yet, a written list—of soothing, happy people who can help you regain your footing when a crisis occurs. Solutions to life's problems come much more easily when we aren't burdened by despair.

As you take action and fine-tune your attitude, remember that humor leads a sensitive, sheltered existence. It must be allowed to happen. It can't be forced. As anyone knows who's ever had a joke fall flat, humor is totally and utterly subjective. What *I* think is funny may just as easily leave *you* scratching your head. We have one friend who never missed a rerun of the TV comedy *The Golden Girls*, for example, and another who absolutely couldn't abide the show. Humor is not an equal opportunity employer.

Each of us is well served by cultivating our individual funny bones: tacking up cartoons that make us smile, telling jokes or anecdotes that point out life's ironies, going to movies that make us laugh, or watching TV shows that strike us as amusing. Once we have a better understanding and appreciation of our own sense of humor, it'll be much easier to make use of it when we really need it.

So what makes *you* laugh? Give this question some "serious" thought, then take some time to make a list of people or activities that you find funny. Your roster might include specific movies, TV shows, or books. It might list a favorite comedian or novelty act, a certain cartoonist or social commentator. What makes you laugh aloud may be your four-year-old grandson, a neighbor's kitten, or a longtime buddy. Whatever it is, try to integrate it into your life on a regular basis. "Humor is contagious and laughter is infectious," concludes writer and physician William Fry. "Both are good for your health."

CHAPTER TWELVE

THE SECRET OF CREATIVITY

CREATIVITY IS A WONDROUS THING. It is the full, reborn expression of each individual human spirit, to be cherished, nourished, and cultivated. Although it is precious and extraordinary, creativity is also an attribute not only of the great and the gifted, not just of the young and vibrant, but of everyone.

As we age, rather than becoming less creative and open to change, we can become more so. Our later years are often accompanied by an enriched sense of self and a greater flexibility of attitude.

Most of us associate creativity with the making of items that are both exceptional and tangible: a painting, book, sculpture, song, house, or even computer chip. Dictionaries define creativity as the ability or power to create, to cause to exist, or invent, and it may or may not refer to something physical. But because our culture places a high value on the product that is the end result of a creative act, many of us grow up with the misconception that creativity is a rare gift available only to a privileged few.

Nothing could be further from the truth. Creativity, we believe, is a state of mind, an openness to life. It is a term that can be applied to making a meal as easily as writing a poem, to talking with a grandchild as well as molding a piece of clay. Being creative involves taking a stance toward life that allows every act, no matter how mundane and familiar, to become fresh and interesting.

We don't want to diminish the importance of activities ordinarily thought of as creative, like writing, painting, playing an instrument, or singing. We encourage their pursuit and praise their rewards. At the same time, we recognize that appreciation of less traditional creative activities can change our lives dramatically and broaden our expectations of ourselves.

Being creative isn't always easy. Expanding our thoughts and actions beyond routines and habits often requires great discipline and struggle. Sometimes we resort to an original way of thinking because of difficult circumstances that push us to approach a situation in a new and unexpected way. As the old saying goes, necessity is the mother of invention. Yet as we get older, we frequently experience physical or financial limitations. We must thus probe our true aspirations and realistically assess what must be done to move our lives forward and continue growing.

We'll discuss these important concepts as we go along. First we'd like you to meet Coulter H., who made profound, and very creative, changes late in life. A career diplomat in the U.S. Foreign Service, Coulter spent thirty years traveling from one overseas embassy to another, always meeting new people and mastering new foreign languages. It was an exciting and fast-moving life, albeit a stressful one.

Gradually crippled by severe arthritis and high blood pressure, at age sixty-one our friend's body was so wracked with pain that he had difficulty moving. Coulter's physician recommended that he retire immediately and, in a moment of candor, told Coulter he might have as little as six months to live. "I was urged to see a physical therapist," Coulter said, "and I began a regular regimen of outpatient exercise. I had no problem with any of this, but it didn't seem to go far enough."

Coulter knew intuitively that the time had come to make a drastic and fundamental change in his demanding lifestyle. The fast pace and unrelenting tension of his chosen occupation were, quite literally, slowly killing him. The decision he was about to make would affect every aspect of his future. "We sometimes ask people, 'What would you do if you found out you had only six months to live?' Well, like everybody else, I never paid much attention to that kind of question. But this time my life was really on the line, and I had to give myself a completely honest answer."

Coulter discovered, unexpectedly, that instead of narrowing his options, staring death in the face actually seemed to open up his range of choices about living. He started taking charge of his life in a whole new way. Coulter set aside some time to look back and reflect on things he'd always wanted to do but had never done. He made a point of quieting his mind and letting pleasant memories drift into his consciousness. "I'd always loved being around animals," Coulter told us, as he prepared coffee in the cluttered kitchen where he now starts and ends each long day. "But because I was always being transferred to some exotic foreign capital, I'd never been able to own so much as a cat. I also started thinking about some of the other things that I'd always liked."

Over a period of several days, it occurred to Coulter that being outdoors and active was something he had always craved. Unfortunately, his office jobs in the Foreign Service hadn't provided this. Coulter was determined to fulfill at least some of his long-held dreams before time ran out on him. Within the next few weeks he bought a run-down farmhouse on several pastoral acres in rural Maryland and made plans to retire there. On the day of our visit to the property, this elegantly mannered retiree appeared very much like the sophisticated foreign attaché he once was, except for his muddy work boots, stained overalls, and rumpled flannel shirt.

"My friends were a little skeptical when they saw the place," Coulter conceded. "The well was caved in, and the house had structural problems. But I like a challenge, and arranging to have these things repaired got my adrenaline pumping and my brain ticking."

The place had come complete with some barnyard animals that demanded daily feeding and watering, a task our friend took on with enthusiasm. Coulter's joints were stiff at first, but within a few weeks the constant activity caused his chronic inflammations to subside. "I think managing the farm actually eased my ailments, because I had to feed my livestock every single day, whether I felt like it or not. The animals needed me!"

Slowly but dramatically, Coulter's health improved. It didn't happen overnight, but he eventually got to the point where he could set aside many of his medicines and end his weekly physical therapy sessions. About a year later, Coulter opened his remodeled fifteen-room farmhouse as a bed-and-breakfast inn. Because it is close to Washington, D.C., the lodge quickly generated plenty of business among young professional couples intrigued by the worldly hotelier with the rustic menagerie. Renovating the ramshackle farm has brought him a new social life as well as a respectable income, thanks to favorable word-of-mouth publicity.

"I get excited every time a new person walks through the front door," confessed Coulter, as he guided us through his well-appointed rooms, each fully furnished with charming antiques. "When people spend the night here, I say to myself, *Let's find out what they're really interested in.* Often I'll sit down and talk with them in the evening. Before you know it, the clock's chiming midnight."

An energetic man who now boasts a sturdy physique, Coulter rises early to gather fresh eggs from his chicken coop, then picks up fresh croissants at a nearby bakery. Later, after his visitors have checked out, he does the laundry, cleans the rooms, and makes the beds. "There are still the animals to take care of," he noted. "I have four cats and two dogs, plus three peacocks, two horses, and a goat. I know it sounds dreadfully mundane, but simply watching these creatures go about their business is a source of great joy for me."

Not all of Coulter's "new" life revolves around his rural bed-and-breakfast. Another fresh interest is volunteer work at a local hospice, where he counsels the terminally ill. Coulter isn't trained formally in this field; his knowledge and sensitivity come from his generous heart and lifelong experience working with people of diverse backgrounds. Coulter told us he was inspired to help others in this way after his wife and only child died in a tragic automobile accident some years before he retired from the Foreign Service. Having dealt with the death of close family members and his own once-precarious health, Coulter is able to celebrate the spirit of life wherever he goes. "I find I'm particularly effective in helping men my own age," he said. "I tell them that even if their days are numbered, there's still a lot of living to be done. I try to provide them with the support and friendship they need."

Through his hospice counseling, Coulter has found that when people face their own mortality, the emphasis in their remaining days invariably shifts to the present. "I can empathize with them," he concluded, "because I am one of those fortunate enough to wake up every morning with a smile, merely because I've been granted another moment, another hour, another day."

Coulter used his imagination, intuition, and intellect to get what he really wanted in life, even when "the experts" were pessimistic about his survival. He regained some measure of his health only after deciding to create a lifestyle that brought him the physical and psychological rewards he was looking for. He cultivated an exceptional gift for listening to others, finding delight both in human companionship and in the companion-ship of nature. The joyful activities Coulter now incorporates into his daily routine have become self-perpetuating: the more happiness these activities bring him, the more he relishes them. And although the various and diverse elements of his lifestyle may seem unrelated, they all are creatively integrated to sustain Coulter's body, mind, and spirit.

This Late Bloomer was at a major crossroads in his life when health circumstances prompted him to make major changes. The rest of us need not wait until we're confronted with a doctor's dire prediction (or some other major crisis) to make creative decisions about the way we want to live. We have the opportunity to make such choices every single day. Recognizing, accepting, and acting on those challenges can bring about enriching changes in our lives. If we pause to reflect, we'll find that creative opportunities, large and small, turn up around every corner. You don't have to change your circumstances as much as Coulter did to approach them more creatively—to see life, as Buddhists teach, "with beginners' eyes."

Although we may not think of it in those terms, being a grandparent, for example, is an enormously creative and challenging activity. The loving, supportive contact between you and the children of your children is an extremely important and often unheralded intergenerational connection. The special relationship between grandparents and grandchildren is unique because, in its best realization, it is based on unconditional love and acceptance.

A grandparent can be a friend, confidant, and mentor as well as a role model and a teacher of what some might call "old-fashioned virtues and values." Through wise and gentle counsel, grandparents can give moral guidance to the developing child. In contrast, parents have the responsibility of feeding, clothing, teaching, and disciplining their children on a daily basis, so they necessarily become the focus of the small and large stresses and strains that occur in any family. Their role is, of course, vitally important, but it is by definition much different from the role played by grandparents.

In our conversations with grandchildren of various ages, we've discovered that the influence of a grandparent on the formation of a person's values is often strong, powerful, and positive. As grandparents, we are among the primary disseminators of our culture, passing along its traditions, rituals, customs, myths, and social mores. The role of cultural disseminator is one that even modern societies need grandparents to play, probably now more than ever in our troubled, fast-paced world. And grandparents are still appreciated.

While dispersal by geography has disrupted the tradition of extended families gathering for Sunday dinner at grandmother's house, relatives still go to great lengths to get together in an intergenerational mix for holidays and vacations. And, for a variety of reasons, thousands of children are being raised part time or even full time by their grandparents.

Unfortunately, our American customs lack rituals or traditions that commemorate the vital role played by its grandmothers and grandfathers. Too often society ignores their contributions or takes them for granted. In contrast, grandparents in Japan rate instant recognition: they traditionally wear red, a color associated with honor. In some African nations, women are bestowed with a special title when their first grandchild is born. It's up to each of us to recognize, without public fanfare, that to be a grandchild of any age, or a grandparent by blood or by choice, is to be a link in that powerful chain of the generations, to love and be loved.

At its best, grandparenting is a wonderfully creative challenge, especially at a time when so much social turmoil and technological innovation have altered the structure of many families. We need grandparents to help give our lives historical perspective and continuity.

"One of my grandfathers came into this world in 1865," recalls David O., a writer and actor born in 1936. "I can remember his telling me about events that occurred in his childhood, just as I now tell my grandchildren about my memory of the bombing of Pearl Harbor. In this way, I've become a repository of experience and history extending all the way back to the Civil War. This connection to history is vitally important in an era in which there seems to be little appreciation of a past beyond yesterday's news."

In a similar fashion, Judith Moyers, wife of television host and producer Bill Moyers, acknowledges her important role as a "connecting link" between generations. "My paternal grandmother poured into me every bit of information about our family's past that she had," Judith told us. "She would sit me down and say, 'Let me tell you about the Smiths,' or 'Let me tell you about the Ashleys.' My grandchildren will have no direct experience with the histories of either of these families, so it's my responsibility to pass them along."

Grandparents, it seems, need grandchildren today just as much as grandchildren need grandparents. Because the world that children inhabit today is so different from the world we inhabit, they can help us understand and appreciate the rapidly changing times we live in. During the same interview session, for instance, Bill Moyers said that having grand-children made him think about the future in a new way. Being able to visualize his grandson living in the twenty-first century "has made issues like the economy and the environ-ment seem more personal and less abstract. As a result, I'm now concerned with such problems not just for all of poster-ity but for my grandson, Henry."

Creative grandparenting can be instrumental in forging a new kind of relationship between grandparents and their own children as well. When a grandparent and grandchild have a special relationship, it rubs off on others. Ethel B. has played an active role in her granddaughter's life since the day the child was born. When Alice was only a few months old, after weeks of being sung to on grandma's knee, Ethel was delighted to hear her grandchild giggle for the very first time. "Sharing experiences like these have not only brought about closer bonding for me with Alice," said Ethel, "they've yielded deeper intimacy with my son and daughter-in-law as well. My kids are as pleased as they can be at the new level of closeness among us all."

In talking to Late Bloomers and their families, we've found that this kind of intimacy often dissolves stereotypes and melts age barriers, bringing about greater appreciation across generations. "She may look old, and she is old," one little girl told us, talking about her grandmother, "but she's not old in my heart."

Clearly, grandparenting can be an enormously creative, challenging, and satisfying experience. Over the years, we've met many "extraordinary ordinary" individuals who have taken a creative approach to their later years. While their experiences may be very different from one another, these Late Bloomers demonstrate a common commitment to open-minded thinking and to experimenting with new ideas and opportunities. They are willing to create themselves anew. They are *engaging* in life, not *retreating* from it.

A case in point is Thelma T., an eighty-year-old widow at the time of our first meeting, who had never danced a step before being persuaded to join an intergenerational troupe called Dancers of the Third Age that performs twice weekly. When we caught up with her, this Late Bloomer had spent eight years expressing herself through modern dance and ballet. "I'd always wanted to dance," Thelma explained, "but it's just something I never did during my fifty-four years of marriage. You see, my husband didn't care for dancing at all."

A retired teacher and government worker who lives in Washington, D.C., Thelma moved, after her spouse died, into a sprawling housing complex for seniors and decided to enroll in an exercise class to keep in shape. She soon discovered that a group of older women were getting together after class to learn dance steps together. "I'll be frank about it: at first I was afraid of failure, so I only watched from the sidelines. It seemed to me that these old ladies were just showing off, trying to behave like young people instead of their own ages. But after watching them a few times it looked as if they were having so much fun that I said, 'What the heck,' and joined right in."

Dancers of the Third Age have performed at schools, churches, and community centers all over the United States and Europe. A recent project involves working with a troupe of much younger dancers, The Dance Exchange, to celebrate the beauty of movement across generations. "When the two groups are dancing together, there seems to be no age gap at all," Thelma marveled. "Whether a partner is twenty-five or eight-five, it merely feels like another person."

In life as in dance, developing a creative approach is often easier if we shift our focus from the *product* to the *process*. To be sure, sometimes the process *does* result in a product, but often it does not. The creating may never be manifested physically; it may exist only in the domain of experience. The process incorporates a way of looking at life, an attitude, that is at once spontaneous, accepting, and nonjudgmental.

Redefining creativity opens the door and lets everyone in. A number of years ago, when he was seventy-seven, we talked with the late composer John Cage about the creative process. The first thing he said was unexpected and memorable. "Unfortunately," Cage began, "too many people think that creativity is something mysterious that belongs only to certain people. That's not true. Everyone has access to it. We all wake up with creative energy."

While certainly proud of his achievements, Cage confessed

that he was no longer concerned about his musical compositions after their completion, only with work that remained to be done. "As I get older," he said, "I find that my interests, rather than lessening in number, multiply instead." These new fascinations come as a result of "being open to the world and to things that happen. So as something new appears in my experience, rather than closing that door, I open it."

Others we've interviewed take a broad view of the creative impulse. Ceramic artist Beatrice Wood, still making art past the age of a hundred, was particularly eloquent. "One can be creative wherever one is," she said. "You don't have to be an artist. Creative persons are those who are open to life and listening to life as it comes to them. You can be creative inside even as you're washing dishes. Creativity is more a state of the *inner* being than the *outer*."

Our creativity isn't enclosed in a box. It's a part of us that's tuned in to the song of life. But because many of us don't think of ourselves as creative, we haven't put much energy into these rather amorphous elements of our personalities. That is why it's often such a challenge to get in touch with our creative impulses and follow them wherever they may lead.

The late Rollo May, a psychotherapist who became well known in his midsixties as author of the best-selling *Courage to Create*, insisted it is foolish to ask people whether they are creative. He said the appropriate questions are, "What do they do, and what do they make?" When we approach creativity in those terms, we realize that it's a capacity we *all* possess, since all of us do and make various things in the course of our lives. "Creativity keeps us fresh, keeps us alive, keeps us moving forward," May told us. "The older we get, the fresher we ought to get. We face our fears . . . and we have the courage to create."

Another Late Bloomer, Tony L., sold his successful electronics consulting business and moved from New York to the west coast at age sixty-seven. After many years of hard work, he looked forward to a life of leisure. For Tony, this meant being "a California playboy": beachcombing and playing golf whenever he pleased. "I found out, however, that the town I moved to had no services for seniors," the silver-haired widower explained during our interview. "Coming from a big city with lots of options for the elderly, I was appalled."

Tony's outrage came to a head when he tried to find some home-repair help for an elderly widow who lived nearby. His neighbor lived on a fixed income and could find no local public assistance that would enable her to fix a faulty furnace. She faced the prospect of a cold, damp winter without heat. So Tony decided to take matters into his own hands. "I couldn't believe that there was no aid program for seniors who were in my neighbor's situation. I started making phone calls to local officials and got the problem solved. Things kind of snowballed from there."

Before long, Tony was hired by the county government to be its first-ever senior services coordinator, a job that demands over forty hours of his time each week. Tony put in place more than two dozen senior-oriented projects, including programs for furnace repair, roof patching, meals-on-wheels for shut-ins, tax preparation, and an emergency taxi system. He even organized a program whereby individuals could donate eyeglasses with outdated prescriptions to the poor, who are then free to try on (and keep) any pair they find in the huge box that sits atop his desk.

Although he occasionally plays golf, Tony says his beach-bumming days are over. "After a few months of retirement," he confessed, "I was fed up. I had to give myself a reason to shave, shower, and get out every morning. I had to have something to do that made a real difference in the lives of others; otherwise, I knew I'd get lazy and go to seed."

Tony makes a point of always working with his office door open. His constituents walk in and out all day long. They stop to swap stories, register complaints, and share information. Most evenings, folks know, they can find Tony at city council or committee meetings, where he's an articulate and compelling advocate for the older residents of the community.

Not everyone can launch a full-time career of championing the interests of their fellow seniors, but the kind of life-affirming spirit demonstrated by Tony can be reflected in everyone's approach to the challenges of aging. Tony's example shows that creativity can be about service as easily as art. Sometimes, however, it is about art, as another Late Bloomer discovered late in his life.

When Esther died, David L. was devastated and bereft. "We were married for more than thirty-five years," the retired corporate lawyer explained during our visit to his Florida home. "Esther and I were always deeply in love. She meant the world to me."

Intellectually, David knew that he would eventually pick up the pieces. He'd carry on without his wife and learn to live fully again. Yet he also knew that he needed to commemorate their long, loving partnership in some tangible way. "I considered several possibilities, but none of them seemed quite right."

Since Esther had died of a massive heart attack, David decided to set up a nonprofit foundation in her name that supports heart disease research at a major east coast medical college. "Despite its tangible significance," David told us, "establishing the fund didn't really satisfy my need to express the deep feelings I felt for Esther. That's when I began writing poetry about her."

Over the course of the next year, David composed more than a dozen poems that dealt with various aspects of his relationship with his wife. Some were filled with sadness, others celebrated the many happy times they spent together. The poems touched on their mutual interests and active social lives. They celebrated the couple's children and their world travels together. Even though he'd never written poetry in his life, composition came relatively easy to David. It was almost as if the poems were writing themselves and he was merely putting them down on paper. "Writing these poems was a cathartic experience for me," said David. "It allowed me to finally release Esther and accept her passing. This was an enormous relief."

Eventually, David decided to share his poetry with friends and family. He asked an artist friend to illustrate his writings and assembled the finished product into a small pamphlet. Photocopies of this collection were sent to anyone who asked. So many people admired what he'd done that David self-published his memorial tribute, *For Esther*, as a bound book. With the enthusiastic encouragement of his friends and children, he continued to write poetry, expanding his focus to include a wide range of topics. "I enjoyed the publishing process so much that I have since produced a second book called *Wit and Whimsy*. It's a collection of verse and artwork in the folk tradition, using my artist friend's line drawings and my most recent poetry."

Although he still misses Esther deeply and holds her memory close to his heart, David has found great satisfaction in the writing and sharing of his poetry. This experience has served as an effective vehicle for processing his grief and sense of loss, at the same time introducing him to a rewarding activity that is helping him grow in important new ways.

Another Late Bloomer, Ralph M., finds personal enrichment by helping mentally retarded adults master the practical skills they need to live on their own. Ralph derives his greatest satisfaction not from the tasks he performs for a social service agency but from the friendships he's made with three mentally retarded young men. "My relationship with these guys is a two-way street," said Ralph, who lives in a large midwestern city. "We laugh, we joke, we hug, we hold hands. I try to show them love, and I get lots of love in return. They are lovely people."

The young men live in a group home, where Ralph spends several hours each week helping his friends learn to cope with the "mainstream" world. This includes everything from dressing appropriately to shopping for groceries and preparing meals. Once or twice a month, the three young fellows accompany Ralph on outings with other residents of the home to parks, museums, ball games, or the zoo. "I spent forty-six years working in the steel industry," Ralph told us, "rising from blueprint boy to vice president. I had no training in this line of work, but I'd always loved interacting with people."

When he first retired, Ralph accepted a volunteer assignment from a social service agency to work with the mentally retarded in an unpaid office job, but he soon tired of the position. The position was important, but it involved more telephone calls, meetings, and paperwork than he cared for. "I wanted something more personal, more direct," Ralph said. "What I'm doing right now is perfect for me. When I see one of the people I work with smile, I know I'm at least partly responsible."

The experiences of people like Ralph show how creativity

271

during our later years can be as varied and unique as each individual. Some Late Bloomers have written novels, joined the Peace Corps, earned college degrees, produced cable TV shows, learned to dance, found strength in religion, and taught needlepoint. We know a retired seventy-nine-year-old schoolteacher who decided to join a walk across the United States to demonstrate support for nuclear disarmament, a cause he supports passionately. We've met a woman in her sixties who spends her spare time making sandwiches for the homeless. An older couple we know has been raising an adolescent grandchild. The list of involvements is endless precisely because the creative energy and imagination of seniors know no bounds.

We can learn from and be inspired by the diverse experiences of others, but we are not meant to imitate their journeys. What is appropriate for one person may be entirely inappropriate for another. Something I dearly love to do may be a crashing bore to you. Exploring our own creative impulses and directions is one of the keys to later-life blooming.

THE SECRET OF CREATIVITY

Finding a creative activity that brings new meaning to our lives and fills our hearts with pleasure provides a healthy perspective on our own aging and continued growth. Studies have shown that such pursuits will likely improve our physical health as well. Our personal manifestation of creativity may take the form of a hobby, a job, a volunteer commitment, a project, or a relationship with other human beings. The possibilities are diverse and endless. This is the secret of creativity.

Nurturing our creative juices is something we can do every day. When we broaden our perspective about the definition of creativity, we begin to approach even the most mundane aspects of life with an open mind and inventive spirit. Our frame of reference expands to include endeavors as basic as preparing a meal or talking with a friend. This isn't meant to suggest that such traditional creative pursuits as painting, sculpting, writing, singing, making jewelry, or playing music are any less important, merely that other activities in everyday life can be approached creatively too. It's a notion of creativity that's *inclusive* rather than *exclusive*.

The secret of creativity is an important tool for becoming a Late Bloomer because it not only *allows* but *encourages* individuals to become more adventurous and confident. It helps them trust and act on their lifetime accumulation of knowledge and experience. A creative approach to later life celebrates new ways of thinking, feeling, and doing. When we are unafraid to create, we are unafraid to change, to grow, and—yes—even to bloom.

The premise of this chapter is that we can use creativity to redesign our lives, because it gives us easier access to our imagination, intuition, and inner dreams. Creativity is the realm that the artist and inventor operate in, but most of the time this level of inspiration and exploration gets buried beneath notions of the way things "should" or "ought to" be. With a shift in attitude, the way you live a single day can be a creative adventure. It's important to realize that you need not be *doing* in order to be creative. You can be daydreaming or free-associating. You can even be watching the way a squirrel moves, observing a flower blossom, or taking in the sunset. All sorts of things can nourish our creativity. They may seem like small experiences, yet they can have a big impact on our inner lives, expanding the space within and fueling the creative impulse.

Being creative in the final third of life is often easier than at any prior age. As we grow older, we tend to be less constrained by the opinions of others and more in tune with our own rhythms and those intuitive feelings some people call "hunches" or "gut instincts." We often feel emboldened to experiment with our own urges and sensibilities. Because we draw pleasure simply from the act of creation, we seek out such experiences. "As you become older," artist George Braques observed, "art and life become the same thing."

Everyone knows that we can't stay young forever; yet we can stay fresh, alive, and aware. We are challenged to discover who and what we are by aging creatively, through a new way of seeing and being in our later years. Living creatively encourages us to know ourselves better and to celebrate that knowledge more fully. When realized, creativity brings a spark of "newness" to life, an exciting glimpse of the unexpected. When we engage our imagination, a sense of the possible beckons us forward. Through this process, the human spirit is revived, restored, and filled once more with hope. "It's not that the artist is a special kind of person," reminds art critic Amanda Coomaraswamy, "it is that each person is a special kind of artist."

HOW TO ACT ON THIS SECRET

How do we start flexing our imagination to redesign our own lifestyle, guided by a broadened definition of creativity?

In addition to the techniques of brainstorming, talking, writing, and reflecting described in earlier chapters, a good way to get in touch with our innate creativity is through affirmations, those positive statements used to support changes in attitude and outlook. You can compose your own affirmative declarations to suit your individual needs, interests, and desires. Remember, affirmations work best when they are spoken aloud or written down. Repeated use of these statements, over time, will help them become a reality.

Try reciting these affirmation examples. Then make up your own, incorporating whatever language serves you best: "I am experiencing joy and satisfaction as I approach my daily routine with a creative spirit." "I am finding ways to explore my inventiveness by using my intuition and my imagination."

A number of Late Bloomers have told us that the easiest and fastest way to develop creativity is simply to do something you love on a regular basis—daily, if possible. This puts us in touch with our innate creative energy, which invariably surfaces when passions are stirred. We all know the feelings associated with doing what we love, even though we may never have linked such feelings with the creative process. Yet that's what creativity is all about!

Our deepest pleasures may be either planned or spontaneous. They may produce something tangible that we can show others, or they may yield experiences that are meant only for our own pleasure. They might derive from gardening, walking along the seashore, hiking in the woods, playing with a child, writing a letter to a friend, arranging fresh-cut flowers, making earrings, calling a relative, taking a swim, caring for a loved one, or reading a good book. You may love to sing or play your favorite music, lead bird-watching field trips, draw pictures, refinish furniture, read stories to your grandchildren, do crossword puzzles, or lend a hand at a social service agency. Whatever it is, find a way to do it. Engaging in activities we genuinely love is truly a creative act and energizes us like small bolts of lightning. Indeed, those activities can make us feel radiantly youthful and fully alive. Through them, we can discover and explore new options that may prove even more satisfying. The path to personal fulfillment, the late scholar Joseph Campbell often pointed out, is "following your bliss."

Like anything else in life, repetition helps. If we consciously practice creative acts that fulfill us, we'll develop a closer identification with the underlying process and appreciate our own abilities more fully. Our outlook on life will change. We'll start to accept the idea that we, too, are creative beings, like the artists, architects, scientists, and other so-called exceptional people we've heard about. Our confidence will grow, our horizons expand, and we'll begin to initiate other creative activities, along with practicing the many inherently creative acts we've long engaged in without fully realizing it.

Here's one last important observation about the creative process. Silence and simplicity can be as creative as what we label "activity." Frequently, when our outer world shrinks, our inner world blossoms. It is often in this inner space that our most meaningful inspiration emerges through quiet and solitude. "The more we are willing to free our beliefs for active questioning and reframing," author Mary Baird Carlsen has observed, "the more we are able to play with ideas . . . and the more we can incorporate into ourselves a lifestyle that can be called creative."

CHAPTER THIRTEEN

THE SECRET OF GARDENING

Many surveys have confirmed that gardening is one of the world's most popular pastimes. One study estimated that a third of all American adults tend gardens. It is something we can do on acres of land or in a single flowerpot. Enormously flexible, gardening is a hobby that demands widely variable amounts of time, energy, resources, and concentration, and has the advantage of being home centered. Its tangible rewards include beautiful blossoms and pleasing greenery as well as fruits and vegetables.

Thousands of books have been written about the *external* aspects of gardening, about what can be done to make a plot of land healthier, prettier, or more productive. Yet few words have been devoted to exploring the *internal* satisfactions of gardening: what it nourishes in the gardener's heart and soul.

"It's all about life," suggests author and poet May Sarton, an avid gardener who refuses to permit recurring health problems to keep her indoors for any longer than necessary.

"Flowers are so beautiful; they're a tremendous aesthetic pleasure. And they have the whole sequence of life in them, from the bud to death and then growth again." Being close to nature every day, Sarton believes, gives her psychic strength. "Not being able to dig for a year, after my stroke, was very hard for me psychologically," Sarton told us. "I lost something from not being close to the earth."

The plants and blossoms of one's garden are not simply an end product but also a vehicle that delivers profound meanings and deep satisfactions that go beyond the experiential delights of a colorful bouquet or ripe, juicy tomato. Through our conversations with a number of passionate gardeners, we've heard firsthand about how gardens can tie us intimately to the cycles of nature, the life-sustaining interplay of the elements, and the healing power of growing things. As fragile but essential elements in the natural universe, the plants in our gardens link us to a complex web of life that goes far beyond our comprehension—but not our appreciation.

"The person who loves a garden," someone wise once wrote, "has a reverence for all creatures. The person who loves a garden loves the joys of simple living and the peace on which no one can put a price."

Gardening is a very creative activity, one that allows us to be playful, inspired, nurturing, expressive, and imaginative. Making a garden is an innocent, leisurely delight. Gardens are as different as the people who shape and tend them. Here's an inspiring example:

On any sunny day between May and October, you're apt to find Dorothy D. toiling in a five-acre vegetable garden that overlooks the Mississippi River in rural Minnesota. "I spend 99.44 percent of my time out here during summer months," smiled Dorothy, as we stood knee-deep in yellow bush beans, in her garden near the frame house where she's lived all of her seventy years. "This used to be a tree farm," she added, gesturing across a hundred rows of carefully tended carrots, cucumbers, tomatoes, and onions. "Ever since I retired, I've been using this land of mine to grow food for the needy."

A childless widow whose husband died eighteen years ago, Dorothy lives with two cats and a dog on her tranquil homestead. She gets up early and goes to bed late, spending the long hours in between wearing a floppy straw hat and tending her beets, broccoli, and other vegetables. "Once a week, during fall harvest, I load what I've picked into my station wagon and drive north to the Twin Cities," she explained. "I deliver my produce to three or four community centers that help people in need. I give away every bit of food that I grow."

Dorothy is the first to admit that hers is an unusual lifestyle for anyone, but especially for a woman of her age. "You see, for me, working in the garden is a little like meditating," she said. "Or you might just as easily say it's my way of praying, of getting close to God."

Dorothy was quick to add that her life wasn't always this way. For more than four decades she worked at a high school in the nearby village, teaching English and social sciences to tenth graders. During this time she lived at home with her husband, Steven, and her Scandinavian-immigrant parents. Pulling together as an extended family, they raised and sold Norway pines that are used as Christmas trees. They also grew vegetables in a small plot near the farmhouse. "Gardening is something I was always good at," Dorothy told us. "My father taught me everything he knew."

Her mother passed away while Dorothy was in her thirties,

and her husband Steven died of heart disease soon after. Dorothy stayed at the farm to look after her ailing father, who became an invalid at age sixty-five and was housebound for another fifteen years. "I guess the reason I did so well with growing things was that I had to stay close to home all the time in order to take care of Dad," said Dorothy. "I always figured I'd better put that time to good use."

It was an isolated existence. By the time her father died six years ago, Dorothy was eager to become more involved in the community at large. Although she didn't really mind being alone, it had always been important for her to feel useful to others.

She thought first about volunteering her time and talents at a nearby hospital, where one of her longtime friends was employed as a nurse. "But I decided that it wasn't the way I could best serve myself and others," explained Dorothy, whose generous nature and green thumb are known equally well for miles around. "Then it occurred to me that everybody has to eat, and since I'd been growing a garden each summer for many years, I might as well expand it and make that my main activity."

Dorothy is fortunate enough to enjoy excellent health and brags that she's never been sick for more than a day at a time. Except for a handful of heavy tasks, like tilling and fertilizing the soil, she works her land by herself. While many people over seventy might feel exhausted just thinking about single-handedly farming a five-acre plot, Dorothy is thrilled by the challenge. "It's a wonderful feeling," she told us, her sky-blue eyes aglow with excitement. "I'm surrounded by beautiful ever-greens and flowers. No artist could paint with the colors I see in nature every single day. I am filled with such an inner peace to know that God has given us all of this to enjoy. I'm alone out here, content in my serenity. It's a very enlightened feeling."

There's no question that Dorothy's greatest satisfaction comes when she sees the faces of hungry people light up when she delivers her big loads of farm-fresh produce. "It's so rewarding," she told us, explaining that most of the food goes to the homeless, unemployed immigrant families, and low-income elderly. "I get a warm, contented feeling way down deep inside."

Dorothy has pared down her other activities to "the bare essentials," focusing primarily on growing her vegetables and socializing with a few dear friends. Work on her vegetable garden begins in February, when seeds are ordered from a catalog, and continues without a break until the first frost of October. During winter months, when the land lies fallow under a blanket of snow, Dorothy sews baptismal dresses that are used in ceremonies at her Lutheran church. "You can't take your bank account or fame or material possessions with you when you die," she stressed. "In the twilight of life, I believe we have to think about what really matters—to go one step higher. In my opinion, retirement means reaching out to whoever needs help."

Although Dorothy has fond memories of her many years of marriage and long career as a schoolteacher, she insists that her happiest days have all come in the six years since retirement. Dorothy thinks more often and more deeply about spiritual things now. "I do this to make my life worthwhile," she said of her gardening and giveaways. "Being in my garden brings me so much closer to God." She maintains an almost childlike sense of wonder about the miracle of life, as it is revealed each season through the birth, maturity, and death of her thousands of individual plants.

Like many older people, Dorothy has chosen to let go of a number of long-held attachments and judgments, preferring to keep her days relatively simple and her intentions single minded. She good-naturedly dismisses the quizzical looks others sometimes give her when she explains how she lives. She's secure in her conviction that helping others through gardening is what makes her happiest. Dorothy has designed her retirement in a way that balances her physical abilities, intellectual talents, and spiritual desires.

Balancing the needs of mind, body, and spirit may take a very different form in your case, although many older people, including some you might never suspect, seem especially attracted to the self-renewing satisfactions of gardening. Essayist E. B. White and his wife Katharine, the longtime fiction editor for *The New Yorker*, cultivated tulip bulbs avidly after they'd retired to Maine. Actor Eddie Albert, star of numerous movies and TV shows, grows mouth-watering sweet corn in the large organic garden he tends outside his southern California home. "Losing contact with nature," says Albert, "is like throwing gold into the sea and losing it. Sometimes I walk outside in the middle of the night just to talk to my flowers and trees, telling them how much they're appreciated. I might tell the olive tree, for example, how glad I am that it let my children climb into its branches, or the maple how spectacular its colors are in the fall."

Many people use gardening as a form of self-expression and long-term sharing, fashioning something that will remain for others to appreciate. Others employ gardening as a kind of therapeutic lifeline, a calming source of consolation and support. The practice allows them to step away from the noise, distractions, and confusion of the mechanical world into one that is simple, basic, and harmonious.

"The natural world has always been a means of survival for me," poet and lifelong gardener Stanley Kunitz told us in an interview. "It has given me something I could trust, and could never betray me. It responds to my ministrations, and it is beautiful. I love the marvelous returns of one's labors and the beauty of what grows. I can't wait to get up in the morning to see what happened in my garden during the night."

This responsive, interactive dimension of gardening—seeing living things react positively to our nurturing actions—can help build our self-esteem and boost our pride. Like a gentle, caring parent, one tends a garden with unconditional love, hoping for the best. Some people go so far as to talk to their plants, while others play music for them. Most gardeners say they feel a close bonding with their plants that is personal, even intimate, in some fundamental ways. For many, like Dorothy, working in the garden is a kind of meditation, a way of relating to nature on a primitive, visceral level.

"I think it's a basic, biological connection," declares Diane G., a sixty-year-old schoolteacher who has gardened since she was a young girl. "Growing things is what we humans are meant to do, going all the way back to the Garden of Eden. It's a very deep, rewarding, creative relationship we have with the earth, the plants, the smells, the air, the water, and the light. I know that, for me, a garden is my best friend."

Diane's parents didn't particularly encourage her gardening, although one of her grandmothers fired her with an enthusiasm for growing vegetables that remains undiminished. Members of her immediate family, including her husband, have always been indifferent to gardens, and it's an interest she's shared with few friends. Nevertheless, Diane's garden has always been a source of joy for her, and she spends many hours puttering in it every week. "If I have the choice of reading a book, sitting in a cozy chair by the fire, or digging outdoors with a hoe," Diane said, "I'll choose the hoe every time."

Diane especially enjoys the solitude of her garden, which she says is a welcome respite from her busy, hectic working hours. At school she comes into contact with a hundred or more students each day, and her time alone in the evening allows her thoughts to settle and her tensions to dissipate. Picking flowers, watering plants, and pruning branches somehow free her to act like a carefree kid again instead of maintaining the role of the authority figure that seems needed at work. In this regard, Diane likes to quote the French scientist Marie Curie, who once wrote: "All my life through, the new sights of nature made me rejoice as a child."

During the past few years Diane has dealt with several personal tragedies, including the sudden death of two grown sons. During these times, as at other critical junctures in her life, she has found gardening to be a source of healing and consolation. "Working with the plants and soil somehow soothes my grief and helps me heal," she explained. "I think this is because the life cycles of plants remind me that whatever else happens in any individual's life, the natural rhythms of life will still go on. The seasons keep repeating themselves; birth and death are always there if you simply look around you."

Describing the sequences in the life of a flower, Diane points out that "even when it dies it is beautiful. When a flower drops its petals you see that inner part that you wouldn't see when it's alive. You enjoy a flower until it withers and dies, and that's what happens with people too." In the final analysis, says Diane, "gardening is a supremely creative act. I don't regard it as a job or duty; it's something I do strictly for my own pleasure. I have nothing but positive feelings when I'm working in the garden. How often can you say that about something?"

One of our interview subjects, a professional landscaper who switched careers in midlife, pointed out that gardening is for most of its practitioners a noncompetitive activity that allows and encourages them to create an environment that suits their individual preferences. They garden in their own way, at their own pace, for their own reasons.

"When you garden," she explained, "you explore yourself and learn a thousand different things. You come to grips not only with your own personal creativity but with your individual level of concentration, of caring, and of tolerance. And because most people work in their gardens alone, gardening is also about coming to grips with silence and solitude, making these a source of solace instead of feeling imprisoned by them."

Many people feel restored by their gardening in part because they see direct, positive results from their efforts— something that may not be the case in their daily interactions with families, friends, and work. A plant not only doesn't nag or talk back, it doesn't ignore us or walk away. It responds to our attention without passing judgment. It simply responds. Nurturing a plant, helping it grow and flourish, is a way of affirming our own existence and asserting our self-worth. Having a garden that both depends on us and reacts to us can help satisfy a basic desire to be connected to, and needed by, other living things. "I feel that every bud is a prayer, and every flower is a smile," one Late Bloomer said. "They give me something to live for, something to cherish."

Some gardeners enjoy creating a source of shade, beauty, or nourishment that can be shared with others, even if those others will never be known to them. In India, for example, the story is told of an old man who was digging a hole to plant a breadfruit tree when a young neighbor stopped and stared with a puzzled expression on his face. "How long will it take that tree to bear fruit?" the neighbor asked.

"Oh, about twenty-five or thirty years," the old man answered, pausing from his labor and wiping the sweat from his brow.

"But why are you planting it, then?" the younger fellow wanted to know. "You'll be long gone by then!"

"Yes, that's true," he replied. "Yet when I was a small child I ate breadfruit from a tree someone before me had planted. It is my duty to do the same for the children who come after me."

This appreciation for the continuity of the inevitable life cycles, the connectedness of all living things, is a common occurrence among gardeners. The soul is satisfied by the business of creating new life, because it knows that those who come later will rejoice in that life. There is an acceptance of birth and death, because both are always present in any garden. And there is an acceptance of and appreciation for nature's seemingly infinite beauty as well.

"Our eldest daughter was married in our garden last year," Rose D. disclosed during an interview at her North Carolina home. "My husband and I worked so hard in order to get it ready, yet there was such a joy in that. We knew it would be very beautiful for her wedding, and we knew that the images of our flowers would never be forgotten." Rose told us that whenever she walks in her garden now, part of her remembers the happiness of her daughter's wedding day. She also talked about feeling linked to her grandfather, who shared his considerable gardening expertise with Rose as she was growing up. "I look at an apple tree he planted, and I can't help thinking about him," said Rose. "I see Grandpa harvesting apples in the fall, wearing his straw hat and overalls. That image always makes me smile."

Like the old Indian man who planted the breadfruit tree for the next generation of children, our friend Rose recently planted some lilac bushes, knowing she will probably not see them grow to maturity. "The idea of leaving something lovely behind is important to me," she explained. "It doesn't matter whether I see it or not. I'm happy today knowing that it will be here for someone else to enjoy tomorrow." Like most gardeners we've met, Rose feels renewed and restored by her cultivation of the earth, and that renewal enhances many other dimensions of her daily life.

THE SECRET OF GARDENING

The secret of gardening is its ability to connect us to many important aspects of the natural world—and our place in it. When we are connected by a garden to the intrinsic rhythm and beauty of nature, we are better able to fully actualize ourselves. In short, we learn much about blooming from first-hand observation of this process among plants.

Gardening appeals to human beings on many levels. Some are more obvious than others. Through this activity we experience the aesthetic pleasures of beautiful flowers and verdant greenery as well as the utilitarian harvests of fruits and vegetables. Yet gardening also links us to higher truths, recovers our awareness of the universe, and reminds us of nature's most fundamental laws. One of the secrets of gardening, as it applies to Late Bloomers, is its capacity to teach. "Plants communicate universal life qualities to those who tend them, displaying rhythms different from those of the man-built environment," wrote horticulturist Charles A. Lewis in an anthology entitled *The Meaning of Gardening.* "In order to become involved in the microcosm of the garden, one must leave the outer world at the garden gate."

Gardens have special meaning because they transcend time, place, and culture. They link us to our collective and primeval past, serving as records of our creative expression, private beliefs, and public values. Working in a garden is often distinctly humbling because it teaches us that nature always has its own plan, one more diverse and complicated than ours. After talking with many avid gardeners, our view is that gardens can, and often do, reflect our thinking about who we are.

Gardening secrets help us "bloom" late in life by giving us a calm, quiet place to contemplate our inner world in a supportive environment and in a creative, nurturing, and open-minded manner. In the garden—if we take time to watch and listen carefully—we can often find pathways to the sources of our deepest satisfaction and greatest fulfillment.

It's obvious that many gardeners have deeply held feelings about their gardens that go beyond the pragmatic, although these feelings are often unspoken. It seems that, for whatever reason, we find it easier to talk about weeds or the weather than the connectedness to life cycles we may feel when we closely observe a new seed sprout, a flower blossom, or an old plant wither. Yet it's important not to discount or overlook these inner responses to a garden. Our lives are richer when these experiences are embraced and celebrated.

HOW TO ACT ON THIS SECRET

If you already have a garden, we encourage you to look beyond the practical, strictly physical aspects of its care and maintenance. Explore the notion that gardening can become an opportunity for profound inner growth. Get in touch with the way you experience your garden, in every aspect and dimension. And as you nourish your plants, don't be surprised if they nourish you back.

As we pointed out at the beginning of this chapter, little has been published about the appreciation of gardening on an experiential level, particularly as it relates to our spiritual beliefs or personal philosophies of life. Feel free to articulate some of these feelings among friends and acquaintances. Dare to shift the scope and tenor of conversations about gardening. Not everybody will want to talk about their experience of gardening in this way, but we can assure you that some people will. And as you explore this internal dimension together, the depth and meaning of your shared feelings and experiences will expand immeasurably.

Those who aren't yet gardeners need not feel left out. We haven't talked in this chapter about how to get involved in gardening, should you be interested. Here, now, are some practical suggestions that may help you get started.

If you don't have a garden and would like to start one, or if you'd like to expand the one you already have, you can find many resources readily available. Libraries and bookstores offer many books (and sometimes videotapes) on the subject, and a few national PBS television series about gardening are available on videotape for rental. Plant nurseries can be found from coast to coast, and their employees are trained to help gardeners at every level of experience and ability. Many clubs, government agencies, and community college classes deal directly with garden topics, from the broad to the specific, for the novice as well as the expert.

If you're starting out, an important first step is to evaluate how much space you have available for plants and how much time you're willing to devote to their care. The possibilities are virtually limitless, ranging from a single low-maintenance indoor plant to extensive outdoor gardens that demand daily attention. You can grow things in simple window boxes or balcony pots, or on a small patch of ground outside your bedroom window. If you have no room at all, you may find that your town offers "community gardens" where individuals can work the soil on public or donated land.

Once you've made a basic decision on where you'll cultivate your plants, the process of selecting and obtaining them gets a lot easier. You'll quickly discover that choices are dictated to a large extent by soil, light, weather, and aesthetics as well as personal preferences. You may be interested exclusively in growing vegetables, for example, or in long-stem flowers that can be cut for indoor vases. Your location may be too cold for some plants, too hot for others.

Whether or not we're active gardeners, the internal dimensions of the garden experience are as close as a walk in a park, a visit to an arboretum, or the admiration of someone else's yard. For our purposes as Late Bloomers, the important thing is not the closeness of our involvement in the physical act of gardening but the metaphysical and sometimes even spiritual encounters with nature that gardening affords.

No matter what kinds of practical choices we make, it's clear that gardening will enhance our inner lives and enrich our spirits. We're reminded of an eloquent meditation on nature by the English poet William Blake:

> To see a world in a grain of sand
> And a heaven in a wildflower,
> Hold infinity in the palm of your hand
> And eternity in an hour.

CHAPTER FOURTEEN

THE SECRET OF SPIRITUALITY

IN THE BIBLE, THE BOOK OF ECCLESIASTES assures us that "to everything there is a season." Our premise in this chapter is that some of life's most valuable activities are well suited for that season of life we might call winter, when more days lie behind than ahead. It's our belief that at this time of life some very special exploration and personal growth—an inner journey that melds wisdom and experience with awareness—often take place.

For many, however, the notion of taking time for serious introspection is uncomfortable. This aversion to spiritual and existential matters can be traced, religion scholar Phillip Berman believes, to our heritage of Puritanism and pragmatism.

"We are, after all, a practical people," Berman writes in his book *The Search for Meaning*. "We want answers, not problems. . . . When dealing with moral and spiritual matters we deal with mysteries—the insolubility of which we find deeply

292

discomforting. Much of what we call American life is about this discomfort, and the manifold ways we seek to deny it or avoid it. Our capital-driven society discourages reflection in order to encourage consumption."

The "third age," as the French refer to life's later years, is measured neither by the energy and ascendancy of youth nor by the acquisitiveness and productivity of midlife. This final phase has been characterized by some observers as an emphasis on *being* rather than on *doing* or *having*. As we get older we often prefer a simpler, calmer existence that cultivates and nourishes a rich and satisfying inner life. "I live in that solitude which is painful in youth, but delicious in the years of maturity," wrote Albert Einstein, as the famous physicist embarked on a later-life career as a distinguished writer and philosopher.

Each of us has known at least one person who shared Einstein's attitude, the kind of person poet May Sarton has called "life-enhancing to the end," the sort who "look on old age as something marvelous, to be attained as all good things are, because of a passionate commitment to life."

While praise of age is rare in a youth-oriented society like ours, other cultures have for thousands of years celebrated this idea. Older Native Americans, for instance, are often venerated for having earned, through their many years of living, the special privilege of studying ancient art forms and time-honored rituals, and of teaching sacred dances and handing down oral history to those who are younger. Elders in many Asian countries serve as "keepers of the flame," making sure that cultural values remain intact and that the deeper meaning of life is continually examined. It is still the practice among many religious traditions to defer to older scholars and spiritual leaders when the most profound moral and philosophical questions arise. In many cultures around the world, the emergence of the maturing elderly from a phase of "doing" to that of "being" is not only respected but revered. These cultures recognize that older people have a kind of divine purpose to fulfill, a timeless obligation to future generations.

Unfortunately, traditions of respect for later life have shallow roots in modern America, a society that is only now in the process of redefining "retirement" after generations of dismissing its older citizens as "over the hill." Our collective attitude still seems to be that remaining active, distracted, and materialistic is superior to a life of reflection, introspection, and contemplation. The younger generation doesn't seem to know what to do with old folks and tends to discount and ignore them.

In our society, the young tend to look for meaning in the "exterior world" of physical things, financial rewards, and status. When we're in our thirties, forties, and fifties, our lives are often too busy and stressful to find the quiet time or the psychic space necessary to probe the "inner world." Yet we've met many Late Bloomers who've taken advantage of their free time and slower pace to concentrate on exactly that. Their retirement has felt, as one sixty-seven-year-old described it, like exiting the fast lane of an eight-lane freeway and driving down a peaceful country road. In our youth, it seems, we're surrounded by scenery that flies by in a blur. And despite youth's common misconception that growth is lacking among the aged, the exact opposite is often true, as older people take advantage of their free time and depth of experience to seek, cultivate, and enjoy higher truths.

"My wife and I find ourselves taking walks together to savor the subtle beauty of a sunset," Bob M. told us, adding that his new appreciation of such pleasures has prompted him to take up nature photography.

"When I was young I thought I'd live forever," recalled seventy-one-year-old Marian W. "Now that I know how short life is, I feel much closer to God."

"After my recent divorce, I thought my world had ended," said Vera G., age sixty-nine. "I recently went back to church for the first time since I was married. It's become so important to me that I've volunteered to become the new organist."

"I used to be a very active woman, involved in everything you can think of," confided Mary H., a recent widow at seventy-nine. "I'm a quiet person now. Meditation has become a vital and satisfying part of my daily life."

"I now see a spiritual dimension in everything I do," a retired business executive named Morris O. told us. "That's something I would never have said before age sixty."

The late-blooming process often involves a multi-dimensional exploration of the inner world through reflection, contemplation, and reminiscence. During this phase of life, many of us, perhaps unconsciously, review our values and reevaluate our priorities. As we age, we may finally have the time, inclination, and wisdom to explore parts of ourselves that we didn't pay much attention to when we were younger.

Some of us are direct about this, asking ourselves such basic questions as "What is the meaning of life?" or "Why am I here?" Others, for example, feel the desire to go back to church for the first time in thirty or forty years, enjoying the fellowship and ritual of religious services. Some find themselves exploring new faiths or forms of worship. Still others express inner changes in their outward behavior, simplifying or altering their daily routines as they set new goals or priorities, such as spending more time with loved ones.

Each Late Bloomer with whom we've talked with about spirituality has mentioned the presence of "a higher power" in his or her life, although each describes and defines it differently. Some refer to a humanlike deity with a long white beard, others to an almost mystical unseen energy. Others feel they are linked in some way to a "light," an inner voice, or "the power of the universe." Some view God as the sacred in every human, others as nature itself. Many shared with us a feeling of connectedness, some to all that exists in the universe, some to all living things. Clearly, these are highly subjective and deeply personal matters.

The Late Bloomers described in this chapter are not limited to those who embrace traditional or organized religion nor to those who espouse a narrow interpretation of what is spiritual. We are sticking to a broad definition of spirituality as not having to do with the tangible or material, but with the nature of the sacred. We like the way psychologist John-Raphael Staude expands this definition to include "the personal quest for truth and right living." It has less to do with previously learned answers than with a personal process of honest searching, questioning, and developing our own answers. It pervades our whole lives, not merely how we act, or don't act, in moments of worship, reverence, or prayer.

Education consultant Paula Payne Hardin takes this notion a step further in her book *What Are You Doing with the Rest of Your Life?* pointing out that spiritual experiences "are not necessarily religious. Religions usually develop because a special teacher or prophet connected to the spiritual life suggested certain rules and beliefs, which became institutionalized. Spirituality, on the other hand, goes beyond religion to encompass the whole living web we call earth, including our feelings, choices, thoughts, and questions." A religious experience is by definition spiritual, but a spiritual experience is not necessarily religious.

Whatever your particular spiritual or religious beliefs, we hope you'll draw inspiration from the enthusiasm, gratitude, and appreciation our Late Bloomers express for this important (but rarely discussed) "positive" about aging: the opportunity to grow, in a spiritual dimension, through a more complete awareness of both the outer world and the inner self.

"As you grow spiritually," author Sanaya Roman reminds us in *Spiritual Growth: Being Your Higher Self,* "you will understand your life's purpose." Within this context, we offer a few Late Bloomer stories that illustrate the spectrum of possibilities that exist for exploring and embracing our "inner life" as we get older. We've deliberately avoided making judgments about the worthiness of the values and beliefs they've expressed, and we recognize that some will be more appropriate role models for you than others. As a Catholic, Jew, Protestant, Muslim, Buddhist, agnostic, or atheist—whatever label applies—you'll obviously have your own feelings about doctrine and dogma. What's common among these individuals, and many other Late Bloomers we've met, is their profound appreciation that their lives are part of the enormous web that makes up the universe. They accept themselves as components of a much bigger whole and are striving constantly to understand more fully the nature of that very special relationship.

The ceramic sculptures of California artist Beatrice Wood

have delighted collectors for more than a half century. Although in her late nineties at the time of our visit, Beatrice was still living in the modest home with a studio where she has for three decades created figures, vases, and bowls. Located far from the noisy city, this secluded retreat nourishes Beatrice's creative impulses as well as her spirit.

The artist learned a valuable lesson in the connectedness of all human beings when, during a three-day hospital stay for a minor ailment, she shared a room with "a toothless old crone" who mumbled to herself all night. During the day, the woman chattered incessantly to no one in particular. "I couldn't sleep, so I was angry and tried to avoid her," Beatrice recalled. "But I could see she was lonely and needed someone to talk to. So I said to myself, *I must be more decent to her.*" When afternoon arrived, "I got off my high horse and listened to her. She'd had a heart attack and was all alone, scared to death, and in a state of crisis."

The next day, before checking out of the hospital, Beatrice sat on her roommate's bed and, out of kindness, patiently endured her frightened prattle. She promised to call the woman every day. "I could tell that this really meant something to her," said Beatrice. "She felt absolutely bereft and alone." The next day, Beatrice stopped by for a visit. "I didn't want to spend any time with this sick old person, but I forced myself to go see her anyway. She had appreciated so much that I, a stranger, was willing to befriend her."

Beatrice sat on the bed, took the woman's hand, and gazed into her eyes. "And this ugly, toothless woman, to my astonishment, was beautiful. There was no wall between us. We are all really one, and that oneness is what I touched in that special moment." When Beatrice telephoned the next morning, she was told that her new friend had passed on during the night. "Yet I was sure this lonely old woman died knowing somebody cared," Beatrice told us. "You see, I threw my arrogance of 'the artist who does not wish to be disturbed' into the ashcan, and, without a wall, met another human being. And that ugly human being became beautiful. This is one of the most important experiences and lessons of my life."

Her compassionate response to a dying stranger helped Beatrice feel a closer bond to humanity than she'd felt when she was a brash young artist, struggling to assert her identity and fulfill her ambitions. Now imbued with humility, gratitude, and forgiveness, Beatrice felt connected to the essence of another person. She was struck by the universal truth that physical beauty is temporary and confined, while the beauty of one's inner spirit is timeless and pervasive. The former divides us, while the latter brings us together.

Simplicity and solitude are vital for a person like Beatrice Wood, because when the mind is quiet and still, ideas and inspiration most easily make themselves known. Such tranquillity is valuable to any of us who are directing energy and attention inward: asking ourselves questions about life's meaning, mulling over our experiences, listening to our intuition, and allowing our imaginations to roam.

In this discussion, we define "turning inward" to mean enriching one's sense of self, probing new depths of understanding, promoting personal wisdom, and enhancing spiritual and psychological well-being. This "going within" is often an attempt to make sense of our lives and to clarify our relationship to the universe. For some, this is exemplified by deeper involvement in their chosen religious institution. For others, this kind of self-examination reveals itself through journal keeping or the writing of reminiscences. For still others, the introspective process takes the form of meditation or prayer, opening the door to greater levels of self-understanding and spiritual awareness.

It's important to know that there are no "right answers" in the search for spiritual truths, so it would be presumptuous for us, as authors, to suggest any. Nor is any single approach intrinsically more valuable or appropriate than another. The crucial point is to explore these dimensions of life for yourself, in your own time and your own way.

Our friend Don K., for example, has chosen during his later years to focus much time and energy, directly and deliberately, on his personal spiritual growth. This process has greatly enhanced and deepened the quality of our friend's daily life. "I've devoted the last three years to my own search for truth," revealed this soft-spoken fifty-five-year-old, who left the Roman Catholic church nearly two decades ago and is actively seeking a new "faith community" to fill his need for the rites and rituals of organized religion.

In order to concentrate more fully on inner growth, Don has been on what he calls a "spiritual sabbatical" for the last three years. He's taken unpaid leave from his job at a North Carolina university to embark on a search for spiritual truth. "It's the best gift I think I could have given myself," Don declared, when we got together one afternoon in the wooded foothills of the Appalachian Mountains. "I think of myself right now as a sort of searcher, on the move and looking for answers."

Although Don has always been interested in spiritual matters, his perspectives began to change after becoming the director of a rural health service for the homebound elderly. "I've been inspired by my contact with people much older than I am. Many are asking, 'Why am I here?' and they're responding in ways that are far less dogmatic and more universal than I ever expected."

The willingness of the elderly to explore life's purpose, ethics, and values impressed Don so much that he decided to take time off without pay to create a more meaningful life in his own outer world by expanding his inner universe. "I was raised with the idea that 'if it's not Catholic, it's not going to fly,' " he told us, recalling boyhood priests who warned him against playing basketball at the YMCA for fear his faith would be shaken by contact with non-Catholics. "My parents were very strict, very traditional," Don continued. "I was an active parishioner but, as I got older, found that many of my ideas were out of favor with the Vatican. So by my midthirties I'd abandoned the church."

Now Don is searching actively for belief systems that might replenish those needs. He's perused shelves full of books, attended many workshops and seminars, and carefully examined his own feelings through prayer, meditation, dialogue, and group discussion. "I've also treated myself to some unstructured exploration," he said. "For instance, I went out to New Mexico to visit a number of Native American sacred sites. While I was there, I happened to spend a lot of time with some Jewish friends who shared the perspectives offered by their faith. I've been trying to see well beyond the limits I'd previously imposed on myself."

Don has also kept a "spiritual journal" in which he's recorded a wide range of personal reflections and insights. It is intended for no one's eyes but his own. Don started writing this journal after deciding he needed to store all the inspiring, thought-provoking facts and quotations that stood out in the books he was reading. Then he began adding to the journal his own observations and feelings, along with relevant newspaper articles and pertinent anecdotes from his life.

"I look on this journal as a private space," he explained, "a place to befriend myself and develop a deeper appreciation of my own life. I reflect each evening on the events of the day and their significance to me from a spiritual perspective. In the morning, I sometimes jot down dreams I've had, or things that have occurred to me as I was drifting off to sleep the night before. I often outline the highlights of conversations I've had about spiritual topics. And of course I always keep a list of books I've been reading." Sometimes Don reviews events from the far-distant past, writing as many as fifteen pages at a time about particularly significant turning points in his life. This "life review," as he calls it, often provides fresh insight into his previously unexamined actions by casting them in a new light.

Don's journal keeping prompted him to take a fresh look at Catholicism. In reviewing what he'd written, he realized that there was much about the church that was still very important to him. After years of rejecting the traditions he grew up with, Don now feels some affinity for Vatican theology. "I have much in common with certain Catholic thinkers," he explained, "although they tend to be the biggest mavericks. I have a Trappist monk teacher, for example, who is much more independent in his views than the Pope would like him to be." With the guidance of this Trappist mentor, Don has developed a form of daily meditation that both men feel will help him maintain a more personal relationship with God. For at least twenty minutes each morning and evening, Don intentionally quiets his mind and gets in tune with what he refers to as the "intuitive messages" that emanate from his spiritual center.

"I believe our intuition is really a voice to us from God," he said. "Our higher self is a link with some kind of divine power, and I really don't think it matters what you label it. My feeling is that you can't hear God if you're talking all the time or endlessly busy, so I'm deliberately reducing the unnecessary distractions in my life." One direct result of Don's spiritual journey is his newfound conviction that "every religious tradition deserves respect, that all have truths. What's really most important for me now is discovering my own personal truth."

Don has concluded that the best preparation for later life is learning how to live your present life. He believes the appropriate response to basic questions like "Who am I?" are always carried within us. We can hear them, he says, once we've learned how to have a heart-to-heart talk with the most important person in our lives: our self.

B. J. Hateley, author of *Telling Your Story, Exploring Your Faith*, agrees that quests like Don's are undertaken "to satisfy the hunger for understanding one's world, the history of that world, and one's place in it. They nourish the psyche and the soul." A specialist in human relations, Hateley points out that many of us are too busy during our preretirement years to embark on "spiritual journeys." Our mature years often represent our first real opportunity for a deep and sustained look inward. For many older people, this is a search for what connects them to larger truths and makes them greater than the mere sum of their experiences. It's a journey that many of us cannot make when we are younger because we simply don't have access to the self-knowledge—some might call it wisdom—that accrues with age. We can't know what we haven't experienced. "Because this spiritual journey is private, most of us rarely talk about it," Hateley noted. "But that doesn't make it any less important."

Many spiritual and religious leaders have said that the essence of the spiritual path is connection first and foremost to one's self, and through that self to others, to the earth, and ultimately to the universe. This is what Beatrice Wood discovered when she was able to put her "separateness" aside and feel empathy toward a distraught woman who lay dying without friends or family to comfort her. This is what Don K. found when he made a deliberate commitment to explore his inner world.

Through such challenging experiences we learn that spirituality is present each day of our lives, even if we're unaware of it. And it is this everyday spirituality, whether it's examined or not, that infuses our essential psychological being and guides our response to the world.

Awareness of our spiritual selves frequently increases when we reach a point in life where we no longer feel compelled to compare our accomplishments and possessions with those of others or invest energy in "socially appropriate" behavior. At the same time, we can often express more freely our most immediate and sincere inner voice; a voice that speaks not from selfishness and posturing but from the natural melding of mind, body, and spirit into a fully realized human being. Think of this as the part of ourselves that lives fully immersed in the present moment, in unabridged appreciation of being aware and alive. Think of this as the essence, the "now-ness," of who we are.

"You must reach old age before you can understand the meaning—the splendid, absolute, unchallengeable, and irreplaceable meaning—of the word 'today,'" French philosopher Paul Claudel wrote after he'd reached his eighties. This existential approach to life is not widely acknowledged or discussed, yet it often takes on profound significance as the end of life nears.

The late Eve Merriam, a poet and playwright who wrote more than fifty books, echoed the view held by many older people that life becomes more precious in our later years and more appreciated as a result. "A love for the ordinary—not the extraordinary—is what is most important as one ages," said Eve, who was seventy-four at the time of our interview. "To get the joy out of the daily-ness, that's what struck me when I hit my sixties. I thought to myself, *Good heavens, I'm getting so much pleasure out of my breakfast. I didn't know grapefruit juice could taste so good!* It's really amazing, as though some kind of slight film over the world has been stripped away and there is a clarity that I didn't have before."

Eve discovered in her later years that many of her perceptions became much sharper and clearer, as she took more time to savor simple pleasures. In a sense, her outer life became narrower while her inner life grew deeper. She committed herself to living more fully today rather than tomorrow. Through this process, Eve learned to focus on what mattered most to her.

"I finally learned to pare away things that didn't interest me much," Eve Merriam said, explaining how she had stopped putting energy into relationships or activities that weren't especially rewarding. "Now I pick and choose very carefully."

What does "today" mean to you? How would you express this simple little word's implications for the way you experience and carry out your own life? Is your response significantly different from what it would have been twenty, ten, or even five years ago? If so, how?

As your appreciation of the present moment deepens, you may not feel a need to alter your life dramatically in order to accommodate your deepening spiritual perspectives, although some people do make radical changes. The late Joseph Campbell, a professor of comparative mythology, emphasized that major lifestyle changes do not result automatically from increased spiritual awareness, nor should they. According to Campbell, heightened spiritual awareness may result in doing "more of the same," but from a different perspective. For some of us, it may mean lying on a backyard hammock with a stack of books, or renewing the commitment to a career we cherish. It may prompt a devotion to helping others, a trip to the Grand Canyon, or a summer on an archaeological dig. Campbell's essential message was that a search for personal spiritual meaning leads individuals in different directions. Self-knowledge and heightened spiritual awareness will draw you, consciously or otherwise, toward whatever path is most appropriate and enriching for you.

One Late Bloomer whose decisions were affected dramatically through deep and probing introspection is a self-described "spiritual pilgrim" named Shirley W., who has the distinction of becoming one of the first women ordained into the priesthood of the Episcopal church. When we met her, at age seventy-two, she was serving a five-year appointment as dean of the Episcopal School for Deacons, located in a tranquil suburban community east of San Francisco.

"Rev Shirley," as she's known, describes her position as a demanding full-time job that involves administration, teaching, and preaching. Being dean of the Episcopal seminary is immensely satisfying and rewarding, she adds quickly, representing the fulfillment of a passionately held goal.

"I was about fifty when I first considered a more serious involvement in the church," Rev Shirley told us. "At that time

Episcopals didn't allow women to be ordained, so I knew that my opportunities were limited."

Rev Shirley would seem to have an unlikely background for a keeper of the sacrament. An Army veteran and the mother of four children, this imposing yet soft-voiced woman was happily married and living in a middle-class tract home at the time of her calling. Although she'd enjoyed a long, successful career as a college professor specializing in physical therapy, Rev Shirley had felt a certain "incompleteness" in her life. "I've always been deeply religious, even as a child," she explained. "But I got married pretty early and started working. There wasn't enough time to get more involved in the church. After my kids were grown and my husband retired, I became rather bored with teaching and was looking for another career."

During her middle years, serving the church became more important to Shirley, and as she got older spirituality took center stage. She met with her parish priest, who described a program that trained "auxiliary ministers," a kind of unpaid volunteer staff working for high-ranking church officials. "I agreed casually to pursue this. At the time becoming an auxiliary minister didn't mean much to me. But after I'd started taking the necessary classes, I decided to go for the highest position then offered to women."

After becoming a deaconess in 1970, at age fifty-five, Shirley enrolled in an Episcopal seminary and was fully ordained in 1977, the same year the church reversed its policy and allowed women to become priests. Having retired from her college teaching job, she was appointed the following summer to take charge of the School of Deacons.

Rev Shirley says becoming ordained "is a whole different

thing" for someone her age; most become priests around twenty-seven years of age. She's reached the conclusion, however, that "seminary candidates should not join the priesthood until they are older," citing her experiences as a wife, mother, and "working civilian" as positive assets when dealing with parishioners.

During her spiritual journey, Rev Shirley has had more than her share of health problems, including a close call with cancer. And delicate surgery thirty years ago to remove a life-threatening brain tumor left her face partly paralyzed. "At first I was shattered by this," said Rev Shirley. "I was a shy person and didn't even want to go out in public with one side of my face drooping down. I spent an entire summer practicing my speech, which had been affected adversely. But in some ways, I've used my paralysis to my advantage."

Because younger priests often have not yet had to cope with such traumas, Rev Shirley says, many older churchgoers find it difficult to seek counseling from them. "A lot of people feel easier talking to someone of my age," she told us. "I'm able to respond better, since I've experienced many of the same things they're experiencing: problems associated with marriage, separation, divorce, rearing children, disability, death and dying, for instance. I at least know how those events have made me feel."

Although she is often preoccupied with the rather mundane details of running a school, Rev Shirley feels secure in the knowledge that her late-chosen career is worthwhile, that her service to others makes a positive difference. "I get the sense that my whole life has pointed toward this outcome and that every lesson I've learned was taught me so that I could do this job better. I feel that God called me to become a priest, and I'll be perfectly happy to be one until I die. This is my work, and this is my play."

Rev Shirley feels lucky to have found her true calling while she was still healthy and energetic enough to pursue it. In her voice is a sense of peace and contentment, a joy that comes from knowing her place in the cosmic scheme of things.

Many of the psychologists, sociologists, and other experts who've studied aging detect a pattern in the stories of such Late Bloomers as Rev Shirley. They report that older people often respond to a growing awareness of their own mortality by placing a higher priority on their spiritual fulfillment. "Urgency gives way to growing," aging consultant Phillip Berman points out. "Aging forces us to develop deeper resources of patience as well as the tolerance to accept uncertainty." Through this age-related process, our focus shifts from self-centeredness toward a connectedness with the whole. We are freed from our absorption with ourselves. That is why, as we get older, being of service "to the good of the whole" often has greater appeal. Among many people the impulse to serve is virtually unconscious, as if helping others were simply "the right thing to do," the fulfillment of a responsibility to pay for what's been provided them throughout their lives.

Invariably, Late Bloomers involved in service-oriented activities have told us that they get back more than they give. "The joy and enrichment is in the giving," insisted one couple, who volunteer almost all of their spare time at a local hospital. "It connects us to people, to humanity. That's where the satisfaction comes from."

When our giving comes from a place beyond separateness, our service to others replenishes and rewards itself. In this context, we give less for personal reasons than out of spontaneous caring and compassion. In short, we give out of love, which transcends the self.

"Our impulses to care for one another often seem instinctive," Ram Dass and Paul Gorman remind us in their book *How Can I Help?* "The more we're able to act on [these impulses] freely, the more opportunity we have to feel whole and be helpful." Through conscious service to others, they point out, we "not only relieve suffering but grow in wisdom, experience greater unity, and have a good time while we're doing it."

How and when you might be of service is obviously a personal decision, as the stories in this book have demonstrated. Much has been written about the available options and approaches, and we encourage readers who are interested to take full advantage of these resources. A commitment to serving others can enhance the richness of one's life and help balance the ongoing interconnectedness of one's body, mind, and spirit. We have come to believe that spiritual growth occurs most readily when we experience more love and compassion, open our hearts and minds, and respond to the human needs that surround us.

Whether it happens to be work or service, play or learning, many of our Late Bloomers describe a sense of timelessness—an experience of total immersion and involvement—that takes over when they're deeply engrossed in a favorite activity they feel passionately about, one that allows them to feel completely alive. This transcendence may occur during virtually any sort of endeavor that captures our attention fully, whether it's gardening, walking, cooking, meditating, studying, working in a later-life career, laughing with a friend, holding hands with a loved one, helping someone in need, or making a work of art.

When we do what we love and value most, the activity seems unforced, and we lose awareness of the passage of time. Late Bloomers often emphasize that the only time we really have is the here and now, and that we will miss the present if we worry too much about the past or the future. When this shift in focus occurs—from obsession with the passage of time to the preciousness of the present moment—our attitudes toward death may also change.

"If we have learned to live in the present, there is no room in our minds for dying," the late psychoanalyst Ben Weininger once wrote. "We fear dying because we have not consciously lived fully and life seems incomplete. If one is fully alive and living every moment, there is nothing to miss by dying."

This recognition that living occurs in the present may account for the desire expressed by many older people to simplify and streamline their lives, focusing on experience rather than acquisition. When mature individuals come to know what makes them happiest—whether it's making hooked rugs, sailing on cruise ships, loving and being loved, making sandwiches for the homeless, or baby-sitting their grandchildren—many of them are eager to rid themselves of such "unnecessary distractions" as unwanted material possessions, relationships that no longer nourish either party, and once-interesting activities that now feel like chores.

"Older people often learn to travel light," explains gerontologist Tom Cole. "Lightening behavior," he says, is often related directly to a search for inner peace, an acceptance of one's limitations, a feeling of connection with other human beings, and an understanding of God—or whatever we choose to call the divine power of the universe. Yet even after we've simplified our lives and made an effort to get in touch with our deepest and most meaningful sources of satisfaction by living as fully as possible in the present, we must still deal with our mortality. And, as social historian Mark Gerzon pointed out in his book *Coming into Our Own,* "until we accept death, with an open heart, our own souls will be as strangers to us."

How we feel about and deal with death depends to a great extent on how we've felt and dealt with life. The inevitability of our own demise therefore affects each of us in widely different ways. Paradoxically, the feelings of many younger people frequently revolve around the mystery, apprehension, and fear of death, while those who are older often accept death more easily and are less frightened by it. On the whole, ours is still a death-denying society; the subject is something we don't discuss easily or comfortably.

Today, however, a growing number of people believe that talking openly about their own mortality and our natural place in the life cycle can enrich the quality of life and make it more meaningful. Hundreds of older people have told us, in various ways, that they've come to a kind of resolution and inner peace about their mortality. Most of these individuals are frightened not of the actual event of death but of the implications of a chronic illness or a lingering dependence on others. They've moved past the fear of dying to a place where they're more free to experience life. They're committed more than ever to celebrating life's depth and fullness, hour by hour and day by day.

"If you can face and understand your ultimate death," Elisabeth Kübler-Ross pointed out in *Death: The Final Stage of Growth,* "you can learn to face and productively deal with each change that presents itself in your life. You can understand the search for your own self—the ultimate goal of growth."

Several persons we've come to know have been made aware, by doctors, that they're living out their last days. These individuals have told us they're open and willing to share with those who will survive them their thoughts and feelings about their dying. Death is the last event in a life that others can participate in lovingly, and a dying person often takes comfort in discussing his or her deepest feelings about death with those whom they love and trust, or with caring professionals. These conversations are often consoling and enriching for everyone involved. They help us feel more at ease with dying, even when our own deaths seem far in the future.

One day we broached the subject with a terminally ill friend, who had been suffering for eight years with incurable cancer. "I think preparation for death means preparation for being alive," said Margie, who had thought a great deal about her own mortality. "What I would define as 'the normalcy of living' has to include a thread of dying."

Margie felt exasperated by people who didn't want to acknowledge her impending death. During her losing battle against cancer she'd discovered that some people refuse to ever deal with their mortality. One of the lessons the illness had taught her was that "death is a partner" that follows us everywhere, even if we don't acknowledge its shadowy presence. "Death is a part of life," she reminded us. "Death is meant to be accepted, so that we are then free to live more fully." When we accept our corporeal existence as finite, Margie and other Late Bloomers have told us, living in the present gets easier.

"By skirting around the edges of what really happens, we find ourselves unprepared for our death," contends E. Jane

Mall, who wrote *And God Created Wrinkles* when she was in her seventies. "I prefer to face that fact now, and be as prepared for it as possible. Old age is our final stage of life and is inevitably going to lead to death. . . . If we prepare ourselves, we will remove the fear and perhaps, in the doing, teach young people some good things."

How can you integrate an awareness of your mortality into daily life? There's no single answer to this question, for the simple reason that everyone's response will be intensely personal and highly individual. Many people, as they grow older, make themselves more comfortable about dying by placing their later lives within the context of something larger and more powerful. They may have faith in a life after death, for example, or of joining God in heaven. Perhaps they believe in some form of reincarnation, in an eternal life of the soul, or in a coming together of the collective human spirit. Others see their lives on earth as their only form of existence, to be lived morally and well.

Many Late Bloomers accept their mature years as the logical culmination of a natural cycle, comparable to the seasons of the year. For them, maturity (and all it offers) directly follows midlife, as autumn follows summer. A heightened awareness and acceptance of this inevitability doesn't have to deplete the value of the time that remains; it can, in fact, enhance time's value. Each person treasures every precious hour and tries to live it fully, with a sense of dignity and purpose. As one Late Bloomer put it, "it's not death I fear as much as living a life that's incomplete."

The world's religious traditions have reflected on this phenomenon for thousands of years, and there is growing recognition of the universality of their wisdom. The transformative power of unconditional acceptance—of taking in all that life has to offer, including death—is a theme sounded in some Western and most Eastern spiritual practices. "I find I am now nearer the attitude called *wu-shih*, recommended by the Zen masters," wrote Edward Fischer in *Life in the Afternoon.* "*Wu-shih* means accepting birth, death, and everything in between with no fuss."

If our encounters with Late Bloomers have taught us a single truth, it's that one's attitude toward death reflects one's attitude toward life, and vice versa. In order to learn how to die, we must first learn how to live.

THE SECRET OF SPIRITUALITY

Like the people whom poet May Sarton calls "life-enhancers," the Late Bloomers in this book are not escapists or Pollyannas. Nor are they blessed with unusually good luck, perfect health, or fat bank accounts. They are, with few exceptions, "regular folks" who've learned to be realistic about the losses they've endured and the finite aspect of their lives on this planet. They know that compromises, setbacks, and unfairness are inevitable realities in the course of life. Yet they have little use for cynicism and disenchantment, hostility and helplessness.

What distinguishes the men and women of these pages is their understanding of the secret of spirituality. This secret is simple, yet powerful: as human beings, we are all connected to the sacred, through the living web we call the earth, which includes our choices, feelings, thoughts, and questions. When we acknowledge and accept the inherent sacredness of the universe, we are free to live more fully, more deeply, and with greater satisfaction.

We've seen in these pages how Late Bloomers are stimulated, challenged, and impassioned by the prospect of living as fully and joyously as possible. They are aware of the fragile, finite dimensions of their own existence as physical beings, and they accept their connectedness in space and time to the rest of the universe. They accept the balanced relationship between body, mind, and spirit that promotes growth of the whole person. They take life seriously, but never at the expense of being truly alive.

In this chapter, we've stressed the importance of synthesizing a profound and purposeful sense of one's place in time, space, and the universe, and we suggest that this is a vital dimension of spiritual awareness. Spirituality connects us not only with the universe but with our planet, the people around us, our selves, and all that is sacred to us. In short, it infuses our lives with a deeper understanding of what we're doing here. It is this multidimensional quest for life's intrinsic meaning, through the awareness and appreciation of spiritual values, that is perhaps the most important secret of becoming a Late Bloomer.

We are reminded of the writing of a particularly inspiring psychologist whose words encourage us to value the internal journey of our later years. Florida Scott-Maxwell reflected at age ninety-four that "a long life makes me feel nearer truth, and I want to tell people approaching and perhaps fearing age that it is also a time of discovery. If, at the end of your life, you have only yourself, it is much. Look, and you will find."

HOW TO ACT ON THIS SECRET

Many people are by nature or inclination not consciously introspective, and may seldom, if ever, make a concentrated and deliberate effort to reflect on "the meaning of life." They may prefer to manifest their spiritual or religious beliefs in the way they live each day: by sharing, volunteering, and doing good works, for example. They may express deeply held philosophies and values through one of the so-called creative arts, such as singing, making music, performing on stage, writing, or painting.

We encourage you to contemplate, through whatever means fits your personality and style, your own such feelings about what goes on at the very center of who you are and how you relate to the world. This essential "core of self" can capture our attention and find expression even in the midst of life's dullest routines. While we're folding laundry, for example, we may mull over a need to make sense of the world and our place in it. Spirituality will become part of our daily lives if we adopt an attitude that welcomes it, that opens our hearts and minds to it. You'll find that revelations come as easily in the shower or bathtub as in the library or classroom.

While an ongoing commitment to self-actualization is the key ingredient in this recipe for change, there are some practical and pragmatic things we can do that will often make the process more accessible.

One approach is to get involved in some form of service to others, as many people described in earlier chapters have done. For many Late Bloomers, helping others—giving of one's self—is a deeply spiritual activity because it connects them to their own higher purposes as human beings. They experience great joy and satisfaction in linking themselves to the world at large and to generations that will follow them, much like the old man who planted a breadfruit tree so that the generations after him could enjoy its fruit. Serving others fulfills a desire to give something back to a world that has already given much to us.

Many Late Bloomers have stressed to us the perceived advantages of keeping a spiritual journal or diary as an effective tool for learning more about themselves. Whether this activity is formalized seems not to matter, since these thoughts are recorded primarily for the benefit of your personal growth and need not be seen by anyone else. Simply jotting down words or sentence fragments works as well for some people as writing carefully structured essays does for others. The important thing is to establish a self-dialogue through the process of writing about what matters most, a process that is itself often revealing.

You may also find it useful to engage in something called "life review," a reflective activity through which an individual looks back on his or her life and articulates it in some form, such as a scrapbook, autobiography, photo collection, or dramatic rendering. One older couple we know actually created a theatrical presentation based on the peaks and valleys of their lives. These life reviews may be strictly personal and shared with nobody else, or they may be circulated among close friends or relatives, or with a spouse. You might wish to share recollections of your experiences and feelings with a small group of contemporaries, at a family reunion, or in some form of memoir writing. The life-review process is often rewarding because it puts events into perspective and infuses them with meaning, providing a view of our accomplishments and feelings of self-worth that we can incorporate into our futures.

Another technique is to ask specific, probing questions of ourselves that may not have definitive answers. They may instead stimulate deep reflection and perhaps some helpful discussion among family members and friends. In later life, we've found that heightening our spiritual awareness gets easier once we've asked ourselves some basic questions, which might include: "What to me makes life feel as if it's worth living?" "When I feel particularly enthralled by something, what meaning does it hold?" "Looking back over my life, what patterns do I see in what I have cherished and valued the most?" "What are my deepest fears?" "When and where do I feel most connected to all living things?" "What feelings and thoughts surface when I think about death and dying?"

Another strategy for increased self-awareness is to play detective with yourself: watching how you act when visiting relatives, interacting with friends, playing with children, mingling with strangers, or staying home alone or with your spouse.

Above all, pay attention to what you pay attention to. Notice, for example, what conversation topics are most likely to spark your interest. What traits do you first notice in other people? What do you feel when you see a child, a puppy, a garden, a sunrise, the Milky Way on a clear night? When do you feel nourished, appreciated, loved? What do you feel when you're quiet, busy, thinking, reading, meditating, or serving others? What do you feel when it's warm and sunny, cold and rainy? Where do you feel most "in touch" with yourself: the countryside, the city, in church, visiting friends, or while learning something new? What does your inner voice say to you in moments of solitude?

As you ponder these questions, remember that this dimension of personal growth is always available to us, at any time and place. Only recently has our society begun to accept the idea that the spirit is an integral partner with the mind and body. It is now clear that mind, body, and spirit are to be seen not as separate parts of the whole human but as being intimately connected.

We believe that the answers you come upon during the course of your spiritual journey will help you to better understand your thoughts and actions as well as your own unique "inner world." These responses will, in turn, have an enormous impact on your choices, interests, activities, and interactions, while framing the attitude you hold as you face each new day.

CHAPTER FIFTEEN

AFTERTHOUGHTS

THROUGHOUT THIS BOOK, the collective "we" has been used to reflect the views of the co-authors. At this point it may surprise you to learn that we are not Siamese twins joined at the computer, but two people with very different backgrounds and life experiences. Here's how the experience of writing this book has influenced our attitudes toward our own aging.

AFTERTHOUGHTS FROM
CONNIE GOLDMAN

There's a bit of common wisdom that I've heard expressed many times during my life: "We always teach what we need to learn." I now understand the truth and subtlety of that phrase, for as the pages of this book have piled up, I've realized how the process of writing *Secrets of Becoming a Late*

Bloomer has become a major ingredient in my own transition into various phases of maturity.

I recall an anecdote about the Roman scholar Cicero who, after composing a work entitled *On Old Age,* declared that the exercise had "not only wiped away all the annoyances of old age, but rendered it easy and pleasing." I would probably replace Cicero's "easy and pleasing" with "rewarding and inspiring." There's no question that I've grown enormously through the experience of integrating my Late Bloomer stories into this book. I can state with sincerity and candor that I now see the various stages of my own aging process not as a crisis but as a quest. I accept with greater ease my gray hair and wrinkles as outward manifestations of my continuing inward development as well as acquisition of experience and wisdom.

Getting to this place has not been easy.

I'll explain why by sharing one last Late Bloomer story— a personal one. Several years ago, when I was a staff reporter at National Public Radio, I began a series of interviews on the subject of retirement. I was the daughter of aging parents, a divorced mother of three grown children, and a first-time grandmother. I was in mid-life. Admiring and respecting elders was not something I had learned from the older adults in my family. In fact, most of them stated openly that they hated to be with old people. My relatives proceeded to devote enormous amounts of energy to denying, resisting, and out-maneuvering the aging process. Within this context, I decided to gear my retirement-related interviews to exploring, through the collection of personal stories, the way people from all walks of life coped with the changes and challenges of their aging.

My first and most important discovery was that in spite of the fear of aging and discounted value of older persons in our blatantly youth-oriented society, hundreds of older citizens were willing to share stories that reflected an attitude in praise of age. My strength as a reporter has always been my ability to present the drama of personal experience. With great determination that soon burned within me as a passion, I decided that someone—namely, Connie Goldman—needed to tell the world that there were lots of folks out there who regarded their own aging as rewarding, exciting, and meaningful. I heard inspirational tales from older individuals who overcame limitations, accepted new challenges, examined values, and contemplated the meaning of life. These words were from the real experts on aging, those who had actually been there.

Such individuals graciously shared their secrets of later-life blooming, each confirming that the focus ought to be not on what we lose with age but on what we may gain. Each recalled that as one door closed in their lives, another inevitably opened. Whether an experience in a Late Bloomer's life was happy or sad, joyous or stressful, there was always an implicit message that, at any age, life gives us opportunities to learn and grow. For more than two decades, this has been the inherent message of my writing, radio broadcasts, and public speaking.

We never know what experience, incident, or encounter may alter the course of our lives. These "Late Bloomer" interviews changed mine forever. How fortunate I was to meet and talk with those who truly believed that the rest of life was the best of life. Their personal accounts reflected acceptance, humor, courage, and spiritual depth. In their later years they had transcended many of the fearful and ageist attitudes that I believe are still deeply ingrained in our culture today.

There's no end to this last story I've shared; my life is still a work in progress. Every day, it seems, I learn fresh truths. As I move through my seventies, exploring new horizons in my busy external life—as well as the quiet times I've learned to enjoy—I understand and appreciate each year of my life with greater gratitude.

Although the title of this book may suggest there are some profound secrets to becoming a Late Bloomer, I confess that there really is no rulebook, no chartered path, and no secret formula. Allow me instead to offer some words that you can freely borrow, taken from my interview with television personality Hugh Downs: "Aging is like a piece of fruit, you can go from green to rotten without ever ripening—and that's tragic. For myself, I hope to keep ripening until it's my time to go."

Welcome to the challenge of becoming a Late Bloomer!

AFTERTHOUGHTS FROM RICHARD MAHLER

Life looks different at fifty-six than at thirty-nine. I was Jack Benny's age when I co-wrote the first edition of this book in 1990. It's an understatement to say that things have changed. For one, I am now immersed in a youth-oriented pop culture whose self-absorbed members will wonder: "Who is Jack Benny? And what's so special about him—or Richard Mahler, for that matter—being thirty-nine years old?"

You have to be middle-aged, of course, in order to appreciate fully life's many nuances. The same goes for "late" middle age or "early" old age or whatever the heck we're labeled at any given point along the arc of life. For me, thirty-nine was a time of intense focus on building a career, enjoying a newly purchased home, exploring the world, and (as a single man) enjoying exciting romantic relationships. I ate, drank, and made merry, without much thought of the future. I never set foot in a gym, rarely saw a doctor, and thought the only I.R.A. was in Northern Ireland. The good times seemed as though they would go on forever. The stories in this book seemed far removed from my direct experience.

As Connie and I revised our manuscript in 2007, I was chronologically qualified to many "seniors only" privileges, including a residence at Leisure World or a discounted stay at Motel 6. But I don't need numbers to remind me that I've grown older. My stiff joints, deep wrinkles, gray hair, and burdensome bifocals announce this each day. I now am careful about what I eat, have mastered the elliptical trainer, and contribute as much as I can to an Individual Retirement Account. At fifty-six, my aging can no longer be avoided or denied.

I've discovered good stuff about growing older, too. I am not so impatient with people since I've come to greater acceptance of everyone's foibles and frailties—including mine. I'm more mindful of the preciousness of life, now that I've lost loved ones. It's become easier to know my own truths rather than be swayed by the opinions of others. And I better appreciate the priceless value of friends and family members who've remained loyal to me for decades at a stretch.

One of the unexpected "good things" that's happened to me since Connie and I first wrote this book is that its strategies for positive aging have never felt so relevant. During the intervening sixteen years I have changed my residence three times, shifted gears in my profession, lost a parent and favorite aunt, written eleven other books, discovered the Internet, traveled the world, and shifted from partnership to bachelorhood more times than I care to admit—or would have anticipated. I have, in sum, learned to be a Late Bloomer.

As we put this edition to bed, I find myself reinventing myself in a new home in a place where I've never spent more than two weeks. There are friends and opportunities waiting to be discovered. Is it a little scary? You bet! Is it exciting? Oh yeah! Will I be jumping into fresh challenges another sixteen years from now? Of this, I have no doubt. You see, once you allow yourself to blossom, it's virtually impossible to reverse the process.

I wish you, dear reader, good health and the very best of luck. If you get a chance, please send me an e-mail message and let me know how the late-blooming process is unfolding for you. I can be reached through my website: www.RichardMahler.com.

ABOUT THE AUTHORS

CONNIE GOLDMAN is a former daily and weekend host of National Public Radio's "All Things Considered" and an NPR arts reporter. Her mission for the past quarter of a century has been to write, speak, and produce public radio specials about transitions in midlife and the years beyond. Her focus is on deepening and growing in the second half of life and embracing the changes that come with the passing years. She is the author or co-author of several books, including *The Ageless Spirit, The Gifts of Caregiving: Stories of Hardship, Hope and Healing,* and *Late-Life Love: Romance and New Relationships in Later Years.* In addition to *Secrets of Becoming a Late-Bloomer,* Connie has also co-authored *Tending the Earth, Mending the Spirit: The Healing Gifts of Gardening* with Richard Mahler. More information is available on her website at www.congoldman.org.

RICHARD MAHLER has authored or co-authored twelve books, including *Stillness: Daily Gifts of Solitude* and *Santa Fe Memories*. Specializing in personal growth, the environment, and travel, his articles have appeared in hundreds of magazines and newspapers as well as on the Internet. Richard teaches "Mindfulness-Based Stress Reduction," an eight-week course incorporating yoga, meditation, and other techniques. His features and commentaries have aired on National Public Radio, CBS, Pacifica, Canadian Broadcasting Corp., Voice of America, and Public Radio International among other outlets. He is the former news director of KPFK-FM Los Angeles and wrote the popular *Un Poco de Todo* column for the *Albuquerque Journal*. Richard lives in a small town in the mountains of southern New Mexico. Learn more about his work at www.RichardMahler.com.